CCAR Journal
The Reform Jewish Quarterly

Contents

FROM THE EDITOR
At the Gates 1
Guest Editor: Rabbi Shira Koch Epstein

IN MEMORY OF RABBI DAVID ELLENSON, Z"L
Soaring on Two Wings: Solomon Schechter, Kaufmann Kohler, and Rabbinic Education at the Turn of the Twentieth Century 4
Rabbi Lisa J. Grushcow, DPhil

Exploring Tradition and Modernity: Ellenson on Holdheim 21
Rabbi Michael Marmur, PhD

David Ellenson: The Passionate and Practical Zionist 35
Rabbi Naamah Kelman

The Halachah of Artichokes *alla Giudia*: Wrestling Tradition and Modernity, Israel and the Diaspora, in Tribute to David Ellenson. 44
Rabbi Joseph A. Skloot, PhD

Borowitz, Durkheim, and Ellenson: Covenantal Theology and Collective Effervescence in Conversation 50
Rabbi Liz P.G. Hirsch

Israeli, Reform, Halachic: Practical Meanings of Rabbi Ellenson's Approach for Israeli Jews 62
Rabbi Benjamin Minich

CONTENTS

Keeping His Dream Alive: The Loving Legacy of David Ellenson 68
Rabbi Robert N. Levine, DD

Rabbi Dr. David Ellenson, *z"l*: A Kind Visionary and a Visionary of Kindness 77
Rabbi Asher Lopatin

Senior Sermon: *Parashat Tzav* 79
Hannah Ellenson

General Articles

A Contemporary Controversy: Pope Pius and World War II 85
Rabbi Daniel Polish

The Footnote—Reading Spinoza's *Ethics*: The End of Medieval Thought 94
Rabbi Paul Golomb

The Truth Judge or the True Judge? 103
Daniel M. Berry and Rabbi Lori Cohen

Jacob Schiff, the RPB, and My Retirement 113
Rabbi Alan Henkin

CCAR Responsum 5784.1

Photographic Images on Tombstones 134
CCAR Responsa Committee, Rabbi Joan S. Friedman, Chair

True Forgiveness: A Responsum and Two Case Studies 144
Rabbi Marc J. Rosenstein

Responding to Moral Injury: The Healing Power of Jewish Texts, Teachings and Practices 153
Rabbi Kim S. Geringer and Rabbi Nancy H. Wiener

When Sons Disappoint: The Consequences of Filial Failure in the *Tanach* 169
Rabbi Barry L. Schwartz

CONTENTS

Book Reviews

A Life of Psalms in Jewish Late Antiquity 186
by Dr. A.J. Berkovitz
Reviewed by Eden Glaser

*Judaism Is About Love: Recovering the Heart of
   Jewish Life*... 190
by Rabbi Shai Held
Reviewed by Rabbi Sam Pollak

*Books Like Sapphires: From the Library of Congress
   Judaica Collection* 193
by Ann Brener
Reviewed by Jordan Finkin

*Holy Rebellion: Religious Feminism and the Transformation
   of Judaism and Women's Rights in Israel* 196
by Ronit Irshai and Tanya Zion-Waldoks
Reviewed by Rabbi Sara Zober

*Reading Reform Responsa: Jewish Tradition, Reform
   Rabbis, and Today's Issues*........................... 199
by Rabbi Mark Washofsky, PhD
Reviewed by Rabbi A. Brian Stoller

Poetry

Wicked Problems 205
Miriam Flock

Jacob in Luz 210
Janet Ruth Heller

To See the Divine Face and Live—Or Not! 212
Rabbi Stephen S. Pearce

Springtime.. 216
Wayne Norman Cochran

1 Tishrei 217
Jessica Greenbaum

A Poem for Purim...................................... 218
Rabbi Natalie Louise Shribman

CONTENTS

The Synagogue of the Sea 220
Elegy: Forest Wildfires 2023 220
Saving Eden. 221
Roger Nash

Kfar Aza 222
Sharon Rogoff

The Diameter of the Massacres 224
Rabbi Karen Bender

Poor God. 226
Paul Raboff

Englischer Garten, 1922 227
Nathaniel Lachenmeyer

Savta 229
War and All. 230
Rinat Harel

Love and Lice 231
Rabbi Dr. Israel Zoberman

Dead Sons 232
What Happened at Mount Sinai 232
Rabbi Adam D. Fisher

Elegy in Reverse for Yom Kippur 234
Rabbi William (Bill) Cutter

At the Gates

Included in this special issue, in addition to regular articles, book reviews, poetry, and a Reform responsum, are pieces in memory of our beloved teacher, Rabbi Dr. David Ellenson, z"l. I am so grateful to Rabbi Shira Koch Epstein who has served as guest editor for this special volume.

I (Edwin Goldberg) was fortunate to have David as my teacher in Los Angeles, and words will never adequately express the lessons he shared with me and my class. My favorite moments were when he would stop whatever he was teaching and say he was going to share something not on point but important for any future rabbi (or educated Jew) to know. Of course, his stories were also legendary. I especially loved the tale about how, growing up in Newport News, Virginia, his father would take him to Orthodox services on the holidays. He would tell David not to look at the *kohanim* when they blessed the congregation, lest he see the *Shechinah*. "If you look once, David, you will go blind. And if you look twice, you will die." When David asked, "If I am blind, how can I look twice?" he received a slap from his dad. And in David's telling, that's when he became a Reform Jew!

At home in all Jewish worlds, not to mention the basketball stands, David's warmth and humanity will continue to inspire us and teach us. He was and remains the ultimate text person.

In fashioning this collection in memory of Rabbi Ellenson, Rabbi Koch Epstein writes:

> *"It is the 24th of Kislev, one of the darkest days of the year, when we cannot wait to bring in the light of Hanukkah—and I just received the call that my teacher, my mentor, my rabbi, David Ellenson, has died. I was meant to meet with him today."*

It felt impossible when I wrote those words, and it's still hard to fully grasp that he is no longer here. For so long, David's voice was a constant—a source of wisdom, comfort, and challenge. As

I wrote then, "I know that I am but one of a legion of his students who call him 'my rabbi,' and will share their memories of him and continue to transmit his wisdom." The pieces in this issue of the *Journal* are among the many ways we are carrying his teachings forward into the world.

David's leadership at HUC-JIR and in the Reform Movement went beyond guiding institutions; it was about guiding people. He understood that our work as rabbis and Jewish leaders is to bring big ideas into our lives in ways that make them real and impactful. His scholarship was never an end but a means to live more fully, thoughtfully, and compassionately.

David's voice held both the weight of our tradition and the tenderness of our most human struggles. He gave us a way to see the world that is both rigorous and generous. In an often-fragmented world, he was a living example of how to weave scholarship and life into something whole and sacred.

When I think about David's legacy, I am reminded of the many conversations we had—whether in classrooms, hallways, or at Barney Greengrass over a Diet Coke. He taught me that being a rabbi isn't just about knowing texts; it's about living them and making our tradition meaningful in the messy realities of daily life, both for ourselves and our communities.

This issue of the *Journal* reflects that legacy. The essays are written by colleagues profoundly influenced by David's teachings, exploring themes central to his work: modernity, liturgy, halachah and responsa, Zionism, theology, feminism, and the ongoing dialogue between theory and practice. These are not just academic explorations; they are reflections on what it means to lead, teach, and live as Jews in the world today.

As I published in the JTA last December, "We Jews follow blessings with action, words with deeds. When we say 'may his memory be for a blessing,' we rabbis can make it so when we learn and build upon David's Torah; seek to extend his boundless love as we offer guidance with affirmation and pastoral care with empathy; to have open-eyed, spiritually attuned, and proactive care for Israel and the Jewish people; to ensure that our actions and commitments reflect our highest values . . ."

AT THE GATES

"May we, the students who learned from, who loved, and who experienced the love of our rabbi, David Ellenson, continue to build upon, to share, and to animate his *d'varim*, his words and deeds, and together strengthen the monument that will serve as his memorial and legacy."

—Rabbi Shira Koch Epstein

Please note this correction: The article "Pervasive Sorrow: Disenfranchised Grief, October 7th, and the Power of Jewish Ritual" in the Spring/Summer 2024 issue of CCAR Journal *was coauthored by Rabbi Lauren Ben-Shoshan, MARE, and Betsy Stone, PhD.*

In Memory of Rabbi David Ellenson, z"l

Soaring on Two Wings: Solomon Schechter, Kaufmann Kohler, and Rabbinic Education at the Turn of the Twentieth Century[1]

Rabbi Lisa J. Grushcow, DPhil

This essay is offered in grateful tribute to Rabbi Dr. David Ellenson, z"l, President of Hebrew Union College-Jewish Institute of Religion from 2001 until 2013. He epitomized a commitment to Reform rabbinic education, a passion for scholarship, and a love of his students. In his friendship with Rabbi Dr. Ismar Schorsch, president of the Jewish Theological Seminary from 1986 until 2006, we perhaps saw a modern incarnation of Kohler and Schechter's connection. In this, as in so much else, he was a model for a generation of rabbis, this author included.

In 1915 and 1916, two books appeared in print which can best be described as twins. Both were published by Ark Publishing in Cincinnati, with similar brown cloth covers and gold embossed titles, the names of the authors in the bottom right corners. Both had frontispieces with photographs of the authors, bearded and bespectacled, gazing off into the distance, with their signatures underneath. Both were compilations of addresses representing significant thinking on the questions of American Judaism in the early twentieth century, as written by the presidents of the two major non-Orthodox rabbinical seminaries of the time. The first book was *Seminary Addresses and Other Papers* by Solomon Schechter, President of the Jewish Theological Seminary of America. And the second was *Hebrew Union College and Other Addresses* by Kaufmann

---

RABBI LISA J. GRUSHCOW, DPhil (NY '03) is Senior Rabbi of Temple Emanu-El-Beth Sholom in Montreal. She is the author of *Writing the Wayward Wife: Rabbinic Interpretations of Sotah*, editor of *The Sacred Encounter: Jewish Perspectives on Sexuality*, and coeditor with Rabbi Joseph Skloot of *Communities of Meaning: Conversations on Modern Jewish Life Inspired by Rabbi Larry Hoffman*.

Kohler, President of the Hebrew Union College.[2] Comparing these books, and especially the visions of rabbinic education which they contain, gives us the opportunity to revisit these voices from over one hundred years ago, and to reflect on the issues with which these two seminary presidents struggled—some of which we are still navigating today.

The issues we see these leaders exploring are fundamental to rabbinic education. Their shared question, ultimately, is what rabbis should study, and why. For Schechter and Kohler, this overarching question contained four others. First was an urgent question of the turn of the twentieth century, namely, how Biblical criticism should be approached in a Jewish seminary setting. Second was a timeless question of rabbinic education: how to teach unlimited topics in limited time. Third was an existential question of whether scholarship is an end in itself or rather a means to an end. And fourth was an enduring challenge: Are there important rabbinic skills that cannot be taught, and how should practical and pastoral care be incorporated into rabbinic training? All these questions were pivotal at the time that Schechter and Kohler were writing, trying to establish modern rabbinic seminaries rather than traditional *yeshivot*, to meet the needs of an emergent American Judaism.

To explore these topics, two essays—one by each author—are key, for it is in them that Schechter and Kohler lay out their visions for their respective institutions. We will focus on Schechter's Inaugural Address at JTS, delivered on November 20, 1902, titled, "The Charter of the Seminary," and Kohler's Inaugural Address at HUC, "What a Jewish Institution of Learning Should Be," delivered just under a year later, on October 18, 1903.

Before we turn to these addresses, though, let us take a moment with their authors. Born in Moldavia (now Romania) in 1847, Solomon Schechter was born into a Chasidic family; he studied at a more modern Orthodox rabbinical college in Vienna, and then was trained in the academic study of Judaism at the Hochschule fur die Wissenschaft des Judentums at the University of Berlin. In 1882, he went to London as the Rabbinics tutor of Claude Montefiore, and then was appointed to teach as Lecturer in Talmudics at Cambridge University. Through his years in England, he rose to prominence as a public intellectual and a scholar. It was at Cambridge, in "an inner circle of Cambridge outsiders," that he met and befriended two Scottish

Presbyterian self-made scholars and adventurers, Agnes Smith Lewis and Margaret Gibson, who showed him the *genizah* fragment that led him to Cairo.[3] At the same time, through the 1890s, he was courted by a group of lay leaders of the Jewish Theological Seminary (including many New York Reform Jews) to help them remake their institution, and it was under their auspices that he crossed the ocean to become president of the newly re-established Jewish Theological Seminary of America in 1902. Although his initial focus was not denominationally defined, his leadership was formative in establishing the United Synagogue of America, the Conservative umbrella organization. He died in 1915 after giving a lecture at which he collapsed; lying down at home, he asked his wife Mathilde for a book, saying "I can't just lie down here doing nothing."[4]

Kaufmann Kohler was born in Bavaria in 1843 to a rabbinic family. His approach to Judaism was initially influenced by the modern Orthodoxy of Samson Raphael Hirsch, under whom he studied, but his academic studies at German universities, particularly in Biblical criticism, brought him to the more radical Reform approach of his mentor Abraham Geiger.[5] He continued to be a scholar throughout his life, and published widely in both Biblical criticism and comparative studies of Judaism and Christianity, writing on Jesus, Paul, and Christian origins. He came to America in 1869 to accept a pulpit first in Detroit, then in Chicago, and ultimately in New York, where he succeeded his father-in-law David Einhorn as rabbi of Beth El in 1879. Kohler was the convenor and force behind the Pittsburgh Platform of 1885. Kohler was also involved in significant turn-of-the-century projects in American Jewry, such as the Jewish Publication Society (alongside Schechter) and the Jewish Encyclopedia. Kohler was called to the presidency of the Hebrew Union College in Cincinnati in 1903, a call that some see as a response to Schechter's appointment.[6] Kohler left his mark in increasing the academic rigor of the College in the German *Wissenschaft* model, and also insisting on incorporating piety, with daily and Shabbat services, before he retired in 1921.[8]

Schechter and Kohler were in conversation with each other not only in print but in person, as public figures and leading voices for their own movements and institutions. Kohler was present when Schechter dedicated the new Seminary buildings in New York in 1903. Schechter was present when Kohler dedicated the new HUC buildings in Cincinnati in 1913, and delivered a speech titled "His Majesty's Opposition," the penultimate essay in his collection. Poignantly, the final essay in Kohler's collection is his obituary for Solomon Schechter, who died at the end of 1915; among his many memorials was a special service in the Hebrew Union College Chapel at which Kohler spoke.

The relationship between the two men, however, goes back to 1901, when Schechter was still a professor in Cambridge and Kohler visited him there. Here is Kohler's account of that visit, dating from his memorial remarks in 1915:

> Two years before [Schecter] received this call [to JTS], I was privileged to spend a glorious day with him at Cambridge, and we both found that, notwithstanding all our difference of opinion, we had so much in common, and that we felt especially deeply concerned in the imperative need of a positive Jewish theology for our time, the importance of which is so lamentably underrated by the average Jewish scholar. We realized alike the demand for a constructive system of Jewish thought, which should be at the same time an impregnable fortress of defense against the Church dogma and the Christian interpretation of Scripture on the one hand, and against the ravages of a destructive Bible Criticism and a rampant skepticism and unbelief on the other.[9]

At a banquet honoring Kohler in 1903, Schechter recalled the Cambridge visit as follows:

> There is no scarcity in that ancient seat of learning, "full of sages and scribes," of learned conversation. But the day with Dr. Kohler was one of the most delightful I have ever experienced in that place....We probably differed in a good many points, and please God we shall differ in many more—but this did not prevent our short acquaintance from ripening at once into what might approach friendship....He also delights to engage in what he considers the "Battles of the Lord," and Judaism has need for men of valor.[10]

Schechter's address, given soon after both he and Kohler were appointed heads of their respective institutions, is titled, "Higher Criticism— Higher Anti-Semitism." This brings us to the first topic, that of what rabbis should learn and why, beginning with Biblical criticism.

It is hard for us to appreciate the significance of this issue at that time. Schechter and Kohler, both trained in the scholarly *Wissenschaft des Judentums* tradition, were trying to bring academic methodology and insights to their rabbinic institutions. Both saw America as the center for the future of Jewish scholarship, and they wanted to bring the best of European scholarly traditions to flourish in this new soil. Kohler had written a doctoral dissertation on Jacob's blessing, which was radical at the time in terms of its usage of higher criticism, so much so that he could not find a pulpit in Germany and left for America.[11] Schechter, meanwhile, had published his scholarly edition of the rabbinic text, *Avot D'Rabbi Natan*, which was the first critical edition of any work of rabbinic literature.[12] Both men were open to the insights of Biblical scholarship; their criticism was of the Christian domination of the field, which used modern theories of evolution to support theological assumptions of supercessionism. They both expressed the deep concern that the tools of Biblical criticism were being used as weapons to dismiss Judaism as unsophisticated and outdated. As Schechter wrote, "[W]e must gather our forces and fight the enemy; and Dr. Kohler, by his wide learning, contagious enthusiasm and noble character, is the right man in the right place to marshal a part of these forces, which may, by the blessing of God, help us to victory."[13]

Significantly, Biblical criticism is the first issue that both Schechter and Kohler addressed in their opening remarks as presidents of their respective institutions (after they both praise their predecessors and thank their donors; *plus ça change, plus c'est la même chose*), and they did so by asking what rabbinical students should study, and to what end. Schechter noted that the charter of the Seminary is "for the perpetuation of the tenets of the Jewish religion, the cultivation of Hebrew literature, the pursuit of Biblical and archaeological research, the advancement of Jewish scholarship, the establishment of a library and for the education and training of Jewish rabbis and teachers."[14] He then was quick to note that this statement requires midrash, and went on to interpret what it meant in terms of rabbinic education.

Kohler too saw the primary importance of setting the course of rabbinic study, asking: "But what is the Torah which Israel is commissioned to teach and to propagate? And what should a Seat of Jewish Learning be to the Jewish community and to the world at large? These are, I think, the two pivoted questions which I, as one who is expected to mould the character and destiny of a large body of American Israel, ought to answer today."[15]

First and foremost, the two presidents agreed that Biblical criticism could not be ignored. In "Higher Criticism— Highter Anti-Semitism," Schechter is passionate about the need to reclaim the Bible, and this means both fending off antisemitic Christian criticism and also building Jewish scholarship.[16] In his opening address at JTS, his emphasis is on Biblical criticism as a new intellectual approach, which like all new approaches, has its perils but also holds great potential:

> Mark, too, that there is no intellectual wave that breaks upon our mental horizon, which, disastrous as it may appear to us, will not have some beneficial effect in the end. It may wreak desolation when it comes; it may leave the beach strewn with loathsome monsters when it recedes, but at the same time it will deposit a residue of fresh matter, often fruitful and fructifying.[17]

Kohler, like Schechter, argued that "it is foolish and wrong to evade the discussion of vexatious problems of the day."[18] Unlike Schechter, he was more explicit in his opening address about the responsibility of the rabbi to learn about Biblical criticism as an issue not just of scholarship but of faith:

> You fail to train men of power for the ministry, if you ignore or simply condemn the Higher Biblical Criticism and Comparative Religion and Law as detrimental to the faith or to reverence for the Bible…Never before was the path of the preacher beset with such difficulties, such struggles and doubts of today. Questions which formerly occupied only the mind of the scholar in his study have become the great concern of all thinking people. Each day discloses some long-hidden document in the earth or some startling phenomenon in the sky or the sea that threatens to undermine the very groundwork of faith and calls for a resetting of the Bible and a reconstruction of the whole idea of Revelation and Creation. The issue today is no longer between Reform and Orthodox, but between a world with God and a world without God.[19]

It is important to note that Kohler added "Comparative Religion and Law" to Biblical criticism as a subject that must be studied. Kohler was a scholar of early Christianity and deeply invested in the topic, as shown by his many articles in the *Jewish Encyclopedia* related to Christian origins; in contrast with the argument of Christian scholars of the time that Christianity represented a spiritual evolution from primitive Judaism, Kohler made the case that Christianity represents a deterioration of Judaism's original power.[20] For Schechter, it was more important to maintain focus on Jewish studies, including Biblical criticism but not extending to the study of Christianity. Overall, however, these differences pale beside the similar insistence of both Schechter and Kohler that their students must engage with Biblical criticism, and build up Judaism to meet the moment with scholarly integrity and faith.

Biblical criticism was at the curricular forefront, but far from the only subject.[21] How was one to teach millennia of texts and traditions in limited time? Schechter felt this problem especially acutely. For him, the "minister of religion" is charged with teaching religion, and so, "He should know everything Jewish—Bible, Talmud, Midrash, Liturgy, Jewish ethics and Jewish philosophy; Jewish history and Jewish mysticism, and even Jewish folklore. None of these subjects, with its various ramifications, should be entirely strange to him."[22] The problem, of course, is clear:

> We cannot, naturally, hope to carry the student through all these vast fields of learning the cultivation of which humanity has now worked for nearly four thousand years. But this fact must not prevent us from making the attempt to bring the students on terms of acquaintance at least with all those manifestations of Jewish life and Jewish thought which may prove useful to them as future ministers, and suggestive and stimulating to them as prospective scholars.[23]

This question of *what* to teach is inextricably connected with *why* we teach. What is the vision for the rabbi who emerges from his studies? What is the scope and purpose of rabbinic learning? Here, perhaps, one sees the impact of the two presidents' backgrounds. Before being called to lead JTS, Schechter had worked primarily in academic contexts; Kohler came from thirty-four years as a congregational rabbi, during which time he also published widely as a scholar.

Schecter is clear that the rabbi not only can, but should, also be a scholar, writing: "It is hardly necessary to remark that the Jewish ministry and Jewish scholarship are not irreconcilable. The usefulness of a minister does not increase in an *inverse ratio* to his knowledge..."²⁴ For Schechter, then, learning is meant to be both "useful" to rabbis' ministry and also "suggestive" for their scholarship. Earlier in his address, even before turning to the issue of curriculum, he is clear about the central importance of research. It is worth quoting from this section of the speech at length, as it makes clear that for Schechter, Jewish scholarship is not just an intellectual exercise but a deeply spiritual endeavor:

> The crown and climax of all learning is research. The object of this searching is truth—that truth which gives unity to history and harmony to the phenomena of nature, and brings order into a universe in which the naked eye perceives only strife and chance... the student not only re-examines the old sources, but is on the constant lookout for fresh material and new fields of exploration. These enable him to supply a link here and to fill out a gap there, thus contributing his humble share to the sum total of truth, which by the grace of God, is in a process of constant self-revelation.
>
> ...the sensation we experience in our work is not unlike that which should accompany our devotions. Every discovery of an ancient document giving evidence of a bygone world is, if undertaken in the right spirit—that if, for the honor of God and the truth and not for the glory of self—an act of resurrection in miniature. How the past suddenly rushes in upon you with all its joys and woes! And there is a spark of a human soul like yours come to light again after a disappearance of centuries, crying for sympathy and mercy....You dare not neglect the appeal and slay this soul again. Unless you choose to become another Cain you must be the keeper of your brother and give him a fair hearing. You pray with him if he happens to be a liturgist; you grieve with him if the impress left by him on your mind is that of suffering; you fight for him if his voice is that of ardent partisanship, and you even doubt with him if the garb in which he makes his appearance is that on an honest skeptic—"Souls can only be kissed through the medium of sympathy."²⁵

Here we see Schechter the scholar, up to his elbows in fragments from the Cairo Genizah, bringing those lives to light. To abandon scholarship would be a catastrophe comparable to the destruction of the Temple:

> "Every generation," the sacred Rabbis say, "which did not live to see the rebuilding of the Holy Temple must consider itself as

if it had witnessed its destruction." Similarly we may say that every age which has not made some essential contribution to the erection of the Temple of Truth and real *Wissenschaft* is bound to look upon itself as if it had been instrumental in its demolition. For it is these fresh contributions and the opening of new sources, with the new currents they create, that keep the intellectual and spiritual atmosphere in motion and impart to it life and vigor. But when, through mental inertia and moral sloth, these fresh sources are allowed to dry, stagnation and decay are sure to set in. The same things happen which came to pass when Israel's sanctuary was consumed in fire.[26]

Kohler spoke equally powerfully about the purpose of rabbinic learning, but to a different end. One can imagine he was responding directly to Schechter in putting forward a different vision for rabbinic studies at HUC. Kohler, unlike Schechter, actually had the experience of simultaneously being a scholar and a pulpit rabbi, and this perhaps shaped his emphasis.[27] For Kohler, this was a moment of unique opportunity, and it called for an entirely new approach: "A new generation, thoroughly American in education, culture, and tastes, sits in the pew waiting for inspiration from the pulpit...."[28] This is the Torah that the rabbinic student must learn and teach, engaging with "the great religious and philosophical problems of the age,"[29] rather than getting lost in minutiae. Kohler had no patience for a narrow focus on scholarship:

> The men that have gone forth from these seminaries may possibly have enriched the learned world with a treatise on some obscure Hebrew, Arabic or Samaritan work, and turned out to be fine linguists, perchance, or archaeologists and palaeographers well versed in literature and able to handle manuscripts and palimpsest, but they have missed their vocation. They fail to impart life to the dry bones of Judaism. They lack the power of a great, all-enrapturing, all-vivifying truth. There is nothing of the prophetic spirit in them to make Judaism a power for an age weakened by doubt and chilled by apathy...
>
> The theological school must be the power-house to supply pulpit and people with the dynamic force of an all-ruling, all-electrifying religious truth. It is not enough that Bible and Talmud, Halakah and Haggadah, Hellenic and Arabic literature, Philosophy and Cabala, History and Literature, Liturgy and Homiletics be taught; they must all be turned into vitalizing sparks of truth...

In very fact, it is as a means of conveying power and spiritual force that certain portions of the Halakah and almost the whole of the Haggadah should be taught, and not for mere mental gymnastics. For thousands of years the treasures of coal lay an inert and seemingly worthless substance in the bowels of the earth, until the scanning eye of genius turned them into sources of power.[30]

For Schechter, it seemed the task of the scholar—and the scholarly rabbi—was to dig up the diamonds of our tradition, dusting them off and bringing them to the light of day. For Kohler, the task was more transformative. It is the modern era, and modern rabbinic education, that will turn the coal into treasure. This is an area in which we see some of the most significant differences between these two leaders.

Moreover, for Kohler, new times call for new sources of wisdom. Whereas for Schechter "the religion in which the Jewish ministry must be specifically and purely Jewish, without adulteration,"[31] for Kohler, there is a need to explicitly seek out other influences. Like other Jewish thinkers before him,[32] he grounded his approach to education in the story of Moses. Even if one *could* learn everything Jewish wisdom contains, it would still be insufficient:

> Rabbinical scholarship alone, however extensive, even inclusive of medieval philosophy, all the lofty thought of a R. Joshua ben Hananiah and R. Meir, if a Maimuni and Crescas, fails to solve the vital problems for the seeker after truth to-day…He must, in other words, like Moses in the house of Pharaoh, receive the nurturing sap of life from the mother, the faith that gave him life, while the surrounding world offers him all the educating influences to render him a child of the age. Only then can he with a clear and firm Jewish convictions and principles be a staff of support to those ready to fall and a power to lead the erring and wayward.[33]

Above all else, for Kohler, it is imperative to think big:

> An age of distraction and discrepancies like ours requires the power of a positive conviction and intensity of faith. Reform Judaism stands for a religion of power which alone saves man when in doubt and trial. Reform Judaism broke the shackles of ceremonialism and legalism, because, following the lead of the

prophets, it declared Judaism not to be a system of laws and statutes, but the law of truth and righteousness.[34]

It is in this time and this place that "the Jewish theological school [may] be expected to become a lighthouse to illumine the path of all seekers after truth…a true laboratory of Jewish thought, an authoritative power to reconstruct the history of the world and reclaim for the Jew his rights and his titles as factor of civilization."[35] For Kohler, not only is there no time to focus on the minutiae of ritual and laws; rather, to do so would be antithetical to the purpose of rabbinic education. Rabbis need to think big, and to focus too closely on Schechter's ancient documents would risk losing sight of the forest for the trees. Kohler's rabbinic curriculum is meant to be a means to an end, to bring powerful Torah to American Judaism. Even though he himself was a serious scholar in addition to having been a congregational rabbi, Kohler's aim was to create rabbis who could translate Jewish texts into powerful messages for their audiences. Schechter certainly wanted his ordinees to have an impact on their communities, but he also advocated for their rabbinates to include scholarly contributions, as an intellectual and spiritual goal.[36]

This then leads to a final challenge concerning rabbinic training. Schechter and Kohler come into the presidency of their respective institutions with sweeping visions for the future of Judaism in America. Like leaders before and since, however, both worried about the ability of their students to meet their aspirations. This leads us to our final comparison. Both presidents were acutely aware that no matter how many brilliant scholars they added to their faculty, no matter how much philanthropic support they garnered,[37] and no matter how hard they worked to design the curriculum—not everything could be taught.

Here is how Schechter introduced the issue:

> Another problem presenting itself is how we are to teach the subject or thing called Life. I hardly need say that by Life I do not understand skill in arranging socials and other attractions, or ingenuity in inventing sermon headings. This is not Life. Everything tending to what is common or sensational must need starve our better selves and ultimately result in spiritual death. What I mean by this term is the capacity for dealing with those occasions in our earthly career, which, by reason of intense joys or

overwhelming sorrow or the tender sympathy which they evoke, crowd years into moments, and form, so to speak, portions of life in condensation.[38]

Schechter acknowledges that such "sacraments" have always been the domain of Catholic clergy, and that Protestant seminaries were teaching these skills; "but it must be confessed that we are still somewhat behind."[39] Why? Because in traditional Judaism, this work was not limited to the clergy. Rather, it was undertaken by voluntary sacred societies, "and the very fact of a man's joining them testified to his fitness to engage in works of mercy and loving-kindness. But a man may show the most brilliant record of undergraduate days and yet be utterly wanting in tact, delicacy, patience, sympathy, forbearance and similar qualities necessary for the office of pastor."[40] Schechter both acknowledged and lamented the professionalization of this pastoral role, and expressed concern about students who might not be well-suited for it. On top of this, he referred to "parents and guardians [who] still object to their sons or wards attending funerals instead of lectures."[41] Of his entire address, this is the area in which Schechter seems to show the most uncertainty as to the best path forward, saying: "The support has to be created. The circumstances require it. But, as I have said, the experiment is risky, and we can only pray with the Psalmist that God lead us in the path of righteousness for His name's sake."[42]

It is perhaps indicative of the differences between the emergent Reform and Conservative movements to this day that Kohler showed more optimism here that a solution could be found. At the turn of the twentieth century, the Reform Movement was more willing to embrace the teaching of practical rabbinics and pastoral care:

> All the knowledge the future Rabbi acquires must be subordinate to the higher task of practical communal service which he is expected to assume…The study of sociology and the science of charity are as indispensable equipments for him who is to be the spiritual leader of a congregation, as are pedagogics and psychology and homiletics to him who is to conduct a Sabbath-school and occupy a pulpit.[43]

Kohler was confident that his students can and should be trained to acquire these skills. His apprehension, however, was that their souls would not be sufficiently sympathetic to those who they would serve:

> Ought, then, he who is to bring the divine message of comfort and blessing to hearts and homes in affliction and happiness, ought the young aspirant to the ministry not learn in due time to unfold these deeper powers of the soul with which he is to perform his holy task as priest and shepherd of his flock in order to enable him to offer healing and tonic of the spirit to those that are in trouble and woe? There must be a religious atmosphere about a Jewish seat of learning which gives warmth to the heart and wings to the emotional nature of man.[44]

Strikingly, he was worried that the American-born young reformers who entered HUC had not been raised in a religious atmosphere, and as a result, they "are callous, inclined to a rationalism which chills the heart and blunts the finer tendrils of the soul."[45] Because of this, the role of the College in educating them must be moral and spiritual, as well as intellectual and professional:

> Over against the cold intellectualism which tends to undermine reverence for authority, faith and the longing for God in prayer… we must institute regular religious exercises, devotional readings and other modes up spiritual uplifting. The future Jewish minister must learn how to wing the soul up to God in prayer.[46]

For Kohler, then, rabbinic education requires training in pastoral care, but also spiritual growth. One of Kohler's most significant (and controversial) contributions to life at HUC was to institute regular prayer.[47] Both the fact that it *had* to be instituted—and that Kohler thought it was imperative to do so—says a great deal about this moment in Reform Jewish history, and the different challenges that Kohler and Schechter faced.

Schechter and Kohler each took on the challenge of educating rabbis for a new era. Trained in European scholarship, both tried to bring their approaches to America, while recognizing changing realities. Their ideologies were different, but they knew that there was much that united them. They each struggled to answer difficult questions, which remain with us today, over a century later. What should a rabbi learn? How do we nurture spirituality alongside intellect? How can we be inspired, and how might we inspire? The writing of Solomon Schechter and Kaufmann Kohler, and their connection to each other, is one such source of inspiration. Kohler, in his tribute to Schechter, wrote: "Judaism always had, and in fact will always need, its two opposing forces, Conservative and Progressive…just as the bird while soaring along the sky needs its two wings to fly steadily onward."[48] Schechter and Kohler, each guiding a wing, helped North American Judaism soar into the twentieth century. Their words are worth revisiting as we make our way through the twenty-first.

Notes

1. I am indebted to the Oxford Centre for Hebrew and Jewish Studies for my time there as a visiting scholar from January through March of 2024, where I first delved into Schechter's ideas concerning rabbinic education. As a newcomer to this field, I am grateful to those who contributed to my research and writing (see notes 4 and 34), while all mistakes remain of course my own.
2. Unless otherwise indicated, citations of both Schechter and Kohler in this essay refer to those two respective volumes, and in particular, their opening addresses: "The Charter of the Seminary" by Schechter (1915), 9–34 (originally delivered as his inaugural address in 1902), and "The Hebrew Union College Inaugural Address" by Kohler (1916), 11–30 (originally delivered in 1903).
3. Janet Soskice, *Sisters at Sinai: How Two Lady Adventurers Found the Hidden Gospels* (London: Vintage, 2010), 106; see also chapter 25, on Gibson and Lewis, the Cairo Genizah, and Schechter.
4. Mathilde Schechter, who deserves her own book, was the founder of the Women's League for Conservative Judaism. The story about her husband asking her for a book before his death is cited in "A Jewish Polymath with a Gift for Friendship" https://www.cam.ac.uk/research/features/solomon-schechter-1847-1915-a-jewish-polymath-with-a-gift-for-friendship. On Schechter's time in Cambridge, see Stefan C. Reif, "Giblews, Jews, and Geniza Views," *Journal of Jewish Studies* 55:2 (Autumn 2004): 332–46; and on his call to America, Abraham J. Karp, "Solomon Schechter Comes to America," *American Jewish Historical Quarterly* 53:1, 44–62. See too Jack Wertheimer, *Tradition Renewed: A History of the Jewish Theological Seminary of America* (Jewish Theological Seminary of America, 1997), especially Mel Scult, "Schechter's Seminary," v.1, 45–102. There are biographies of Schechter by Norman Bentwich (1938) and Azriel Eisenberg (1965), and more recent scholarship, much of which is still unpublished, David Starr (Columbia University dissertation, 2003) and Matthew Lagrone (University of Toronto dissertation, 2008). I am grateful to both

Starr and Lagrone for their generosity in sharing their work, which has influenced my own.

5. Yaakov Ariel, "A German Rabbi and Scholar in America: Kaufmann Kohler and the Shaping of American Jewish Theological and Intellectual Agendas," *European Judaism* 45:2 (Autumn 2012): 59–77. Ariel notes that Kohler was representative of his time and place, insofar as "[w]hile at the turn of the nineteenth century most German Jews were traditionalists, by the end of the century most of them were not" (61). In addition to discussing Kohler's contributions at length, Ariel also notes both similarities and differences between Kohler and Schechter, in terms of both their backgrounds and their legacies. As opposed to Schechter, to my knowledge, a full biography of Kohler is yet to be written. I am grateful to Joseph Skloot for his help in contextualizing Kohler's life and thought. A note on spelling: one sees both "Kaufmann" and "Kaufman" in the literature; for this essay, the spelling used is "Kaufmann," following his signature under his photograph in his 1916 publication—that being said, his name on the title page of the same publication reads "Kaufman."

6. In "American Jewish Scholarship: A Survey, In Honor of the Centenary of Kaufmann Kohler" *American Jewish Yearbook* (1944), Ismar Elbogen writes: "The reorganization of the Jewish Theological Seminary was a challenge to the Hebrew Union College, which met it by offering the vacant presidency to the most outstanding scholar in the American Reform movement, Kaufmann Kohler…His aim was to raise the academic standards of the institution and to stimulate the faculty to scholarly endeavor" (56–57). Like Schechter the year before, Kohler's first move was to recruit European-trained scholars to his faculty.

7. Ariel, 70–71. As Ariel notes, these measures were not universally popular at the College.

8. Ariel, 72–73.

9. Kohler, 331.

10. Schechter, 35.

11. For a contemporaneous source on this, see Cyrus Adler's article on Kaufmann Kohler in the *Jewish Encyclopedia*, published during Kohler's lifetime. See also Ariel on Kohler's scholarship (62) and how his embrace of *Wissenschaft* took HUC in a different direction from I. M. Wise, who opposed Biblical criticism (70).

12. Theodor Dunkelgrün, "Solomon Schechter: A Jewish Scholar in Victorian England (1882–1902), *Jewish Historical Studies* 48:1 (2016): 1–8.

13. Schechter, 39.

14. Schechter, 13.

15. Kohler, 13.

16. When speaking at HUC ten years later in his address "His Majesty's Opposition," Schechter said the memorable line, "We cannot have our love letters written for us" (Schechter, 242).
17. Schechter, 15–16.
18. Kohler, 18.
19. Kohler, 18.
20. Ariel, 67–68.
21. Here I must include Schechter's splendid comment on how studying the construction of Biblical texts was important, but that in emphasizing Biblical criticism, we risk approaching the text without the ability to be shaped by it. In 1904, for an address delivered at the Biennial Meeting of JTS, Schechter writes: "One reason for deferring this course of lectures [on the Bible] to a later stage in the schedule is that we find it advisable that our pupils should first know something of the Bible before they learn everything about the Bible. But I must tell you distinctly that with all the allowance we are making for Bible criticism and modern requirement, we are not prepared to reconstruct the Bible in accordance with every whim of the latest commentator. *If I have any hope for myself and for those who are to be trained in this institution, it is that the Bible will reconstruct us*" (Schechter, 56, emphasis mine).
22. Schechter, 19.
23. Schechter, 20.
24. Schechter, 20.
25. Schechter, 16–18.
26. Schechter, 18.
27. See Ariel: "For Kohler, his work as a rabbi, a Reform leader, a theologian, an initiator of scholarship and a writer on Jewish and Christian history, were inseparably intertwined" (60).
28. Kohler, 14.
29. Kohler, 15.
30. Kohler, 16–17.
31. Schechter, 21.
32. See, for example, Philo, *The Life of Moses I* (V:18–24), and René Bloch's discussion in "Alexandria in Pharaonic Egypt: Projections in *de Vita Mosis*" in his book *Ancient Jewish Diaspora: Essays on Hellenism* (Brill, 2022). Bloch writes: "Philo's Moses passes...the best possible curriculum of his time. He studies with both Egyptian and Greek professors; in the end, however, in his search for truth he finds his own way, leaving both behind. This is very much Philo's understanding of Judaism: it surpasses the teaching of others, but it is, at the same time, very much dependent on foreign impulses" (34).
33. Kohler, 18–19.

34. Kohler, 20. I am indebted to Joseph Skloot for the idea that Kohler, like our own teacher Larry Hoffman, encouraged his students to "think bigly." See Hoffman's reflections on his retirement at https://blog.lawrenceahoffman.com/2018/10/28/i-am-retiring-because-why-what-i-really-do/, in which he writes: "Think big," I tell my students, or, preferably, "Think bigly"—they remember it better that way."
35. Kohler, 25–26.
36. Here it is worth sharing Schechter's words when speaking at the JTS graduation of 1910: "The Rabbi is expected to 'do things.' Upon this we are all agreed; but he should also have the opportunity to think things" (Schechter, 198). He expanded on this theme in his address "The Test the Rabbi Should Apply" (Schechter, 195–205), in which he encouraged rabbis to contribute actively to scholarship. For a more contemporary reflection on the role of the rabbi, see Larry Hoffman's recollection of Gunther Plaut instructing his assistant to tell those who called early in the morning that, "The rabbi cannot speak right now; he is busy thinking" (https://blog.lawrenceahoffman.com/2018/10/28/i-am-retiring-because-why-what-i-really-do/).
37. Perhaps with a little envy, Kohler referred to JTS as "enjoying the support of princes in Israel, princes in philanthropy as well as in wealth and influence," while positioning HUC as "a democratic and therefore truly American institution appealing to all Israelites of the land for aid" (30). Later on, Schechter insisted on the importance of building dormitories for JTS students in New York so it could compete with HUC housing in Cincinnati.
38. Schechter, 27.
39. Schechter, 27.
40. Schechter, 29–30.
41. Schechter, 30.
42. Schechter, 31.
43. Kohler, 28–29.
44. Kohler, 27.
45. Kohler, 27.
46. Kohler, 27.
47. Ariel, 71.
48. Kohler, 335.

Exploring Tradition and Modernity: Ellenson on Holdheim

Rabbi Michael Marmur, PhD

David Ellenson's Hebrew name was not David, but rather Zvi Dov. Both of these are animal names, the gazelle and the bear respectively. David had within him qualities of both (he would have been delighted and amused to be compared to a gazelle). He certainly displayed nimbleness in his intellect, sensitivity in his relationships, and grace in his writing. In a further meaning relating to beauty, the word *zvi* became associated with Israel: the land is described as *eretz hatzvi* and *nachalat hatzvi*, and in a famous Biblical eulogy the term *hatzvi yisrael* is employed.[1] This first name appropriately evokes, then, a capacity to cover much ground with grace and alacrity as well as a deep commitment to the land and people of Israel.

David's bear-like qualities (of the cuddly rather than the grizzly variety) were evident to those who were taught by him or worked with him. As a friend and colleague, many have attested that he was warm, accepting, engaged, and comforting. So many people considered themselves a true friend of David's, and so many were right. In considering his contributions as a scholar, however, it is not the gazelle and the bear—but two quite different animals who come to mind.

A fox, according to the ancient Greek poet Archilochus, knows many things, but a hedgehog knows one big thing. This distinction, employed by Isaiah Berlin in the 1950s in a different context,[2]

RABBI MICHAEL MARMUR, PhD (J '92) is Associate Professor of Jewish Theology at Hebrew Union College–Jewish Institute of Religion, Jerusalem. Among his publications are *American Jewish Thought Since 1934*, co-edited with David Ellenson. Michael served as Dean of the Jerusalem School and Provost of the College-Institute under David. His new work, *Living the Letters: An Alphabet of Emerging Jewish Thought*, is due for publication by Palgrave Macmillan in 2025.

is appropriate when seeking to appraise the scholarly and intellectual achievements of David Ellenson. As a person he was neither wily and scheming like a fox nor prickly like a hedgehog. In his scholarship, however, David was both a fox and a hedgehog. He certainly knew many things, wearing lightly his intense grounding both in Rabbinic tradition, most particularly responsa literature, and in the work of foundational thinkers in fields such as history, sociology, and legal theory. Reading through his bibliography one is struck by the range of topics he covered, among them rabbis and the rabbinate, seminaries, denominationalism, feminism, Israel, law, liturgy, theology, conversion, marriage, and much more.

Nevertheless, there was a hedgehog-like quality to his prodigious academic output, concern with a major theme to which his various essays provided variations, illustrations, and illuminations. The Big Story concerned the encounter of traditional Judaism with modernity in Europe, America, and Israel in the course of over two centuries. In his 1990 work on Esriel Hildesheimer, to cite one example, he quoted the words of Peter Berger to give voice to this paradigmatic encounter of Judaism with modernity:

> In the situation of the ghetto…it would have been absurd to say that an individual *chose* to be a Jew. To be Jewish was a taken-for-granted given of the individual's existence, ongoingly reaffirmed with ringing certainty by everyone in the individual's milieu.… There was the theoretical possibility of conversion to Christianity, but the social pressures against this were so strong that it was realized in very few cases.…The coming of emancipation changed all this. For more and more individuals it became a viable project to step outside the Jewish community. Suddenly, to be Jewish [and how to be Jewish] emerged as one choice among others.[3]

In a 2014 essay in the *CCAR Journal*, David credited Eugene Borowitz for providing him with

> an intellectual-theological framework for analyzing the "intellectual arrangements" different Jewish thinkers and movements have advanced over the past two hundred years in their diverse attempts to affirm Jewish meaning in a world where being Jewish is no longer required. My entire scholarly and intellectual project has been informed by my attempts to understand how different Jewish individuals and groups have responded to this challenge…[4]

Ellenson explored this encounter between tradition and modernity with hedgehog-like focus. It came to expression in almost all of his voluminous literary output, as well as in his teaching, and indeed in his efforts as an institutional leader and a public intellectual. However, he rarely settled for abstract generalizations. He was drawn to specific iterations of this broad question, and perhaps for that reason the academic article was his favored vehicle of expression. He preferred to analyze a specific episode, correspondence, or responsum rather than pontificate about some Grand Narrative.

The hedgehog and the fox played a dual role not only in David's scholarly endeavors. They were also present to a significant degree in his teaching and in his institutional leadership. In the latter capacity, he knew the big thing—that the College must continue to train students to lead their communities and to be critical readers of the tradition—while immersing himself in the many smaller things. That is why he often knew the names and life stories of people he had met only cursorily, and why he mastered financial and administrative details when such mastery was demanded. The *k'lal*, important though it was, never obscured the *p'rat*. The overarching vision was underpinned by facts and details. Indeed, the general was constituted by countless iterations of the specific, and his fox-like eye was drawn to details when he deemed them germane to a wider picture.

David's predilection for the particular did not imply a lack of sophistication. Apart from his grounding in philosophy, sociology, and related disciplines, David's writings also exemplified close attention to the interplay between different genres and epochs. Many of his articles can be compared to stories in which the action is taking place in parallel in a number of different time periods. Biblical, Rabbinic and medieval motifs would often be interwoven with figures from the nineteenth and early twentieth century and contemporary figures. Ellenson's historical sensibilities would not allow him to present these various voices in an undifferentiated manner. Rather, he would allow each distinct strand its own pride of place in the tapestry of his scholarship.

While Ellenson's doctoral work focused on Esriel Hildesheimer (1820–1899), a great figure of modern Orthodoxy, Ellenson was also interested in some of the founders of the Reform Movement. Perhaps the most radical of all of them, Samuel Holdheim (1806–1860), features in Ellenson's work in a number of contexts. He penned the entry on Holdheim (along with some other figures of nineteenth-century Judaism) for the 1987 *Encyclopaedia of Religion*. In three paragraphs he described Holdheim's traditional background, his attraction to secular culture, and his position as a leader of the extremist faction of the emerging Reform Movement.[5] Noting his distinction between the perishable shell of Jewish teachings and their everlasting kernel, Ellenson also described his political and social engagement. In that piece Ellenson cited a declaration of Holdheim that articulated his willingness to separate himself from the thrust of Jewish tradition in the name of a new understanding of ethics: "The Talmud speaks with the ideology of its own time, and for that time it was right. I speak from the higher ideology of my time, and for this age I am right."[6]

The original context of this strident affirmation, which appears in Holdheim's 1845 work *The Ceremonial Law in the Messianic Era*, is informative. Holdheim took issue with the prevalent trend to portray Jews of earlier eras as proto-Reformers. Holdheim was convinced that it was preferable to embrace one's present ideological commitments without attempting to cull decontextualized prooftexts from the tradition.

In 1846 as Chief Rabbi in Mecklenburg-Schwerin, Holdheim criticized the position of Samuel Adler from this very perspective concerning the status of women in Jewish tradition: "Instead of emancipating the religious consciousness of the present…from the Talmud and of declaring the freedom of contemporary religiosity and its right to hold its ground toward the Talmud, [Adler] imports the Talmud into the modern religious consciousness. Thereby two of the most incompatible, most hostile elements appear to be intimately connected and in harmony with each other."[7]

While it has been suggested that Holdheim changed his opinion regarding the criteria by which the wisdom of the ancient Rabbis should be judged,[8] a version of this opinion is to be found in his last work, *Ma'amar Ha-Ishut*. In that Hebrew work, which was published a year after his death, Holdheim's deep grounding in Rabbinic Judaism was on full display. In his preface he surveys his career path, listing the various congregations he had served. He continued:

> …even though I am not considered acceptable in the eyes of most of my brothers, there are many who do follow my discipline and who came to hear the word of God from my lips.[9]

Remarkably, the book includes a version of his earlier brash statement about the veracity of the Talmud, but here it is couched in florid Hebrew prose:

> Be not alarmed, dear reader, and do not judge me harshly for the charge of having established a fixed rule and a steady grounding in the examination of law in general and our ancestors in particular. I brought the sages of the Talmud, may their rest be Eden, before the court of my own reason with the ruler's staff in my hand, accusing them and their generation of going against our views and the views of our generation.[10]

Holdheim argues that he is not guilty of such a charge. His declaration is strident: "I have not come to desecrate our ancestors' memory in the eyes of our generation, but rather to respect and honor them."[11] He argues that no person can ever escape the boundaries established by the times and the milieu in which they live. From our perspective the sages of the Talmud can be described as having perpetrated *sh'gagah*, an unwitting error. To repeat that error in our day, when we know better, is to transform that unintentional mistake into a conscious untruth. To continue to propagate that which we now believe to be untrue is morally unconscionable. To behave in such a way is not to perpetuate Torah but to cancel it.[12]

Holdheim's position was that while there was no basis upon which the sages of yesteryear should be blamed for adopting positions congruent with the spirit of their times, we in our day could not escape culpability for continuing to mouth these ancient assertions as truth. The apologetic tendency to ascribe modern sensibilities to pre-modern figures was wrong in a similar way. It was to rip these persons out of their historical context and thus to do them an injustice.[13] The precise nature of Holdheim's view requires close attention, and it appears to have changed over time, as both Michael Meyer and David Ellenson have argued. In practice, Holdheim judged the sages of the Talmud according to the standards of his own worldview, and was prepared to declare without apology or prevarication whenever he deemed that the values of the Talmud were no longer applicable.

In his analysis of Holdheim on the legal character of marriage, Ellenson employs sociological and historical tools in the spirit of Jacob Katz in order to place Holdheim's approach in historical context. He portrayed Holdheim's concept of *dina d'malkhuta dina* as a response to the polemics of Bruno Bauer, and to some degree Karl Marx as well. Ellenson argued that

> ...Holdheim advanced the position that religion continued to possess a legitimate right to exist in the setting of the modern nation-state. It simply had to demonstrate that it could be confined to the private sphere and would not interfere with the individual citizen's performance of duties for the modern nation-states in the public realm...Holdheim's views on *kinyan* in connection with *dinei kiddushin*, as well as the open stance he took in regard to intermarriage, are paradigmatic of the efforts made by some Jews to be worthy of enfranchisement in the modern state.[14]

Ellenson's analysis of Holdheim's argumentation displays the Ellensonian method to great effect. He explains the debate about *kinyan* in a way designed to make the concept accessible to the non-specialist reader, and points to the essence of the issue at stake. He summarizes Holdheim's argument presented in his 1843 work on rabbinic autonomy thus:

> ...inasmuch as the Talmud forbade *kinyan* of any type to take place on the Sabbath or Jewish holidays, the Talmudic prohibition that specified that a marriage ceremony could not be held on these days of rest demonstrated that *kiddushin* and the act of *kinyan* associated with it were not defined primarily as religious acts.[15]

Systematically, without extravagant criticism or undue adulation, Ellenson the fox presents the logic behind Holdheim's thinking, and links it to the great questions of the day: How are Jews to understand their status and role in a modern state? How is change to be effected?

In a 1999 article on the role of autonomy and norms in Reform Judaism, Ellenson highlighted the figure of Holdheim as an exemplar of a radical position, and cited once again Holdheim's strident declaration concerning the Talmud. Commenting on Holdheim's assertion, something of Ellenson's appreciation and his critique comes to expression:

> In taking this stance, Holdheim expressed both the self-confidence and the hubris that marked the modern temperament. His statement remains the *locus classicus* for the notion that personal

autonomy is *the* foundational principle of Liberal Judaism. In enunciating this position, Holdheim—as much as any other single Reform thinker—established a course that distinguished circles within Reform Judaism for the subsequent century.[16]

Ellenson also devoted an entire paper to Holdheim's understanding of the legal character of Jewish marriage in comparison to the views of Zacharias Frankel (1806–1860). Frankel was a contemporary of Holdheim's, and while Holdheim was "the preeminent spokesman for radical Reform during the nineteenth century", Frankel "was the champion of the traditional wing of Liberal Judaism in nineteenth-century Germany."[17] Comparing their stances on an area of Jewish legal debate provided a means to "illuminate the divisions that distinguishes the Positive-Historical and radical Reform wings of German liberal Judaism."[18] While Holdheim's views and style were distinct to him, David Ellenson saw him as an exemplar of an ideological position he was keen to explore.

In a 2018 interview, Ellenson advanced the theory that all the modern expressions of Judaism constitute responses to a situation pertaining in a post-Spinoza world: the challenge to be authentically Jewish while participating in modernity. Asserting that "the first movement to attempt to do that was the Reform Movement," Ellenson went on to list the founders of the Movement, calling Israel Jacobson its grandfather and then listing Holdheim among its founding fathers:

> …people like Abraham Geiger and Samuel Holdheim in Germany, people like Isaac Mayer Wise and David Einhorn in America, attempted to create a Reform Judaism that would be appropriate to this new cultural setting.[19]

In an important 2016 paper on antinomianism, Ellenson referred to Holdheim and Geiger, each of whom made extensive use of the notion of historical development in order "to promote a position that both weakened the traditional commitment of Judaism to law and promoted a universalistic ethos that downplayed or rejected altogether the importance of Jewish ceremonial law and allowed for full Jewish participation in the world of German civil society and culture."[20] He characterized Holdheim's position as one which robbed Jewish law of its authority in our day, asserting that for Holdheim "the place of law in Judaism was limited temporally to the hoary past when Jews dwelt in the Land of Israel."[21] Ellenson quoted Holdheim's 1843 work on Rabbinic authority as a succinct statement of his position, redolent with radical implications:

> That which is of an absolutely religious character and of a purely religious content in the Mosaic revelation and in the later historical development of Judaism...and which refers to the relationship of human beings to God...has been commanded to the Jew by their God for eternity. But whatever has reference to interhuman relationships of a political, legal, and civil character was originally meant only to apply to the given conditions of such a political and civic existence...Yet it must be totally deprived of its applicability, everywhere and forever, when Jews enter into relationships with other states or...when they live outside the conditions of the particular state for which the law was initially given.[22]

Ellenson's examination of Holdheim's reading of the legal status of marriage was reprinted both in his *After Emancipation* and in Christian Wiese's important collection of articles devoted to Holdheim. Of the many articles penned by David Ellenson in the course of his illustrious career, therefore, his work on Holdheim was one of the most widely circulated.[23]

Recent work on Holdheim's legacy has only made clearer the need for a thorough appreciation of his life and work, alongside other founding figures of Reform. He was perceived as a symbol of radical reform, decried by critics such as Graetz and Zunz as a traitor, and by Orthodox polemicists in even more trenchant terms.[24] Among exponents of Classical Reform, in contrast, he was revered as one of the founding fathers. In any case, it seems hard to contest the judgment of Andreas Gotzmann that Holdheim was "one of the most intriguing figures in the history of German Jewry in the nineteenth century."[25]

Some aspects of Holdheim's life and work made him particularly attractive to David Ellenson. In the middle decades of the nineteenth century we find Holdheim wrestling with the great hedgehog question of the encounter between tradition and modernity. He was profoundly modern in his outlook, prepared to reject structures of authority and assumptions he considered to be at odds with the spirit of the day. His approach to the status of women, for example, showed Holdheim as strident modernist. He declared that

...in Talmudic Judaism women occupy a religious position that is deeply subordinated beneath that of men. Only the altered religious consciousness of the present, set against that of the Talmud, has freed them from it.[26]

Had Holdheim's excoriation of the Talmud and his decisions concerning Shabbat and officiation at intermarriage been motivated by little more than an infatuation with the blessings of modernity, David Ellenson might not have found him so interesting. In fact, his critique was rooted in deep learning, a quality for which Ellenson reserved the highest regard. The fact that figures from Reform history such as Geiger and later Kohler were informed by profound erudition made them of special interest for Ellenson. By all accounts, as a young man Holdheim had been hailed as an *ilui*, a prodigy of Talmud study,[27] and his sermons were "profusely illustrated with talmudic materials."[28]

Throughout his career, David Ellenson was interested in the intersection between intellectual search and institutional leadership. When the story of Ellenson's own decision to take on the burden of the presidency of the College is one day told, the influence of figures like Hildesheimer and Kohler will most likely become apparent. Having spent so much time considering the decisions of individuals who had translated their beliefs and passions into institutional service, David (while keen not to self-mythologize) decided to apply similar criteria to himself. The subjects of his scholarship inspired his own leadership.

While Holdheim's influence was primarily theological, he also held positions of communal leadership in Frankfurt an der Oder, Mecklenburg-Schwerin, and Berlin. His preaching constituted a significant part of his oeuvre. He played a highly influential role in the some of the rabbinical conferences of the 1840s. This dimension of communal leadership would also have attracted Ellenson's attention.

In his scholarship and in his teaching, Ellenson was drawn to polemics. When he found worthy adversaries exchanging conceptual blows, he often sought an opportunity to bring a fox-like example of the hedgehog's big idea. The fact that Jacob Ettlinger and others decried him, that Geiger defended him to Zunz, that Michael Sachs contested his burial in the section of the cemetery reserved for rabbis, all this increased Holdheim's fascination.

Holdheim was a German Jew, but his influence extended beyond Europe. As Ellenson noted, his "approach to Reform found expression in America through the efforts of David Einhorn of Baltimore and later Philadelphia; Holdheim can thus be identified as an architect of the 'classical Reform' position in the United States."[29] In another article, Ellenson cited Holdheim as a leading proponent of the anti-halachic strand within Reform.[30] The transfer of ideas from a European to an American or Israeli setting fascinated David Ellenson, and Holdheim's role in this process was worthy of note.

Zvi Dov Ellenson, as mentioned above, was deeply rooted and engaged in questions of peoplehood and "thick" Jewish engagement. Holdheim's views on these questions seemed to have fluctuated, including both the assertion that the only chosen people was humanity in total and the belief, expressed in his latter years, that Jewish particularity had a value in itself, so long as it was divorced from politics. Ellenson witnessed in his own day the re-emergence of ideas privileging the religious and ethical over the national and cultural dimensions of the Jewish experience, and in general his response was one of great concern. He might have been less alarmed at the implications of these developments had they been expressed with the bold erudition of a Samuel Holdheim.

Liturgy was another of David Ellenson's areas of interest, and here too Holdheim had a significant role to play.[31] The ways in which Reform liturgy became a vehicle for the expression of theological innovation fascinated David, and just as he saw in the study of a responsa a way to explore his hedgehog theme, he also cast his fox-like gaze on the prayerbook as it changed and developed. A story (perhaps apocryphal) told by S.Y. Agnon about Holdheim captures some of the complex dynamic of tradition and change which characterized both Holdheim the subject and Ellenson the researcher:

> Samuel Holdheim was the preacher of the reform house of worship in Berlin. Those were the reformers who shifted the holy Sabbath to the first day of the week. On the Day of Atonement, between the morning and afternoon prayers, when they would take a long recess. Holdheim was accustomed to visit the café close to the synagogue. People were of the opinion that he had gone there to eat and drink, but in fact he went there only to read all those prayers and liturgical poems that he had excised from the High Holyday prayer book of his congregation.[32]

The veracity of the tale may be debatable, but its aptness cannot be denied. Few were as radical in their culling of traditional liturgy as Holdheim, and few were as aware as he of what had been removed. Ellenson himself was no adherent of classical Reform, but he was fascinated by figures such as Holdheim, persons steeped in Jewish tradition in full embrace of the promise of modernity.

The time will surely come when the thinking and actions of David Ellenson will be subject to the scrutiny of scholars seeking to understand how this perennial question played out in the latter part of the twentieth century and the beginning of the twenty-first. Let us hope that this account will notice the paw prints of a great bear, and the graceful dance of a gazelle.

Notes

1. See 2 Samuel 1:19, Isaiah 13:19, Jeremiah 3:19, Ezekiel 10:6, and Daniel 11:16, 41.
2. See Isaiah Berlin, *The Hedgehog and the Fox: An Essay on Tolstoy's View of History* (Simon & Schuster, 1953).
3. Peter Berger, *The Heretical Imperative: Contemporary Possibilities of Religious Affirmation* (Anchor Press, 1979), 29. It is cited in David Ellenson, *Rabbi Esriel Hildesheimer and the Creation of a Modern Jewish Orthodoxy* (University of Alabama Press, 1990), 17, where pp. 31–32 are mentioned. The parenthetic inclusion "and how to be Jewish" is Ellenson's own addition. On page 30 Berger notes that "the Jewish case is just a particularly clear case of a much more general phenomenon," arguing that "the orthodox defines himself as living in a tradition; it is of the very nature of tradition to be taken for granted; this taken-for-grantedness, however, is continually falsified by the experience of living in a modern society."
4. David Ellenson, "At the Turning: Reflections on My Life," *CCAR Journal* 61.4 (2014):101–102.
5. While there is no modern biography of Holdheim, some important articles have been dedicated to him. Immanuel Ritter (1825–1890) served as Holdheim's assistant in the Berlin Reform congregation. See Immanuel H. Ritter, "Samuel Holdheim: The Jewish Reformer," *Jewish Quarterly Review* 1 (1889): 202–15; and David Philipson, "Samuel Holdheim (1806-1906)," in David Philipson, *Centenary Papers And Others* (Ark, 1919), 63–98. A much more recent volume comprises fourteen articles all on aspects of Holdheim's life and work, including Ellenson's discussion of Holdheim and Frankel on marriage. Anyone looking to get a sense of the scope and impact of Holdheim should certainly consult Christian Wiese (ed.), *Redefining Judaism in an*

Age of Emancipation: Comparative Perspectives on Samuel Holdheim (Brill, 2007). That work includes pieces by a number of leading scholars, including Michael Meyer, a colleague for whom David Ellenson had particular respect. For a later popular treatment of Holdheim and his impact, see Michael A. Meyer, "Breaking the Chain: The Radical Thought of Rabbi Samuel Holdheim," in Stanley M. Davids and Leah Hochman, *Re-forming Judaism: Moments of Disruption in Jewish Thought* (CCAR Press, 2023), 165–78. Another HUC faculty member held in high regard by Ellenson was Jakob Petuchowski, who wrote a masterful study of Holdheim in comparison with perhaps his most illustrious Reform contemporary. See Jakob J. Petuchowski, "Abraham Geiger and Samuel Holdheim: Their Differences in Germany and Repercussions in America," *Leo Baeck Institute Yearbook* 22 (1977): 139–59. For an interesting discussion of the way in which Holdheim's championing of an internalized Judaism involved the use of metaphor, see Ralph Bisschops, "Metaphor as the Internalisation of a Ritual, With a Case Study on Samuel Holdheim (1806–1860)", in: Ralph Bisschops and James Francis (eds.), *Metaphor, Canon, and Community—Jewish, Christian, and Islamic Approaches* (Peter Lang, 1999), 284–307.

6. David Ellenson, "Samuel Holdheim," in Mircea Eliade (ed.), *The Encyclopaedia of Religion*, (Macmillan, 1987), vol. 6, 418. Ellenson cited this as it is quoted in W. Gunther Plaut's anthology *The Rise of Reform Judaism*. Plaut notes that these words are taken from Holdheim's 1845 work *The Ceremonial Law in the Messianic Era*.

7. Quoted in Benjamin Baader, *Gender, Judaism and Bourgeois Culture in Germany, 1800–1870* (Indiana University Press, 2006), 71.

8. See Michael A. Meyer, "'Most of My Brethren Find Me Unacceptable': The Controversial Career of Rabbi Samuel Holdheim," in Wiese, *Redefining Judaism*, 17. Meyer argues that in the later phase of his life Holdheim, "who had earlier made the case for historical discontinuity, stressing how different modern religious consciousness was from that of the ancient rabbis, now attempted to find an anchor in the past."

9. Samuel Holdheim, *Ma'amar Ha-Ishut* (Berlin, 1861), no page number.

10. Holdheim, *Ma'amar Ha-Ishut*, 21.

11. Holdheim, *Ma'amar Ha-Ishut*, 22.

12. Holdheim, *Ma'amar Ha-Ishut*, 25.

13. Future research into Holdheim might include a consideration of his historical approach in light of the interpretative strategies proposed a century later by Leo Strauss, who criticized the notion (which he ascribed to Kant) that "it is possible to understand a philosopher better than he understood himself." Leo Strauss, "How To Study Medieval Philosophy," *Interpretation* 23.3 (1996): 321.

14. David Ellenson, "Samuel Holdheim and Zacharias Frankel on the Legal Character of Jewish Marriage: An Overlooked Debate in Nineteenth-Century Liberal Judaism," in Wiese, *Redefining Judaism*, 203–204. For an excellent discussion of Holdheim's understanding of the religious and the political, see Ken Koltun-Fromm, "The Politics of Religion in the Thought of Samuel Holdheim," in Wiese, *Redefining Judaism*, 63–79.
15. David Ellenson, "Samuel Holdheim and Zacharias Frankel," 195–196.
16. David Ellenson, "Autonomy and Norms in Reform Judaism," *CCAR Journal* 46.2 (1999): 22–23.
17. David Ellenson, "Samuel Holdheim and Zacharias Frankel", 191.
18. David Ellenson, "Samuel Holdheim and Zacharias Frankel", 205.
19. For a transcript of the interview, see https://collegecommons.huc.edu/wp-content/uploads/2018/02/Bully-Pulpit-David-Ellenson.pdf.
20. David Ellenson, "Antinomianism and Its Responses in the Nineteenth Century," in Christine Hayes (ed.), *The Cambridge Companion to Judaism and Law* (Cambridge University Press), 262–23.
21. Ellenson, "Antinomianism and Its Responses," 269.
22. Ellenson, "Antinomianism and Its Responses," 269.
23. The article was originally published as "Samuel Holdheim on the Legal Character of Jewish Marriage: A Contemporary Comment on His Position" in Walter Jacob and Moshe Zemer (eds.), *Marriage and Its Obstacles in Jewish Law: Essays and Responsa* (Freehof Institute of Progressive Halakhah, 1999), 1–26.
24. See for example the tract published anonymously by Pinchas Menachem Halperin, *Teshuvot B'anshei Aven* (Frankfurt, 1845), especially 1–2; Zvi Hirsch Chajes, *Minchath Knaoth* (Zolkiew: Saul Meyerhoffer, 1849).
25. Andreas Gotzmann, "From Nationality to Religion: Samuel Holdheim's Path to the Extreme Side of Religious Reform," in Wiese, *Redefining Judaism*, 35.
26. Quoted from Holdheim's 1846 work *The Religious Status of the Female Sex in Talmudic Judaism* in Meyer, "Breaking the Chain," 173.
27. See Meyer, "Most of My Brethren," 8.
28. Petuchowski, "Geiger and Holdheim," 148.
29. David Ellenson, "Samuel Holdheim," 418.
30. David Ellenson and Michael White, "Moshe Zemer's *Halakhah Shefuyah*: An Israeli Vision of Reform and Halakhah," in David Ellenson, *Jewish Meaning in a World of Choice: Studies in Tradition and Modernity* (Jewish Publication Society, 2014), 222.
31. See Klaus Hermann, "Samuel Holdheim and the Prayerbook Reform in Germany," in Wiese, *Redefining Judaism*, 143–68; George

Y. Kohler, "Prayers for the Messiah in the Thought of Early Reform Judaism," in Uri Ehrlich (ed.), *Jewish Prayer: New Perspectives* (Ben Gurion University of the Negev Press, 2016), 5–29, especially 12–18; Margit Schad, "The Problems of Moderate Reform: The History of the Berlin Liturgical Reforms, 1844–1862," in Wiese, *Redefining Judaism*, 169–90.

32. Quoted in Meyer, "Most of My Brethren," 21–22.

David Ellenson: The Passionate and Practical Zionist

Rabbi Naamah Kelman

I was blessed to have worked for David Ellenson in different roles: first under Michael Marmur, when he was dean of the Jerusalem School, and then when Ellenson appointed me to the deanship in 2008. I have chosen to focus my article on his unique form of Zionism, whose ideals were sorely tested during his presidency. He remained absolutely steadfast in his support and vision for the State of Israel. One cannot separate David's Zionism from his religious and ideological perspectives, nor from his scholarly interest. One could say the same about his identifying as a Reform Jew and as a feminist. He saw and lived his life with these multiple and inseparable lenses. This article pays tribute to his Reform Zionism: his ability to embrace the best of our age's universal values as well as his fierce defense of Jewish nationhood. For Ellenson, these were inseparable.

In his presidential inaugural speech on October 13, 2002, Ellenson articulated three major goals in relation to Israel:

1. **The need to protect Israel in times of conflict and danger:**
   Foremost among the commitments that we must now honor is our obligation to our brothers and sisters in Israel. At his inauguration on March 15, 1948, a scant two months before the State of Israel was born, Nelson Glueck recognized that the about to be born State was "literally under fire." However, he went on to state that "to abandon" an embryonic Israel would grant "license to terror." And this Dr. Glueck refused to do. Let me say with pride that my intention is that the destiny of the

---

RABBI NAAMAH KELMAN (J '92) recently retired as Dean of the HUC-JIR Taube Family Jerusalem campus (2009–2023). She was the first woman ordained in Israel in 1992, and she continues to promote feminism, pluralism, and the Israeli Jewish Renaissance.

College-Institute will remain intertwined and interlocked with the fate of our people in the State of Israel, and I intend to do all in my power to enhance the presence and influence of HUC-JIR in Jerusalem by expanding our faculty and increasing our student body in the years ahead so that the promise of our present can reach fruition in the future.

2. **The need for Reform leaders to have a sense of *areivut* worldwide built on the experience of Israel as a world connecting Jewish peoplehood:**
Our students in Cincinnati, Los Angeles, and New York who prepare for careers in the cantorate, communal service, education, and the rabbinate will continue to study in Israel at our Jerusalem campus, and there they will learn the true meaning of *areivut*, the ideal of mutual responsibility that binds Jews worldwide into one people. Our graduates will know that when Jews are in distress in Argentina and Europe or any place on earth that their responsibility to the people Israel is absolute.

3. **The obligation to offer Israelis another religious-spiritual option:**
More than thirty Israeli rabbinic students and dozens of Israeli teachers also currently attend our Jerusalem school, and they constitute the most precious resource we could possibly provide for the growth of liberal Judaism on Israeli soil. In a country where an extremist and coercive form of Judaism on the one hand and a strident and unyielding secularism on the other have provided the only two meaningful options between which Israeli Jews can choose, the need for us to educate native Israelis as rabbis and educators who speak the language of liberal Judaism is urgent. Should we fail in this sacred obligation, history will justifiably condemn us.

David Ellenson's love of the Jewish people was at the heart of his Zionism. And because of that passionate devotion to the people Israel, he was absolutely committed to HUC-JIR students Year in Israel program, as well as expanding the breadth and scope of the Jerusalem campus's impact on Israelis. In all of Ellenson's books and in his hundreds of articles, he is always in conversation with fellow Jews, past and present, and Jews of all denominations and affiliations.

His love and commitment to the safety of Israel, and particularly the Year in Israel program, was sorely tested during the year of the second Intifada, 2002–2003. Throughout that year, with each terror attack in Jerusalem, Ellenson would board the first plane he could to be with HUC students. He refused to budge for as long as possible, and he pressed on to keep the program running. I once witnessed a student confront him, demanding to know what would be the "breaking point" of terror incidents that would shut down the program. "How long must we stay?" the student asked. Ellenson simply answered, "As long as I am the president." At that time, Ellenson confided to the Jerusalem administration that a parent had warned him that "blood would be on his hands" if anything happened to our students. To all, including the board of governors, David said—quietly but firmly—that if there was a decision to shut down the Year in Israel, he would no longer serve as president. To the students, he would repeat: "I am firmly committed to clergy and educators who spend a full academic year in Israel; those are our requirements"—until it was impossible. In March 2002, after the horrific attack on Café Moment, in the heart of the neighborhood where so many students lived, he allowed students to leave Jerusalem.

Ellenson's love for Israel began with his upbringing, but coming to Kibbutz Mishmar HaEmek for eight months, followed by his first year at HUC-JIR at the Jerusalem campus (1972–1973), grounded him—literally and figuratively—in Israel. He was not your classic Youth Movement Zionist, singing and dancing the songs of the *chalutzim*. Ellenson later wrote, "The time in Israel was an exceptional one for me. I felt a wholeness and completion I had never felt before or since—and to this day, I will confess that I feel myself a 'failed Zionist.'" In the preface to his collection of essays,[1] Ellenson describes both his love for and alienation from growing up in Virginia. He writes that he found in Israel a sense of *sh'lemut*, which he explains not so much wholeness but as "normalization." But in fact Ellenson was never a failed Zionist; his Zionism expressed itself ways other than making *aliyah*. His Zionism evolved from his time on kibbutz and then in Jerusalem. The "normalization" he experienced was transformed into his lifelong commitment to making a deep attachment to the State of Israel "normal." Ellenson was comfortable in both modern and classical Hebrew, and this too added to his sense of belonging in Israel. For the Israeli rabbinic students in Jerusalem, his ability to understand them fluently was key to their integration into the greater HUC-JIR world.

As a Reform rabbi and scholar, Ellenson often assessed Reform Zionism. In considering the great divide between the founders of Reform with their embrace of universalism, on the one hand, and the Zionists in our movement with their demand for a particular Jewish nationalism, on the other, he noted how much the gap has closed. However, these tensions continue to inform each other. He wrote in 1995:

> The postures that marked each of these two movements at the turn of the century, and that often led to antagonism between them, are for many no more than a page of history.[2]

His essay continues by analyzing the claim that the Columbus Platform of 1937 was a departure from the Pittsburgh Platform of 1885. In the former, Reform rabbis "affirm the obligation of all Jewry to aid in [Palestine's] upbuilding of a Jewish homeland by endeavoring to make it not only a haven of refuge for the oppressed but also a center of Jewish culture and spiritual life."[3] Ellenson contends that the next clause of the Columbus platform asserted the same universalist beliefs that had been present in the earlier Pittsburgh platform: "We regard it as our historic task to cooperate with all men in the establishment of the kingdom of God, of universal brotherhood, justice, truth and peace on earth." Ellenson thus concludes that "even when Reform came to embrace Zionism, it did so in the light of the universalistic religious categories it had inherited from the nineteenth century."[4] This was affirmed again in the 1976 San Francisco Centenary Perspective, with the affirmation of the State of Israel and the Diaspora: "a people transcends nationalism, even as it affirms it, thereby setting an example for humanity which remains largely concerned with dangerously parochial goals."[5]

Ellenson, as the scholar, analyzed this tension and reviewed other scholars who put forward what they saw as the religious significance of the establishment of the State of Israel. Ellenson was careful not to give religious significance to the establishment of the state, but rather identified the two basic Reform religious impulses as a way to be a Zionist. The Columbus Platform approach affirmed the need, which only became stronger after the Holocaust, for a Jewish state. The universalist impulse demanded that Israel remain true to its prophetic traditions and act as the ideological "check and balance" against xenophobia, racism, and even elements of anti-democratic legislation, which can come with extreme nationalism. Ellenson did not hesitate to be critical, publicly if necessary, when he believed that a focus on Jewishness threatened to suppress democracy, in laws and initiatives undertaken by an increasingly right-wing government.

In 2021, he wrote:

> I would argue that the crux of the moral problem present-day Israel has in balancing its twin commitments to a "Jewish and democratic" state is not simply due to contemporaneous events and causes…Nor is there any doubt that an ever-growing Palestinian minority dwelling within the pre-1967 borders of the State as well as millions more Palestinians living after 1967 under an unwelcome Israeli occupation on the West Bank has further intensified the tensions Israel confronts as it struggles with the question of a "Jewish and democratic" nation.
>
> All this is true. However, anyone who seeks to comprehend the ethical dilemma in the current situation must not see it as the result of the past few years alone. Rather, the challenge of creating a "Jewish and democratic Israel" has its origins in diverse and unresolved ideological and religious conflicts present at the establishment of the State.[6]

In this important article, Ellenson explores what he has identified as the two visions for a Jewish state, starting in 1948. He contrasts the Israeli Declaration of Independence with the writings of Rabbi Isaac Halevi Herzog. In addition, he reviews later attempts to protect the democratic nature of the Jewish state (such as the Basic Law of Human Dignity, 1992) as well as others that threaten the balance (such as the more recent Nation-State Law, 2018). In examining these opposing trends, Ellenson expresses deep concern that Israelis are "becoming more ethnocentric and less liberal."[7]

As much as he loved Israel, Ellenson did not shy away from its current greatest challenges to the democratic-Jewish balance. He asserts that "2.5 million Palestinians on the West Bank are disenfranchised by an Israeli government that controls vital aspects of their daily life. This reality of military occupation and the future possible Israeli annexation of Judea and Samaria only further complicate Israeli efforts to be an egalitarian democracy."[8] Ellenson also critiques Rabbi Herzog's positions vis-a vis minorities and women, in the latter's demand for following Jewish law stringently. If, Ellenson concludes, the anti-democratic currents present in the writings of Herzog and others trends affirming Jewish superiority, Israel will be incapable of realizing its ethical vision as being Jewish and democratic. And this, he adds would be a *chilul HasSem*, a "moral blunder that would stain not only the state but the people of Israel."[9]

Ellenson embodied both of these impulses—the love of the Jewish people and the love of humanity—as well as the passionate belief that one can and must remain a Zionist, because our "Reform religious hopes and vision for the state of Israel."[10] Sadly, these two impulses are increasingly at odds since the war of October 7. The antagonism between these ideals has risen again in sharp focus, and many argue that one must choose between them. David Ellenson would refuse to choose. He was also a student of Modern Orthodoxy, and both Zionist non- Zionist leaning rabbis captivated Ellenson's brilliant mind as well as his huge Jewish heart. Particularly later in his life, the *t'shuvot* and halachic reasoning of Israeli Sephardic rabbis piqued his interest, fueling his passion for Israel as a living and breathing Jewish world where Jewish decisions are made. He viewed these Sephardic *t'shuvot* as more open and "liberal," recognizing the challenges of Jewish power and statehood. For a fuller review of these works see: [11] "Between Jewish Tradition and Modernity: Rethinking an Old Opposition; Essays in Honor of David Ellenson.

Ellenson served as Director of the Schusterman Center of Israel Studies at Brandeis University from 2015 until 2018. In that capacity, he oversaw the annual Seminar that convened international scholars to learn about and teach about Israel. Each summer from 2015 to 2018, he brought this group to HUC-JIR's Jerusalem campus for a Shabbat meal, to learn about our work and the dilemmas we face as Reform Jews in Israel. He showed them Israel, including both accomplishments and challenges.

The last article Ellenson published before his death, "Israeli Democracy and Its System of Checks and Balances: The Testimony Derived from Two Supreme Court Opinions by President Asher Grunis,"[12] examined the workings of the Israeli Supreme Court.

The very title expresses his interests regarding the limits of judicial and political conflicts. The two opinions discussed in the article concerned (1) the efforts of the Knesset's Committee on Elections to bar a certain candidate from running and (2) banning certain political parties' campaign ads. Ellenson offers a fascinating analysis on the judicial process and what defines racism, acts of terrorism, and freedom of speech. Although he does not take any political stand in the article, writing from a position of fascination by the workings of Israel's Supreme Court, he does come across as sympathetic to the efforts to ensure democratic values in Israel.

In Ellenson's first years as president of HUC-JIR, a new trend in Israel was underway. Second- and third-generation Israelis, mostly from socialist secular kibbutzim and moshavim, were searching for the Jewish texts and rituals that their grandparents had so proudly abandoned, and that their parents had been too busy with state building to explore. These younger Israelis began studying, and formed a *bet midrash* at the Midrasha of the Oranim College Center. They reclaimed parts of the liturgy and rituals of weddings and some lifecycle events. Prayer, especially Kabbalat Shabbat, became part of their weekly ritual, as they chose parts of the service and replaced others with the songs of the *chalutzim*. This group was very inspired and supported by Congregation Bnai Jeshrun (BJ) on the Upper West Side of New York, and eventually we Israelis had a Shabbat exchange program with Kol Haneshamah, a leading Reform Congregation in Jerusalem, and the Midrasha.[13] This emerging "movement" later became known as *hitchadshut y'hudit*, representing the innovations and changes the Reform Movement had made over decades and adapting them to Israel. When they were about to celebrate their first bat mitzvah, however, they were at a loss. They asked me to bring a *sefer Torah* and help lead the service. Ellenson was in Israel that Shabbat, and we went to Nahalal—the mother of all moshavot—to attend and support the festivities. David was enchanted. Remembering his days on an extremely secular kibbutz decades earlier, he was deeply touched by the journey of these younger Israelis to reclaim Shabbat and life-cycle rituals. He intuited that it was important for him to embrace this development, even though they were adamantly not Reform. I would venture to say that the same was true of his involvement at the Shalom Hartman Institute over many summers. He was simply drawn to Jewish energy and renewal.

Wearing his institutional mantle very proudly, he could be present and participate in a wide range of Jewish expression, regardless of denomination. At his core, Reform Judaism and Zionism represented renewal and rebirth; not only were they not contradictory, but in fact they fueled each other.

As president, Ellenson was committed to launching new programs on the Jerusalem campus and he found the monies to support them, fortifying the Israeli rabbinic program in significant ways. He arrived in Israel after every terror attack to show his love and support for all of the students, both the North American Year in Israel students and the Israeli students. He supported the founding of a Center for Spiritual Counseling[14], and he helped expand the funding for the joint MA in Jewish Education with Hebrew University. He even raised the funds to refurbish the archways and facades of the buildings. He took a keen interest in all the above and more. David's ease with the Hebrew language cemented his involvement in every aspect of campus life. With Jerusalem glittering in the foreground, after having just ordained a new group of Israeli rabbis, we sang Hatikvah—and his tears flowed. Nothing was more satisfying for him than witnessing what he believed was the promise of the fulfillment of Reform Zionism.

In our last conversation shortly before he was taken from us, David told me that he was planning to compile a book on Zionism. He planned to gather his own articles and thought pieces so that he might, in his own gentle, deeply learned, and thoughtful way, offer us a charge: In these embattled times, when our Reform aspirations for a just and peaceful society are being threatened every day by the ultra-nationalistic government, we must keep doing the work and be *k'lei kodesh*, the vessels to bring a new light to Zion.

Notes

1. David Ellenson, *"Reform Zionism Today"* in *Jewish Meaning in a World of Choice* (Jewish Publication Society, 2014). Pp233-245
2. Reprinted in *Jewish Meaning in a World of Choice*, 234.
3. The vote in Columbus was very close; in fact, it was a tie between those who affirmed and those who opposed. On a personal note, my own grandfather—Rabbi Felix Levy, then president of the CCAR—broke the tie, ushering in a new era.
4. *Jewish Meaning in a World of Choice*, 236.
5. *Jewish Meaning in a World of Choice*, 236.

6. David Ellenson, "The Ethical Conundrum of a Jewish and Democratic State," *Journal of Jewish Ethics* 6.2 (2021): 164–83.
7. Ellenson, "The Ethical Conundrum,"182.
8. Ellenson, "The Ethical Conundrum,"182.
9. Ellenson, "The Ethical Conundrum,"183.
10. *Jewish Meaning in a World of Choice*, 244.
11. For a fuller review of these works, see "Caring for an Intermarried Jew by Converting His Partner: Rabbi Uzziel's Earliest Responsum on Giyur (Salonica, c. 1922)," in *Between Jewish Tradition and Modernity: Rethinking an Old Opposition; Essays in Honor of David Ellenson*, edited by Michael A. Meyer and David Myers (Wayne State University Press, 2014).
12. In *Israel Studies* 28:3 (Fall 2023): 34–49. Asher Grunis and David Ellenson met when they were both graduate students at University of Virginia in the early 1970s, and they remained in contact. Ellenson had great concerns about the so-called Judicial Reform of 2023. His article applauds the work of the Israeli Supreme Court in general, and Justice Grunis in particular.
13. These third-generation of Israelis were astounded that we first-generation *olim* from the Zionist youth movements and Jewish summer camps knew all the verses to many of the classic songs of the *chalutzim*!
14. Ellenson raised the endowment to set up the Blaustein Center for Spiritual Counseling.

The Halachah of Artichokes *alla Giudia*: Wrestling Tradition and Modernity, Israel and the Diaspora, in Tribute to David Ellenson[1]

Rabbi Joseph A. Skloot, PhD

The question of the kashrut of the artichoke, fried whole to a golden, crispy brown and liberally sprinkled with salt, may seem like a small matter, but it is a mainstay of the diet and a symbol of the Jewish community of Rome. The dish, served throughout the city in kosher and non-kosher restaurants alike, is called *carciofi alla giudia*, "artichokes in the Jewish style."

Yet in early 2018, the Chief Rabbinate of the State of Israel issued guidance that artichokes prepared whole were not kosher and could not be imported into the country. The guidance stated: "The hearts of the artichoke are very afflicted with insects and [laboratory] investigation teaches that is not feasible to overcome the problem...."[2] This guidance was echoed forcefully in a statement from the Chief Rabbinate's head of imports, Rabbi Yizhak Arazi, in *Haaretz*: "Artichoke hearts are full of worms. There is no way to clean them as is necessary. They cannot be kosher." To which he added, unequivocally, "This is not our decision. It is the halachah of Judaism."[3]

Notably, despite the fact that the Chief Rabbinate sought to cast itself as the guardian of authoritative and authentic tradition—"the halachah of Judaism," the definite article is impossible to

---

RABBI JOSEPH A. SKLOOT, PhD (NY '10) is the Rabbi Aaron D. Panken Associate Professor of Modern Jewish Intellectual History at HUC-JIR, New York and the author of *First Impressions: Sefer Ḥasidim and Early Modern Hebrew Printing* (Brandeis University Press, 2023). He is a historian of Jewish culture and religious thought in the early modern and modern periods.

ignore—its position was a novel one, and that of Roman Jewry was of venerable vintage. This should not surprise us because, as students of David Ellenson, we have come to understand Orthodoxy as much a phenomenon of modernity as is Reform, and as much given to change and adaptation as other modern movements. In fact, the conflict over *carciofi alla giudia* may be understood as a microcosm of the central debates that defined our teacher David Ellenson's life, career, and scholarship: questions about the ideal relationship of Jewish communities in the diaspora and those of the State of Israel; the definition of modernity and the challenges it poses; and the plasticity and creativity of Jewish law, halachah.

There is no doubt that Jewish dietary laws have long prohibited the consumption of most insects—we need only recall Leviticus 11:29, which prohibits the consumption of *sh'ratzim*, "creeping things." Yet, according to the Jews of Rome, the variety of artichokes long used in the preparation of *carciofi alla giudia* have very compact hearts, which do not permit the entry of insects. The prohibition of *sh'ratzim* simply does not apply. Needless to say, the response to the Chief Rabbinate's pronouncement—in Rome, in Jerusalem, and elsewhere—was swift and sharp. *Haaretz* and the BBC both declared this the start of a new "Artichoke War."[4]

Although the subject of this controversy was especially prickly, controversies of this sort are not new; they are at the heart of disputes over rabbinic jurisdiction, over the validity of local customs that may sometimes seem at variance with the blackletter law, and about the relationship of the State of Israel to diaspora Jewish communities.

When I was a rabbinical student, in preparation for my thesis, David and I studied *hilchot shechitah*, laws of animal slaughter, in the *Shulchan Aruch*. The *Shulchan Aruch* is in fact an amalgam of two works by two different authorities emerging from two different milieus. It was initially composed by R. Yosef Karo, a Sephardic jurist and mystic, in the city of Safed in northern Israel. Karo had the messianic desire to produce a simplified guide to Jewish practice for all Jews, yet his legal guidance, as you might expect, leaned toward the Sephardic tradition. His book was printed for the first time in Venice in 1565. At the same time, R. Moshe Isserles was at work on his own code in the city of Krakow, and when Karo's book was printed, Isserles decided to append his own comments and corrections, written from a decidedly Ashkenazic perspective, to Karo's text. The combined work was printed for the first time in Krakow beginning in 1570, and in the years since it has become the single most authoritative Jewish legal code.

What plays out on an average page of the *Shulchan Aruch* is Karo's desire to fix the law for all Jews, and Isserles's regular rejoinder or caveat. Here's a typical example from one of the passages David and I studied, dealing with the process of drawing blood from meat in order to render it kosher:

> Vinegar into which meat was given once to contract it [in order to extract blood], one does not contract meat in it another time because its power will have grown weak. But all [vinegar] that has not contracted [meat] in it yet, it is permitted to contract in it even if it is not strong.[5]

So wrote Karo. In the Krakow edition of the *Shulchan Aruch* and every edition thereafter, we find Isserles's gloss:

> There are those who say that in this time there are no experts in contracting and it is forbidden to scald [meat] in vinegar. Thus it is customary in these lands [Poland-Lithuania] that no one contract meat in vinegar before salting [it] and no one ought to change this [custom]. In any case, *ex post facto*, it is permitted.[6]

Karo seeks to legalize this process of "contracting meat" with vinegar and make it a fixture of Jewish practice the world over. Isserles, speaking from the authority of his own Polish-Lithuanian community, cites the views of unnamed others, as well as the authoritative custom (*minhag*) of the Jews of Poland, who do not use vinegar in this way—and he thus resists Karo's mandate.

The *Shulchan Aruch* is a testament to power of printing, which allowed one man to dream that the worldwide Jewish community would read the same book and live by it too. Elchanan Reiner has shown how the printing of the *Shulchan Aruch* had a paradoxical effect, however, highlighting new and profound disagreements among Jews.[7] Isserles' commentary is now just one among many that populate the standard page of the *Shulchan Aruch*. In the terms of legal theorists, Karo wished to assert legal centralism (one law for all), but instead his book led to the perpetuation of a legal pluralism (many laws for many), which has existed throughout Jewish history.

Alexander Kaye, David's colleague at Brandeis, has shown in a recent book how the institution of the Chief Rabbinate of the State of Israel, established in the early twentieth century, provoked similar kinds of arguments. It was and is, says Kaye, an enterprise rooted in the philosophy of legal centralism, seeking to stamp out Jewish legal pluralism. The Chief Rabbinate today professes publicly only to assert its authority within the bounds of the Jewish State, but its opinions, as we have seen, carry great force across boundaries.[8]

Considering the story of the beloved Roman *carciofo*, I think David would ask two questions.

First, he would encourage us to think about the implications of this story in the larger context of Judaism's wrestling with modernity. In tribute to him, let me offer one tentative suggestion, recalling one of his favorite thinkers, the sociologist of religion Peter Berger. According to Berger, in pre-modernity lives basically followed the same communally determined scripts; modernity demands, however, that individuals make constant choices. "The modern individual, then, lives in a world of choice, in sharp contrast with the world of fate inhabited by traditional man," Berger wrote.[9] While "traditional man" experienced life as the result of numerous factors outside of their control (an omnipotent God and the ingrained habits and rituals to which they were accustomed), "the modern individual" has to decide what to eat for lunch and whether to take the early or late train. Constant confrontation with choices—what Berger calls the "heretical imperative"—has lead the individual to question everything that once may have seemed unquestionable.[10] To apply this framework to our question: At one time, the Jews of Rome could sit at home and eat their artichokes as they pleased, blissfully unaware that some Jews found the practice improper. But now Jews—Roman Jews, Israeli Jews, modern Jews all—are confronted with the choice: Should I eat this artichoke? They have to take a stand. Writing about such choices, Berger suggests that some people will fundamentally stick to their guns and reject new realities, while others will seek to fashion new worlds that heretofore never existed. The Chief Rabbinate—which we might think at first glance of a conservative institution—is in fact seeking to fashion an unprecedentedly innovative reality in Jewish life and law where regional and local differences are homogenized away. It is, in fact, a force of modernization.

This is one analytical framework, one among many, that we could use to describe this problem. But I think that David, ever so gently, would ask another fundamental question: What does this dynamic mean for the unity of the Jewish people? David believed passionately in a Jewish people that could encompass multiple perspectives, multiple viewpoints. In an op-ed from early in his HUC-JIR presidency, he wrote with remarkable charity about the then-mayor of Jerusalem, "He has every right as an individual to feel that Reform Judaism is wrong." "However," he continued, paraphrasing the modern Orthodox theologian Joseph Soloveitchik and the Mishnah, "all Jews share...a common fate as well as mutual responsibility for one another."[11]

David was a champion of that mutual responsibility, that common destiny, alongside all our glorious differences, of Reform Judaism, and every other kind of Judaism—of our pluralism. There's no better reason to fry up some artichokes in his honor.

Notes

1. It would be an understatement to say that David Ellenson shaped the course of my rabbinate, my career, my life. Our lives intersected in beautiful and surprising ways. As he was for so many, he was my friend, my rabbi, my teacher, and my academic lodestar. I offered a version of this tribute to him at a memorial in January of 2024 at HUC-JIR. The version here has been edited and adapted but it is given in the same spirit as the original, one of grief and gratitude, as well as abiding appreciation for his beloved Rabbi Jacqueline Koch Ellenson and their dear family.
2. "Food Import Procedure/Importer's Guide—From the Procedure File of the National *Kashrut* Division of the Chief Rabbinate of Israel," Chief Rabbinate of the State of Israel, April 2018. https://www.gov.il/BlobFolder/policy/nohaly3/he/éáàà%20îæåï%20-%20îãøéê%20ìéáààï.pdf
3. David Lerner, "Ha-rabanut ha-rashit simna oyev hadash: ha-artishok ha-italki" *Haaretz* (April 9, 2018).
4. David Lerner, "*Ha-yerek shelanu heduk yoteir: milchemet artishok olah shlav,*" *Haaretz* (April 15, 2018); Vittoria Traverso, "Has Rome Declared an Artichoke War?," *BBC Travel* (June 5, 2018, https://www.bbc.co.uk/travel/article/20180604-has-rome-declared-an-artichoke-war).
5. *Shulchan Aruch*, Yoreh deah (Venice, 1565), 67:6.
6. *Shulchan Aruch*, Yoreh deah (Venice, 1578), 67:6.
7. Elchanan Reiner, "The Ashkenazi Elite at the Beginning of the Modern Era: Manuscript Versus Printed Book" in *Polin* 10, ed.

Gershon David Hundert (Littman Library of Jewish Civilization, 1997), 85–98; Elchanan Reiner, "The Rise of an Urban Community: Some Insights on the Transition From the Medieval Ashkenazi to the 16th Century Jewish Community in Poland," *Kwartalnik Historii Żydów* 207 (2003): 363–72.
8. Alexander Kaye, *The Invention of Jewish Theocracy: The Struggle for Legal Authority in Modern Israel* (Oxford University Press 2020).
9. Peter Berger, *The Heretical Imperative* (Anchor Press, 1979), 18.
10. Berger, *The Heretical Imperative*, 28.
11. David Ellenson, "In a Jerusalem Praying for Unity, Sectarianism Widens the Divide," *The Forward* (March 7, 2003).

Borowitz, Durkheim, and Ellenson: Covenantal Theology and Collective Effervescence in Conversation

Rabbi Liz P.G. Hirsch

On Borowitz and Durkheim, in Honor of Ellenson

What does it mean to be a movement? What does it mean to be part of the Reform Jewish Movement today? This is the question that simultaneously keeps me up at night and motivates my work as a rabbi, a Reform Jew, and the leader of Women of Reform Judaism (WRJ), the women's empowerment affiliate of Reform Judaism.

My own path to the rabbinate was heavily influenced by the offerings of the Reform Movement of the 1990s and early 2000s. I attended and worked at URJ camps, traveled to Israel for the first time with the then-Eisendrath International Exchange (EIE), and worked as a Legislative Assistant at the Religious Action Center of Reform Judaism between college and rabbinical school. Along the way, I attended NFTY conventions and URJ biennials. As I participated in these immersive experiences, I learned to articulate my own Jewish values and to view the world through a particular Jewish lens. While this was my personal journey, each step of the way happened in, with, and because of the communities I joined—many of them temporary, limited to a time or place.

As a rabbinic student at HUC-JIR, I took an independent study tutorial with Rabbi David Ellenson (z"l) to examine and integrate the theology of Rabbi Eugene Borowitz (z"l) with the sociological theory of Emile Durkheim. As Borowitz states, "The Jewish self

---

RABBI LIZ P.G. HIRSCH (NY '15) serves as CEO of Women of Reform Judaism. Previously, she was rabbi of Temple Anshe Amunim in Pittsfield, Massachusetts.

lives out the Covenant not only as a self in relation to God, but as part of a living ethnic community."[1] Our individual relationship with God is grounded in the covenantal experience of being in Jewish community. God made that covenant not only with each individual, but with the Jewish people as a whole.

Together, David and I explored the communal aspects of Borowitz's covenantal theology, and how Durkheim's sociological concept of collective effervescence might be in conversation with this cornerstone of Reform Jewish belief. In his kind, supportive way, David shared his thoughts and perspectives and always invited me to respond with my own. Most of his emails or written comments to me during that semester of study included the phrase *"This is very good, and have you considered...?"*

As a tribute to David, in this article I will seek to further integrate these thinkers with his own vision for the experience of the Jewish individual in the context of Jewish community:

> We are persons because we can claim and respond, address and be addressed...neither the solitary individual nor the social aggregate is the essential fact of human existence. The fundamental reality that marks us as persons is that we are formed by God as social creatures. We dwell in community, and in community we meet our fellow human beings and God.[2]

As further tribute to David's thoughtful manner of applying theology to our lived Jewish experiences, I intend to build on these thinkers toward expressing a theology for this moment in time: How might we situate the individual, in community, in relationship with both the Jewish people and with God, in the wake of October 7, in a time of fracture, disruption, and new possibilities? As a female-identified individual and leader of WRJ, I seek to add to this conversation that has largely included the theology and theory of male-identified voices.

Borowitz and Covenant Theology

Rabbi Eugene Borowitz (1924–2016), with whom I also had the distinction to study during his final years, offers a key framework for liberal Judaism: covenant theology. His work was and continues to be core to Reform Jewish ideology of the twentieth and twenty-first centuries. Borowitz first articulated his understanding of covenant theology in 1961 and, as Rabbi Rachel Sabath-Beit Halachmi describes, taught it to generations of rabbis until his death in 2016:

> Covenant theology appreciated the core modern commitment to autonomy of non-Orthodox Jews but also understood that no fully Jewish self is simply an individual self but rather lives in covenant with other Jews....At the core of Borowitz's more developed covenant theology is the idea of a threefold covenant: a Jewish self lives in covenant with God, with the Jewish people (past, present, and future), and with one's self...[3]

In *Renewing the Covenant*, building on his own earlier work and that of earlier nineteenth- and twentieth-century theologians, Borowitz seeks to "intimately correlate God, Israel, and Torah, rendering our Jewish theology holistic."[4] After reviewing other paradigms for structuring Jewish belief, including a Revelation dominated paradigm (Heschel), a Rationalistic model (Cohen and Baeck), a Socially based philosophy (Kaplan[5]), and others, Borowitz introduces his model, which hinges on the Notion of the Jewish Self. As Borowitz asserts, "[w]e need a Jewish theology for those believing non-Orthodox Jews who sense their Jewishness is neither incidental nor marginal to their existence, but essential to it."[6]

Utilizing Franz Rosenzweig's classic God-Torah-Israel triad to articulate his theological framework, a key aspect of his covenant theology emerges from Borowitz's treatment of Israel:

> The nature of peoplehood and Jewish selfhood emerge from this Covenantal relationship, not the one without the other. *Against Buber*, who subordinates peoplehood and Torah to self, the Jewish self stands in relationship with God not in bare individuality but as one of the Covenant people...selfhood is substantially constituted by participation in the Covenant.[7]

For Borowitz, the covenant is made not between God and the Jewish individual alone, but between the Jewish individual in the context of Jewish peoplehood. Specifically, "God and particularity set the context within which people go about making up their own minds...[and] personal autonomy has validity only when exercised in intimate involvement with God as part of one's community relationship with God. For Jews that means as part of the people of Israel's historic relationship with God, the *brit*, or Covenant."[8] The covenant between the Jewish self and God is lived and expressed in community.

Durkheim and Collective Effervescence

The work of Emile Durkheim (1858–1917) is an underpinning of modern sociological theory. He is recognized for his work on the division of labor and on the sociology of religion; the latter is most relevant for integration with Borowitz's covenant theology. Less well known is that Durkheim's father and grandfather were rabbis, and it was presumed that Emile might pursue the rabbinate as well before he turned to his academic path.[9]

There has been some exploration of the influence of Judaism and rabbinic thought on Durkheim's sociological theory. Deborah Dash Moore considers Durkheim's Jewish upbringing through the lens of modern Jewish thought. She believes Durkheim's Jewish upbringing influenced his writings, but she nuances the argument by highlighting Durkheim's connection to the events and intellectual atmosphere of French politics of the late nineteenth century. Moore argues that "Durkheim rejected not his father's values, but 'the limitations of the professional and ethnic role' encasing those norms."[10]

Like Moore, Jacob Jay Lindenthal argues that Durkheim was influenced by his Jewish background, citing his rabbinic lineage and traditional education. He asserts that Durkheim's theories on religion and society were strongly influenced by Jewish beliefs and practices. Lindenthal also provides examples of Jewish ritual that he believes connect to Durkheim's view of the collective and the individual in society. He cites the minyan, noting that in traditional Jewish settings prayer cannot occur without a minimum of ten people. Another example he offers is the *Sh'ma*, noting that this essential prayer is a "proclamation of the unity of God [which] has the latent function of coalescing people into a moral community."[11]

Further study of Durkheim's Jewish background and the connection between the breadth of his works and Jewish theology would provide greater integration between collective effervescence and covenant theology. For me, viewing Durkheim's work as a sociological treatise, without mining it for Jewish influence, already provides a rich way to understand Borowitz's covenantal theology as expressed in a communal religious setting.

Durkheim's study of Australian tribal religion in his major work, *The Elementary Forms of Religious Life* (1912), provides the case studies that led him to coin the term "collective effervescence." Durkheim explains that daily life for these Australian societies alternates between two different phases. At times, the population is dispersed in smaller, independent units, with a focus on economic activities. At other times, a larger population comes together for a religious ceremony, and this is when everything changes:

> The very fact of the concentration acts as an exceptionally powerful stimulant. When they are once come together, a sort of electricity is formed by their collecting which quickly transports them to an extraordinary degree of exaltation...while they express it, they also strengthen it...it is in the midst of these effervescent social environments and out of this effervescence itself that the religious idea seems to be born.[12]

In essence, Durkheim's study of these Australian groups becomes an ideal type. This concept, coined by his contemporary, the sociologist Max Weber, is a tool used to create a simplified version of reality that can be compared and contrasted to other societies and societal phenomenon.[13] We can extend Durkheim's concept of collective effervescence and his idealized type of the Australian societies to understand our own collective religious experiences, such as a shiva minyan[14] or Shabbat service. However, Durkheim's description of the contrasting phases and a large, communal gathering provides an even more powerful framework to understand more temporary gatherings, such as youth programs or North American Reform Movement events. As he explains:

> No society can exist that does not feel the need at regular intervals to sustain and reaffirm the collective feelings and ideas which make its unity and its personality. Now, this moral remaking cannot be achieved except by the means of meetings, assemblies and congregations in which individuals, brought into close contact, reaffirm in common their common feelings...[15]

Unsurprisingly, Durkheim differs from Borowitz regarding particularism and universalism. As detailed above, Borowitz emphasizes that the covenant was made between God and the Jewish people. Durkheim views these gatherings as more similar than not, even while citing their particular faith expressions:

> [T]here is something eternal in religion which is destined to survive all the particular symbols in which religious thought has successively enveloped itself...What essential difference is there between an assembly of Christians commemorating the principal moments of the life of Christ, or of Jews celebrating either the exodus from Egypt or the giving of the ten commandments, and a reunion of citizens commemorating the institution of a new moral or legal system or some great event in national life?[16]

Here, also, the nuanced particularism of Ellenson and Borowitz are relevant for our application of Durkheim. In commenting on a piece by Michael A. Meyer, Ellenson explains, "[Meyer] is careful to point out that he does not reject the notion of autonomy as a Reform ideal. Rather, he, like his colleague Eugene B. Borowitz, opts to construct a contemporary concept of autonomy upon a more communitarian vision of the self that allows for Jewish commitment—'binding' he labels it—to precede 'choice' as the first step in the Reform educational enterprise."[17] Ellenson goes on to quote Meyer, who emphasizes that "a strong sense of the Jewish self securely grounded within the Jewish community and the Jewish religious tradition, requires emphasis on particularity and separation."[18]

Thus, Durkheim's collective effervescence is useful in augmenting how we can describe our own particular collective Jewish experience, firmly based on Borowitz's understanding of the covenant. God is also a crucial piece of this conversation. As Borowitz explains: "Covenant implies a two-sided partnership, the involvement of both people and of God."[19] Ellenson provides us with a deeper look at on the relationship between God, the Jewish individual, and the Jewish people through the lens of covenant theology:

> Our dignity as human beings—our autonomy—derives from the freedom that God has given us. Inasmuch as God is the ground for and creator of all humanity, our auto—our selfhood—cannot escape its social dimensions, its interrelationships to other human beings. For the Jew, this means that the self is actualized through the Covenant that God established with Israel at Sinai. Jewish

selfhood arises within the people of Israel and its Covenant with God. As Borowitz states, "The Jewish self comes before God as one of the Jewish people." God is therefore experienced communally by the Jewish self...[20]

Meeting this Moment as a Movement

How might an integration of covenantal theology and collective effervescence guide us to meet this moment as Reform Jews? Already, Borowitz points the way:

> [B]ecause the Covenant was made primarily with the Jewish *ethnos* and only secondarily with the Jewish *autos*, the Jewish people, its local communities, families, and progeny, remain the immediate channels through which we Jews sacralize existence...[even as] modern life immerses us in an individualistic ethos.[21]

From the isolation of the Covid-19 pandemic to the challenging and divisive responses to October 7 and the enduring war[22] in Israel and Gaza, the North American Jewish community is more fractured and at odds than ever. And yet, as Borowitz and Durkheim emphasize, covenant and community are experienced collectively. For all that we are divided and devoted to our own individual opinions, more than ever we are yearning to be a people in covenant with God and each other. A recent Jewish Federations of North America study reported the following statistics:

> Among Jews who are not members of synagogues...37% say they'd be open to joining one now. The most synagogue interest comes from those who identify as Reform or as having no denomination...41% of...Reform Jews who are unaffiliated are open to joining [a synagogue]...and 43% percent of Jews expressed interest in increasing their engagement with Jewish life.[23]

Through several distinct pathways, we can be a Reform Movement for this exceptional moment:

Youth

When Women of Reform Judaism, the organization that I lead, partnered with the then-UAHC to establish the National Federation of Temple Youth eighty-five years ago, they also sought to meet a moment, and to ensure future Jewish continuity.[24] From changing trends in youth engagement, to varying funding levels, to the isolation of the Covid pandemic, our youth work, particularly through NFTY, has waxed and waned. Our URJ camps consistently embody the best of both Borowitz and Durkheim. They place our young people together, in person—not unlike Durkheim's ideal type of collective effervescence—for a brief period of time. Following Borowitz, they form a temporary covenant, a *b'rit*, of how to live and be together. The results are transformational. Throughout the year, in person, our youth can gather in ways that embrace the best aspects of covenantal theology, collective effervescence, and summer camp.

Gathering, inclusion, and welcoming

Like our youth, Reform Jewish adults also need to gather. So many of us have felt the collective effervescent impact of sharing together in worship, conversation, and study. Technology is a powerful tool to bring us together on a more regular basis, with limited financial or carbon impact from travel. While Durkheim wrote long before the possibility of online community, he demonstrates there is no true replacement for physical proximity:

> A collective feeling cannot be expressed collectively unless a certain order is observed that permits the group's harmonious movements, [thus] these gestures and cries are included to be rhythmic and regulated, and become chants and dances...[25]

We can and we must, in all arms and affiliates of our Movement, find more ways to gather (and chant and dance!) in person, and to make these gatherings accessible, welcoming, and open to all. While finances may be a barrier, our overt or unconscious biases as to whom we welcome into our covenantal collectives are also crucial to consider.

In June 2024, Women of Reform Judaism amended its constitution to open up membership to anyone who identifies as female, nonbinary, or gender fluid, and to those who identify as Jewish and those on a Jewish journey.[26] Women's Rabbinic Network[27] and Hebrew Union College-Jewish Institute of Religion[28] took similar steps toward inclusion in 2024 as well. In order to gather in covenantal, collective communities, we must look toward opening the doors as broadly as possible, and saying yes to all those who wish to be a part of our communities. As I charged those assembled at WRJ's most recent North American gathering, "What if, in this moment of fracture and antisemitism and pain—what if we said YES to everyone who wants to be a part of Jewish life?"[29] This inclusive sentiment is inherently feminist, the next stage of what Ellenson declared over a decade ago: "[I] identify as a Jewish feminist and feel that full enfranchisement of women in the public life of our people was a natural and just way for our tradition to evolve."[30]

Zionism and Peoplehood

Ellenson wrote extensively about Reform Zionism. Here, he integrates covenant theology with the responsibilities and blessings of the Jewish state:

> For liberal Jews like myself, schooled on the theological writings of [Rabbi] Eugene Borowitz...there is another approach to authentic religious Zionism that bridges the divide between the absolute universalism of Classical Reform Judaism and unrestrained messianic religious Zionism...Judaism, as Borowitz points out, holds that there is a reciprocal relationship that obtains between God and human beings in general and between God and the Jewish people. It is a covenantal partnership that calls upon Jews and all to realize that revelation is not static. God addresses humankind at all times, and it is surely the task of the people Israel to hear and respond.[31]

Here, I want to connect Zionism to peoplehood. As Durkheim offers, "whatever affects the part also affects the whole; every influence exerted on an individual is transmitted to his neighbors, to his relatives, to everyone with whom he is connected in any way."[32] Taken with Borowitz's emphasis on a covenant made with the Jews as a collective, we can understand our relationship to the Jewish people—the ones we disagree with, and the ones who disagree with us—as inherently part of the same covenant that we have with God. What's more, we join this covenant together—not as individuals, and not only collectively with the people we like or agree with. This extends to those of differing opinions in North America, and it extends to Jewish people around the world, including those in Israel. Through the lens of Borowitz and Durkheim, a Judaism without all Jewish people—those in Israel and those around the world—does not make sense. We can disagree with individuals, with denominations, with governments, with policies—but if we are to claim a Jewish identity, history, and community, we opt in to a collective covenant, together, all of us. If we start from that point, then we must stay in conversation with each other, rather than choose only to relate to the Jews with whom we most closely agree, at home or abroad.

Where Do We Go from Here?

With gratitude to Rabbis Ellenson and Borowitz, we can look toward a future that embraces our collective, covenantal Reform Movement and brings us into a more connected world, through youth and adult gathering, through expanded views of feminism, Zionism, and putting theology at the center. When we look to these theological underpinnings of liberal Judaism and integrate them with Durkheim's sociological theory, we can envision and create a Reform Movement for future generations—a Movement that celebrates the many and that comes together, as one. Durkheim says it best, perhaps with echoes of our prophets:

> A day will come when our societies will once again experience times of creative effervescence and new ideas will surge up, new formulas will arise that will serve to guide humanity...[33]

Notes

1. Eugene B. Borowitz, "The Autonomous Jewish Self," *Modern Judaism* (February 1984): 45.
2. David Ellenson, "Autonomy and Norms in Reform Judaism," *CCAR Journal* 46:2 (Spring 1999): 25.
3. Rachel Sabath Beit-Halachmi, "Refining the Covenant," in *A Life of Meaning: Embracing Reform Judaism's Sacred Path*, ed. Dana Evan Kaplan (CCAR Press, 2018), 98–99.
4. Eugene B. Borowitz, *Renewing the Covenant: A Theology for the Postmodern Jew* (Jewish Publication Society, 1991), 55.
5. In our initial conversations about our independent study, David and I discussed incorporating the work and thought of Rabbi Mordecai Kaplan and his understanding of Judaism as a civilization into our study of Borowitz and Durkheim. As we decided then, I believe now that Kaplan's work is beyond the scope of this article, although it provides another promising area of future theological and sociological study.

6. Borowitz, *Renewing the Covenant*, 70.
7. Borowitz, *Renewing the Covenant*, 71.
8. Eugene B. Borowitz, *Choices in Modern Jewish Theology: A Partisan Guide*, 2nd ed. (Behrman House, 1995), 292.
9. "Emile Durkheim: His Life and Work (1858–1917)," excerpt from Robert Alun Jones, *Emile Durkheim: An Introduction to Four Major Works* (Sage Publications, 1986), 12–23, https://durkheim.uchicago.edu/Biography.html.
10. Deborah Dash Moore, "David Emile Durkheim and the Jewish Response to Modernity," *Modern Judaism* (October 1986): 287–88.
11. Jacob Jay Lindenthal, "Some Thoughts Regarding the Influence of Traditional Judaism on the Work of Emile Durkheim," *Tradition* 11.2 (Summer 1970): 41–44.
12. Emile Durkheim, *Elementary Forms of Religious Life*, trans. Carol Cosman (Oxford University Press, 2008), 162–64.
13. "Ideal type," in *Encyclopedia Britannica*, https://www.britannica.com/topic/ideal-type.
14. Durkheim offers a fascinating reflection on religious ceremonies "provoked by a sad event" (*Elementary Forms*, 303) that would provide an opportunity to further integrate covenantal theology, collective effervescence, and Jewish mourning practices.
15. Durkheim, *Elementary Forms*, 322.
16. ibid, ibid.
17. Ellenson, "Autonomy and Norms."
18. Michael A. Meyer, "Reflections on the 'Educated Jew' from the Perspective of Reform Judaism," *CCAR Journal* 46, no. 2 (Spring 1999): 7–20.
19. Borowitz, *Choices*, 307.
20. Ellenson, "Autonomy and Norms," 26.
21. Borowitz, *Renewing*, 224.
22. A war that endures at the time of this writing, and we pray, may all soon know safety and peace.
23. Mimi Kravetz, Sarah Eisenman, and David Manchester, "'The Surge,' 'The Core' and more: What you need to know about the explosion of interest in Jewish life," eJewish Philanthrophy, May 9, 2024, https://ejewishphilanthropy.com/what-you-need-to-know-about-the-surge-of-interest-in-jewish-life.
24. Jonathan Krasner, "Dreaming Dreams and Seeing Visions: NFTS and the Early History of the National Federation of Temple Youth," in *Sisterhood: A Centennial History of Women of Reform Judaism*, ed. Carole B. Balin, Dana Herman, Jonathan D. Sarna and Gary Zola (Hebrew Union College Press, 2013).
25. Durkheim, *Elementary Forms*, 323.

26. "Legacy Jewish Women's Organization Expands Membership, Leadership Eligibility Requirements," https://wrj.org/press-room/legacy-jewish-womens-organization-expands-membership-leadership-eligibility-requirements.
27. "Membership," https://womensrabbinicnetwork.org/join-us.
28. Philissa Cramer, "Reform movement to ordain intermarried rabbis, ending longstanding ban," June 20, 2024, https://www.jta.org/2024/06/20/religion/hebrew-union-college-to-admit-and-ordain-rabbinical-students-in-interfaith-relationships-ending-longstanding-ban.
29. Liz P.G. Hirsch, "What If We Said Yes?" July 12, 2024, https://wrj.org/blog/what-if-we-said-yes.
30. David Ellenson, "My Feminist Foremothers," *The Forward* (May 8 2012), https://forward.com/life/155286/my-feminist-foremothers.
31. David Ellenson, "A Religious Zionism for Our Time," *Reform Judaism* 33.4 (Summer 2005): 50.
32. Durkheim, *Elementary Forms,* 263.
33. Durkheim, *Elementary Forms*, 323; see Zechariah 14:9.

Israeli, Reform, Halachic: Practical Meanings of Rabbi Ellenson's Approach for Israeli Jews

Rabbi Benjamin Minich

The complicated relationship between the State of Israel (and before it was founded, the political Zionist movement) and the American Jewry has never been bright and shiny, but it has become even more of a serious challenge in wake of the events of recent months. There is a long list of fair explanations for that complexity, one of them of course being the difficulty of trying to define American Jewry. Obviously, this great national and religious community cannot be defined solely by its geographical provenance. It is greatness not only because of its size, but because of its qualities as well.

The American Jewish community has succeeded more than once to create a compilation of Judaism (not just religion or culture, but as civilization, called so by Rabbi Mordecai Kaplan) and American thought. Naturally, the progressive philosophy of Reform Judaism was more suitable for such processes than the traditionalist Orthodoxy. It brought to the new shores its readiness to share the ancient tradition with modern reality.

From its beginning in nineteenth-century Germany, Reform Judaism considered academic excellence as a given for a rabbi. This started decades before Zionism and modern forms of liberalism emerged, due to emancipation and equal rights granted to Jews in Western Europe. Despite many changes since then, rabbi as a scholar is still an intellectual model for Reform Jews.

RABBI BENJAMIN MINICH (J '19) is Rabbi of Kehilat Daniel in Jaffa and a clergy member at Daniel Centers for Progressive Judaism in Tel Aviv-Jaffa. He is a researcher of modern Jewish philosophy and political theology, married to Elena Minich, and father of three.

Rabbi David Ellenson *z"l* was an exemplar of this aspiration. The son of American modern Orthodox Jewish parents, he achieved the classical Reform Jewish equilibrium of being a true *talmid chacham*, both an outstanding academic scholar and also an openhearted rabbi and teacher. He succeeded in showing his rabbinical students, during their studies and after ordination, the true meaning of the word *moreh*—"teacher"—on their ordination certificates. His approach not only taught Judaism, but also renewed old ideas, making them relevant and helpful for our own day. His ideas were never just theoretical, but ready for use outside the *beit midrash*, in daily rabbinic practice.

American and Israeli: The Practical Meaning of Living in the Jewish State

On the sky on American Reform Zionist leaders, the star of Ellenson was especially shining. His starting point, as always, was to get away from a monistic approach—whether exclusive or universal—towards a multidimensional point of view. Creating syntheses of different approaches was his Torah. Ellenson considered himself as Israeli even without living his everyday life in Israel, giving credit for that to a year he spent at Kibbutz Mishmar HaEmek. He compiled his *yisraeliyut* with "Reform commitment to morality and ethics," demanding the State of Israel to be "the ultimate testing ground for the truth of Jewish teachings and values."[1]

Ellenson recognized the uniqueness of Jewish sovereignty in the State of Israel but did not see it as separate from the history of the people of Israel. For the first time after almost two thousand years of communal self-governance, Jewish civilization stepped up for national self-governance.

Connection to Israeli society through sharing ideas is evident in many ways in Ellenson's work. In his research of contemporary halachic literature, he studied the responsa of Israeli Chief Rabbis Herzog, Unterman, and Goren deeply across a broad range of issues. One such issue was the connection between living in Israel and adjustments to the process of *giyur*, conversion to Judaism.

Rabbi Isaac Herzog, who succeeded Rabbi Abraham Isaac Kook in 1936 as the second Ashkenazic Chief Rabbi of the Land of Israel, advised "special consideration" for the *giyur* process of non-Jewish women who "saved their husbands from death during the Holocaust."[2] This was his way of reinterpreting the idea of *l'shem shamayim*, "for the sake of heaven." Rabbi Herzog's successor, Chief Rabbi Isser Yehuda Unterman, evaluated the possibility of a convert in Israel later turning to idolatry, concluding that this was highly improbable. The next Chief Rabbi, Shlomo Goren (who also served as the first Chief Rabbi of the IDF), "re-converted" a member of secular kibbutz who had previously converted with Rabbi Moshe Zemer, one of the founders of MARAM (the Reform Rabbinical Council in Israel), without imposing significant difficulties on her process. It thus seems that the fact of living in Israel was recognized more than once in their halachic responsa as an important consideration for the conversion process—and this corresponded very much with Ellenson's own set of beliefs. The reality of Jewish majority and sovereignty in the State of Israel challenged Jewish rituals to adjust first. The same would also be correct for Jewish modern culture and ways of life (to which point I will return below).

Rabbi Ellenson also studied the halachic philosophy of former Shas Knesset member Rabbi Haim Amsalem, who built on the work of Chief Israeli Sephardic rabbi Ben Zion Meir Hai Uzziel's concept of *zera yisrael* ("seed of Israel") regarding descendants of Jews not recognized as Jews by traditional halachah (for example, those of patrilineal descent). Ellenson engaged with Amsalem's two books, *Zera Yisrael* and *Mekor Yisrael*, which present as moderate alternative to radical ultra-Orthodox rabbis—have at times cast aspersions on **all** modern-day conversions. The current Chief Rabbinate of Israel has departed from the path of the previously mentioned three chief rabbis, and Amsalem's approach provides a counterpart to its extremism. Amsalem states that his work serves "the best interests of the Jewish people"[3]—which resonates so much with Ellenson's approach. It is not merely a simplified use of Maimonides' *p'sak*, which recognizes any conversion post-factum if all the technical rituals (i.e., circumcision and ritual immersion) have been fulfilled; it reflects a deep concern for the future of the Jewish people.

Ellenson's interest in issues of halachah in the State of Israel went beyond the specific issue of conversion. A broad vision of halachic tradition, taking it many steps toward becoming the tradition of a sovereign nation, can also be found in his reading of a responsum by Rabbi Haim David HaLevi regarding the application of the Talmudic rule "if one comes forth to slay you, forestall by slaying them"[4] not just to private interpersonal law but more broadly to Israeli public policy. He uses his genuine understanding of "a community's interests," nevertheless confirming the rule is applicable only to "actual cases of self-defense."[5]

Ellenson's scholarly approach principle of synthesizing different (sometimes contradictory) values aimed to broaden the horizons of Israeli scholars, to make practical synthesis possible in real-life situations.

Ellenson's Decade-Long Presidency from the Israeli Reform Perspective

Rabbi Ellenson was a profound Zionist, and this was not an empty slogan for him. In 2014, at the end of his presidency of HUC-JIR, he published a draft manifest titled "Reform Zionism Today: A Consideration of First Principles."[6] In his usual manner, Ellenson called to synthesize "both national and religious foundations" to create a new "meaningful sense" and to fulfill the Reform Jewish mission of living in the modern world enriched by tradition. He saw the State of Israel as a "testing ground for the truth of Jewish teachings and values,"[7] with the help of the ancient tradition of pursuing justice united with Reform commitment to morality and ethics. Reform Zionism, as he envisioned it, would represent an "interplay" between particularism and universalism. He declared: "The monism of universalism must be rejected!"[8]

While serving as president of HUC-JIR, Ellenson's attention was necessarily divided between the US campuses and the Israeli campus in Jerusalem—and nobody could complain that they lacked his attention or support. During the fourteen years of Ellenson's presidency, the number of Reform rabbis ordained in Israel doubled and the number of ordained women equalled the number of ordained men. This fact was the practical consequence of the ideas found in Rabbi Ellenson's writings. He wanted to expand and strengthen opportunities for creating change in Israeli society, which sorely needed quality rabbinical training, in which the College-Institute was (and still is) outstanding. However, Reform rabbis, largely outnumbered by the Orthodox colleagues, have been precluded from serving in all the places they would like, and the challenge of numbers still pertains.

It was especially important for Ellenson to create a chain of development of the Israeli Reform tradition, the Israeli liberal halachah. That is why he researched the work of Rabbi Moshe Zemer, one of the founders of the Israeli Reform Rabbinic Council (MARAM) and a founder of Kehilat Kedem (today Beit Daniel) in Tel Aviv. Ellenson saw Zemer's work as an outgrowth of the first Reform rabbis of the Temple in Hamburg in the nineteenth century. Ellenson agreed with Jacob Petuchowski,[9] who had raised the attention of researchers and scholars to the fact that it had been especially important for the earliest Reformers to defend themselves to their Orthodox challengers using the language of halachah. Although today the Reform Judaism is considered "non-halachic," I prefer the use the term "post-halachic"—since we cannot say there is no religious legislation at all in Reform Judaism, even if our perspective is different from a more traditional halachic perspective.

Analyzing his book *Halachah Sh'fuyah*,[10] Ellenson agrees with Zemer's critical explanation of modern Orthodox rabbis choosing to make the path of Jewish law more and more narrow. This approach is wrong, according to both Zemer and to Ellenson. They see the Jewish tradition as a treasure, each part of which can be useful. Using Israeli Orthodox halachic sources, they tried to create the common language of Israeli Judaism. Ellenson has built on Zemer's work and enriched the conversation with important ideas of gender, equal rights, and historical perspective, all of which are so important for Reform Jewish scholarship. Together the compilation created a brand-new point of view on halachah from multiple perspectives—of Reform Zionism and of Jewish national sovereignty—all mindful of advancing the conversation "for the sake of heaven."

Conclusion

Rabbi David Ellenson can be counted as a genuine representative of the special group of *g'dolei ha'dor*, the leaders of the generation. He could not stand aside while the biggest miracle of modern Jewish history—a sovereign state—was taking its first baby steps, in a need of support from anyone able to help. And help he did, as well as he could, and his heart always had a warm corner for Israel.

Unfortunately, Ellenson passed away before the work was finished. But as we learn in Pirkei Avot: *lo alecha ha-m'lakhah ligmor*, "the work is not yours to finish but you are not permitted to leave it aside." Recently, a memorial volume was published for Rabbi Moshe Zemer's tenth yahrzeit, entitled *L'shimkha Na-eh L'zamer*.[11] It reflects on the decades of his work, which is still not finished. The first year without David can and must be the time when we think how we continue David's important mission—the one that was characterized with a deep love, embrace of multiple perspectives, and real scholarship.

A satiric joke says that the best way to ruin a fantasy is to fulfill it, which is the reason that the most Zionist Jews do not live in Israel. Rabbi Ellenson taught us an appropriate way to live outside of Israel keeping it alive and real in our hearts, thoughts, and deeds.

Notes

1. David Ellenson, "Reform Zionism Today: A Consideration of First Principles" (2014) from Gil Troy, ed., *The Zionist Ideas* (Jewish Publication Society, 2018), p. 437.
2. David Ellenson, "National Sovereignty, Jewish Identity, and the "Sake of Heaven," chapter 14 from *Jewish Meaning in a World of Choice: Studies in Tradition and Modernity* (Jewish Publication Society, 2014), 190.
3. David Ellenson, "The Rock from Which They Were Cleft," chapter 16 from *Jewish Meaning in a World of Choice*, 215.
4. Babylonian Talmud, *Sanhedrin* 72a.
5. David Ellenson, "The Talmudic Principle, 'If One Comes Forth to Slay You, Forestall by Slaying Him,' in Israeli Public Policy," chapter 15 from *Jewish Meaning in a World of Choice*, 210.
6. David Ellenson, "Reform Zionism Today: A Consideration of First Principles" (2014) from Gil Troy, ed., *The Zionist Ideas* (Jewish Publication Society, 2018), 436–38.
7. Ellenson, "Reform Zionism Today: A Consideration of First Principles," 437.
8. Ellenson, "Reform Zionism Today: A Consideration of First Principles," 438.
9. Jakob J. Petuchowski, *Prayerbook Reform in Europe: The Liturgy of European Liberal and Reform Judaism* (New York: World Union for Progressive Judaism, 1968).
10. Literally "a sober halachah"; published in English as *Evolving Halakhah: A Progressive Approach to Traditional Jewish Law* (Jewish Lights Publishing, 2003).
11. Kineret Zmora Publications, 2022.

Keeping His Dream Alive: The Loving Legacy of David Ellenson

Rabbi Robert N. Levine, DD

We are still trying to come to terms with all we have lost in the wake of David Ellenson's sudden death on the eve of Chanukah. The entire Jewish world is already missing his brilliant, prodigious, academic output. David was arguably this generation's finest Jewish scholar. His ability to imbue love of text and heritage was unparalleled.

Too many of us already also miss his friendship and willingness to do anything just because you asked. Speaking personally, I lost my best friend of over fifty years and will confess that I still listen to his sonorous voice on my phone with his signature opening, "Oh hi, Robert." Quite clearly, we also lost his incredible leadership and ability to inspire a new generation of clergy and teachers to create and sustain Jewish communities everywhere.

Equally difficult is our quest to understand all we have gained through Rabbi Ellenson's immense legacy. I will not try to tackle this entire task in this short essay, but will focus on one academic and personal dream I believe my friend harbored for most of his life, one that he hoped his many students and disciples would learn from and emulate.

Rabbi Ellenson spoke and wrote often about the seismic changes modernity brought to the entire spectrum of the Jewish community. No longer were Jews expected to owe allegiance to communal norms and standards. No longer did rabbinic authorities have the power to judge and sanction the actions of any individual.

What David well understood is that the vast majority of Jews, irrespective of how traditional or liberal, were dealing with the exact

---

RABBI ROBERT N. LEVINE, DD (NY '77) is Rabbi Emeritus at Congregation Rodeph Sholom in New York, New York.

same sociological conditions and challenges. In his own words: "I feel that virtually all Jews in the modern situation stand at different points along the same continuum and that the overwhelming majority of them—of all denominations and viewpoints—have responded positively and in a common vein to the creative possibilities inherent in a world where Jews are able to affirm both their attachment to western culture and their identity as Jews."[1]

Most fascinating to him was how Orthodox Jews could navigate the complex path between a tradition many believed to be fixed, immutable truth and the everchanging contemporary world. This quest would become the prime focus of his brilliant academic career.

As a young man, David realized how tricky his own journey would be from his small Orthodox shul in Newport News, Virginia to the campuses of William and Mary and the University of Virginia, to the Israel he cherished, back to the coasts of the United States. How, he wondered, would his autobiography affect his Jewish decision-making and relationship choices? As he wrote, "For me, the study of Judaism had become and remains a religious quest, an attempt at self-knowledge and discovery."[2]

That quest found an excellent mentor in his doctoral thesis subject, Rabbi Esriel Hildesheimer, who was a product of the yeshivah world and was also secularly trained at the University of Berlin. Not surprisingly, when he opened his own yeshivah in Berlin, known as the *Rabbinerseminar*, his was the only Orthodox institution that required a prior and significant secular education and expected that education to continue on the university level simultaneously with classical Jewish study. Perhaps even more important was his embrace of *Wissenschaft des Judentums*, which championed the evolution of the Jewish tradition over the course of history. This approach specifically rejected the view that the Jewish system of jurisprudence is unchanging and impervious to time and setting. Contemporary sensibilities and individual discretion thus had a place in the halachic system.

A wonderful example of the use of discretion even while pledging fealty to the halachic system is a responsum Professor Ellenson introduced in *Judaism* magazine in the fall of 1996.[3] Since Jewish institutions could no longer tax their members and enforce penalties for non-compliance, as they once had been able to as part of a medieval Jewish community, they had to resort to modern fundraising methods to meet budgetary needs. Rabbi Elesar Ottensosser (1798–1878) asked Rabbi Hildesheimer if it violated Jewish law to publish the names of donors and the amounts they pledged. Ottensosser clearly was opposed to this practice and quoted Talmudic sources seeking to prove that Jewish law only countenanced anonymous donations, such as: "It is small wonder that our Sages concluded that the secret giver of alms was greater than Moses" (*Bava Batra* 9a); he also cited a number of codes he interpreted as demanding that charitable monies be donated with no public fanfare.

Rabbi Ellenson was clearly fascinated that while Hildesheimer was respectful of the sources Ottensosser marshaled, he countered with decidedly modern sensibilities. Publishing names of donors and the amounts they gave produced impressive results and should not be forbidden, Hildesheimer argued. Moreover, Hildesheimer pointed to our ancestors' endorsement of public bidding for Torah honors. Halachic sources do not impose upon moderns a single set of irrefutable actions. Interpretation of the law is built into the halachic system, as is discretion, argued Hildesheimer. His reply in this responsum asserted that Jewish tradition could endorse the publication of donor names and the amounts they pledged in service of a worthy cause.

Ellenson saw Hildesheimer's decision as a wonderful illustration of how to navigate the tension between tradition and modernity: be deeply respectful of legal sources, never contradict positions that offer no nuance, and bring personal judgment to bear wherever possible to serve the needs of the community in the new world where communal norms could no longer dictate individual actions. Hildesheimer understood the financial pressures modern institutions faced and did all he could to address those worries in a way that ensured their viability and survival.

Clearly, Ellenson was drawn to Orthodox rabbinic authorities who could weigh modern sensibilities and halachic precedence at the same time. There could be no doubt, however, that David was searching for yet another crucial quality in picking his research subjects: humanity. Did these titans of Jewish leadership also possess compassion for the people who would be affected by their legal rulings?

As I had the privilege of co-authoring two articles with Professor Ellenson for the *Journal of Reform Judaism*, I can attest to this abiding concern personally. In "Jewish Tradition, Contemporary Sensibilities, and Halachah: A Responsum by Rabbi David Tzvi Hoffman,"[4] we turned to an important question posed to this leading Orthodox rabbinical authority in Berlin at the turn of the twentieth century: Did a twelve-year-old boy born to a non-Jewish mother and Jewish father, who had been circumcised by a mohel when he was eight days old, have to undergo a *hatafat dam* before being permitted to convert? Hoffman decided that it was unnecessary, citing reasons based on Jewish legal sources, but also added the following: "If there is even a slight fear that the drawing of a drop of blood will injure the lad, *hatafat dam b'rit* need not be performed." Hoffman was as sensitive to the boy's wellbeing as a person, just as he was to proper interpretation of halachic sources.

In the second article we published together, "Rabbi Z. H. Kalischer and a Halachic Approach to Conversion,"[5] we analyzed a responsum by Rabbi Kalischer (1795–1874), one of the leading halachic authorities of nineteenth-century Eastern and Central Europe, issued in reaction to a halachic decision authored by Rabbi Bernard Illowy of New Orleans in 1864. Illowy had ruled that sons born to Jewish fathers and gentile mothers could not be circumcised by a mohel, lest the children be mistakenly identified as Jews. Kalischer responded in a letter to Rabbi Hildesheimer that such children should be circumcised, so that they would have a much easier path to conversion if they chose to do so later in life. Kalischer rather stunningly called the child of a Jewish father and non-Jewish mother *zera kodesh* (holy seed). Dr. Ellenson was quite moved by this attribution. Not only did Kalischer show an understanding for the struggles of modern couples in their personal relationships, but he also showed true feelings for the young boy in this situation. Kalischer's compassion shines through in his legal writing, and Ellenson could shed more than one characteristic tear in the face of this rabbi's humanity.

The last eminent rabbi I will bring forth to illustrate the academic choices Ellenson chose to make is the twentieth-century Orthodox leader Eliezer Berkovitz (1908–1992). This preeminent Jewish thinker and theologian showed true courage in devoting much of his halachic writing and communal involvement to an ultimately unsuccessful effort to establish a *beit din* that would bring together all movements of Judaism. He found no legal sources that forbid his position and he championed a principle that clearly is close to the heart of David Ellenson:

> One of the most serious problems of our day is the widespread ideological fragmentation within the Jewish people. The religious ideologies are numerous. Yet, Judaism in its very essence is not sectarian but the way of life of a people. Indeed, it can be fully realized only by a people. To work for Jewish unity in the spirit of *Ahavat Yisrael*, love of every Jew, in the interest of *K'lal Yisrael*, the reality of the totality of the Jewish people, is an urgent demand of Torah-realization.[6]

So how did Rabbi Ellenson, raised as an Orthodox Jew, who spent much of his academic career immersed in such Orthodox halachic sources and rabbinic authorities, many of whom he held in great esteem, become a Reform Jew, rabbi, and president of HUC-JIR?

His own clearest answer was given in an HUC-JIR podcast. In the interview, Ellenson asserted: "Reform Judaism comports more accurately to authenticity and truth that any of the other movements for me…I have great respect for the halachic tradition…but the way I have come to look at it, from my Reform perspective, is that I see it as an ongoing narrative where each generation of Jews writes a different story in which they attempt to capture what it is they feel God commands in their age."[7] In a CCAR ravblog post, Ellenson confirms this line of thinking: "As a Jew who is commanded every day to remember my bondage and my exodus from Egypt…I cannot forget the books of my Jewish past, nor do I want to. My years as president of the College-Institute had been an extension of my entire life and all my values. I have aspired as a Jew born in America and connected deeply both to Israel and the larger world to place myself and my students in a chain of Jewish tradition that is humane and inclusive."[8]

This brilliant scholar, who had the biggest heart most of us ever knew, was able to choose among the values that have evolved over the centuries, especially those that have emphasized the inclusion of all people who are in search of or in love with Jewish identity. As a Reform Jew, he could respond to the culture and history he had experienced growing up in the South. As Ellenson reflected, "The inequities and evils I witnessed as a child and as a teenager in matters of race and gender and the sense of being an outsider as a

Jew to the gentile culture in which I was raised all left a permanent mark on me."[9]

His experiences motivated his determination to be humane and inclusive as a Jew and a rabbi. They also deeply affected his approach to his students, as both a professor and the president of HUC-JIR. Ellenson firmly believed that the Reform Movement was the best Movement for personal growth, as its adherents were not locked into immutable halachic parameters. Professor Jonathan Sarna quoted Ellenson as saying, "Certainty has never been mine and conflicting emotions and a sense of distance from my surroundings has always marked me," in perhaps the most self-revealing sentence that he ever wrote.[10] The ability to wrestle with various and competing truths is a recipe for personal transformation, but according to Sarna it was also the key both to his denominational eclecticism and to his friendships across the Jewish spectrum (and beyond): "In our charged and polarized time, when so many profess absolute certainties and associate only with men and women of their own kind, David Ellenson found truth and goodness in people of many kinds and they loved him back in return."[11]

In an article entitled "American Jewish Denominationalism: Yesterday, Today, and Tomorrow," Ellenson illustrated how eclectic he was, drawing on his own family life:

> In approaching the topic of Jewish religious denominationalism today, I will begin with an autobiographical "confession." I was raised in an Orthodox synagogue, sent all my children to either Solomon Schechter schools or Camp Ramah, was a member of a Conservative as well as a Reform congregation for another twenty years of my life, am an Associate Member of the Reconstructionist Rabbinical Association, as well as an alumnus of the rabbinical school of the Hebrew Union College-Jewish Institute of Religion, and currently serve as President of the premier educational institution of the Reform movement.[12]

The way he lived his Jewish life had a significant impact on his approach to his students and mentees. Ellenson clearly had a multilayered vision for creating Jewish leaders: they must have a deep knowledge of values-based Jewish tradition, a lifetime of Jewish experiences, and a creative ability to interpret and shape the past so that present and future Jewish communities will be compelling to the changing mores of every generation.

But Ellenson expected more…which brings me to David's dream. Let me share two final quotes, which together will articulate what I believe David truly yearned for. The first is from an interview with the Los Angeles-based *Jewish Journal*. Journalist Julie Gruenbaum Fax asked the question: "With your academic work, your personal worship, and your rabbinic life, you seem to have a foot in every denomination of Judaism. Will you try to use that in some way to bridge the gaps between the movements of Judaism?" David responded as follows:

> I quite actively correspond with a number of Orthodox, Conservative, Reconstructionist, and Reform colleagues…All the movements and all the leaders in their own way are attempting to chart a course for Judaism that they feel is true to authentic Judaism, that is, a response that views the tradition in light of the needs of the modern moment. Even if we disagree on what that should be, we can at least emphasize those approaches that unite us and acknowledge the sincerity and good will that drive concerned persons in each of the movements of the Jewish world.[13]

In a second article, David's close colleague and friend, Rabbi Shirley Idelson observed:

> For all his deep learning, it was David's extraordinary *ahavat yisrael*—the deep love of the Jewish people he exuded at all times and which undergirded his many ideas—that truly powered his leadership. His pluralism stemmed from his love of *klal yisrael*, his Zionism rested on his love of the land and people of Israel. His love for Torah and learning fueled his teaching. He saw feminism and LGBTQ rights as logical extension of his love for justice and equality.
>
> Famous for crying openly in public settings, David taught me the power and effectiveness of unabashedly grounding one's thoughts and deeds in love. In the workplace as well as the broader world, he showed love and respect kind almost always engendered love and respect in return.[14]

David desperately wanted Jews from all denominations to resist the temptation to stay in their own silos, to remain self-satisfied and convinced that they and only they had the Truth, the right way to do Jewish. He wanted us to know each other and feel mutual respect, despite our different approaches to Jewish law and living.

No one modeled this love of all Jews more movingly and completely than did David Ellenson. There could not be a better illustration of this fact than what David Ellenson did on the very last day of his life. He went to an Orthodox *shul*, The Jewish Center, in New York City. Having written an article in a *festschrift* celebrating the leadership of the illustrious former rabbi of the congregation, he was there to pay tribute to his colleague and he was greeted as a true *chaver*.

This is what Jewish unity and pluralism meant to David Ellenson. There is no question in my mind that he hoped others would see and emulate his spectacular example.

Perhaps it is true that for Ellenson "certainty has never been mine," but on this point he was quite certain: the well-being of the Jewish community, now and in the future, depends on *ahavat yisrael*, an abiding love of ALL Jews.

Notes

1. David Ellenson, *After Emancipation: Jewish Religious Responses to Modernity* (Hebrew Union College Press, 2004), 19–20.
2. Ellenson, *After Emancipation*, 18.
3. David Ellenson, "Tzedakah and Fundraising: A 19th Century Response," *Judaism: A Quarterly Journal of Jewish Life and Thought* 45.4 (Fall 1996).
4. Robert N. Levine and David H. Ellenson, "Jewish Tradition, Contemporary Sensibilities, and Halachah: A Responsum by Rabbi David Tzvi Hoffman," in *Journal of Reform Judaism* (Winter 1987): 49–56.
5. Robert Levine and David Ellenson, "Rabbi Z.H. Kalischer and A Halachic Approach to Conversion," in *Journal of Reform Judaism* (Summer 1981): 50–57.
6. Eliezer Berkovits, *Not in Heaven: The Nature and Function of Jewish Law* (Ktav, 1983), 106–7.
7. Joshua Holo, "What Makes Me A Reform Jew," *College Commons Bully Pulpit Podcast*, Hebrew Union College-Jewish Institute of Religion (February 15, 2018).
8. David Ellenson (December 13, 2023), https://ravblog.ccarnet.org/2023/12/rabbi-david-ellenson-at-the-turning-reflections-on-my-life-2014/.
9. David Ellenson, https://ravblog.ccarnet.org/2023/12/rabbi-david-ellenson-at-the-turning-reflections-on-my-life-2014/.
10. Jonathan D. Sarna, "Certainty Has Never Been Mine: The Denominational Eclecticism of David Ellenson," January 7, 2024, https://

thelehrhaus.com/timely-thoughts/certainty-has-never-been-mine-the-denominational-eclecticism-of-david-ellenson/.
11. Sarna, "Certainty Has Never Been Mine."
12. David Ellenson, "American Jewish Denominationalism: Yesterday, Today and Tomorrow," in *The Reconstructionist* 7.2 (Spring 2007): 5.
13. Julie Gruenbaum Fax, "Judaism as Transformation," *Jewish Journal* (June 14, 2001).
14. Shirley Idelson, "Lessons in Leadership from Rabbi David Ellenson, z"l," *eJewishPhilanthropy.com*, December 15, 2023.

Rabbi Dr. David Ellenson, z"l: A Kind Visionary and a Visionary of Kindness

Rabbi Asher Lopatin

Around the world, Jews are still grieving at the loss of a great Jewish leader and thinker, Rabbi David Ellenson, z"l. I was blessed to spend time with Rabbi Ellenson as part of various cohorts I joined, from Wexner to Hartman to just being friends with a lot of Reform rabbis. Eventually, when my career turned toward being president of an Orthodox rabbinical school, Yeshivat Chovevei Torah, I was particularly blessed to be a colleague of his. Of course, YCT was much smaller than Hebrew Union College–Jewish Institute of Religion (which Rabbi Ellenson would always call "the College-Institute"), and of course Rabbi Ellenson never treated me like anyone less than a president of a rabbinical school. I am so glad that he was one of our panelists, representing the Reform Movement, at my installation in 2013, along with my dear friend Rabbi Elka Abrahamson.

I treasure one gesture of kindness that is unique and that will provide an insight into the depth, breadth, and height of his imagination and goodness. When I came to YCT, David was so encouraging! I had a vision of bringing Orthodox, Conservative, and Reform seminaries into one building so we could all share learning space, cross fertilize, and learn from each other's similarities and differences. It was certainly ambitious—and perhaps a crackpot idea.

I did not get much traction for it from anyone. Except David. David not only encouraged the idea, but when I suggested that YCT move into the HUC campus in New York, he actually sent out

---

RABBI ASHER LOPATIN is the rabbi of Kehillat Etz Chayim, an Orthodox synagogue in Oak Park, Michigan, and is the Director of Community Relations at the Jewish Federation of Greater Ann Arbor.

a memo to the senior staff in charge of the building and the organization to see if such a move would be feasible on a logistical level. I saw the carbon copy! I was so touched by his kindness. Whether David really took me seriously or just wanted me to feel good—I guess I will never know. But I was so moved and touched by this gesture—one case where a 'cc' can be the sweetest, most supportive thing in the world!

In the end, nothing came of this—speak to folks on how much effort it took to move a small department of the Reform Movement onto the campus, let alone an Orthodox rabbinical school—but this is a memory that I cherish beyond the Torah, the passion, the love and the joy of Rabbi Ellenson. Maybe in heaven, Rabbi Ellenson, in addition to studying with his beloved Rabbi Hildesheimer of Germany, is also studying with Reform rosh yeshivas of the past along with the great heads of the Orthodox yeshivot and the great Conservative thinkers of years past. I wouldn't be surprised if in heaven, some way of everyone learning together was worked out logistically, theologically, and politically. And maybe one day that will happen. But what is real is the kind vision of a great man, a kindness that leaves an unending impression on me, and will leave an infinite legacy for our world.

May Rabbi Dr. David Ellenson's memory be a blessing for all of us.

Senior Sermon: *Parashat Tzav*

Hannah Ellenson

This senior sermon was delivered by Hannah Ellenson at Hebrew Union College–Jewish Institute of Religion's New York campus on March 28, 2024.

Every Friday night, for as long as I can remember, this has been my family's tradition: we gather around the dining room table that belonged to my paternal grandparents. After my mom lights the Shabbat candles and we kiss each other and everyone sings *Shalom Aleichem*—which until recently—was always started by my dad, we all hold hands, which maybe sounds a little hokey, but usually was a nice moment for us kids to smile at each other because we knew what was coming.

When we were quiet, my parents would bless us, both their children—those related by blood and by love, as my mom likes to say—and those that aren't considered children anymore. They began with *Yesimeich Elohim* and concluded with the words everyone in this room knows well. My parents would recite the Hebrew, followed by,

"May God bless you and keep you.
May God's face shine upon you and be gracious unto you.
May God's face always be lifted up to you
And may you know peace."

Of course, not everyone in this room has had this experience. Perhaps your family didn't have Shabbat dinners. Or maybe your family did, but your relationship with your parents was or is complicated. And you did not feel blessed at their table.

HANNAH ELLENSON is a rabbinical student at Hebrew Union College–Jewish Institute of Religion in New York. She was previously Youth Director at Congregation Rodeph Shalom in New York City and Associate Director at the New Israel Fund.

I'm not sure Aaron's sons did, either. In the *parashah* this week, God gave instructions for Aaron and his sons as part of their ordination as priests:

וּמִפֶּתַח אֹהֶל מוֹעֵד לֹא תֵצְאוּ שִׁבְעַת יָמִים עַד יוֹם מְלֹאת יְמֵי מִלֻּאֵיכֶם כִּי שִׁבְעַת יָמִים יְמַלֵּא אֶת יֶדְכֶם.

"You shall not leave the Tent of Meeting for seven days until the day that your period of ordination is completed for your ordination will require seven days." (Leviticus 8:33)

If they were there for a full week, they must have had Shabbat. Did they sit at a Shabbat table together? Did Aaron's eyes twinkle with pride? Did he bless his kids the way my parents blessed us? I really hope so. But we have no indication that that's what happened.

Here is what we do know: when they emerged from the *Ohel Mo-eid*, which we'll read next week, Aaron and his sons offer four sacrifices: for purification, a burnt offering, well-being, and a meal offering. What is the very next thing Aaron does? וַיִּשָּׂא אַהֲרֹן אֶת יָדָיו אֶל הָעָם וַיְבָרְכֵם "Aaron spontaneously raises his hands over the people and blesses them." (Leviticus 9:22)

What blessing does he recite? No text is provided. We aren't told until much later in *Parashat Naso*, when Aaron is commanded to bless *B'nei Yisrael*. God instructs Moses to tell Aaron and his sons:

כֹּה תְבָרְכוּ אֶת־בְּנֵי יִשְׂרָאֵל אָמוֹר לָהֶם:

"This is how you shall bless the people of Israel:"

יְבָרֶכְךָ יְהוָה וְיִשְׁמְרֶךָ:
יָאֵר יְהוָה פָּנָיו אֵלֶיךָ וִיחֻנֶּךָּ:
יִשָּׂא יְהוָה פָּנָיו אֵלֶיךָ וְיָשֵׂם לְךָ שָׁלוֹם: (Numbers 6:23–26)

While our sages appreciate knowing the words of the blessing, the verse that precedes it, the one with the instruction, has one word that has engendered debate. What does *ko tivarchu* mean? What does it mean to offer the blessing just like "this?" The rabbis aren't sure.

In *Bamidbar Rabbah*, they offer a number of suggestions: Does it mean the blessing needs to be offered in *lashon hakodesh*, the holy language? Must the priests be standing? Must their hands be raised *b'nisuot kapayim*? Can it be used to bless only *Yisrael* or is it for everyone? Should the priest say the blessing looking into the faces of the people?

The rabbis *finally* agree on what *ko tivarchu* means: The blessing must be offered *b'ahavah*—with love: כֹּה תְבָרְכוּ אֶת־בְּנֵי יִשְׂרָאֵל "With love, bless the people Israel." (*Bamidbar Rabbah* 11:4)

A tradition from the Zohar, taught to me by Rabbi Larry Hoffman, goes even further:

כָּל כֹּהֵן דְּהוּא לָא רָחִים לְעַמָּא,

"A priest who does not love his people,

לָא יִפְרוֹס יְדוֹי לְבָרְכָא לְעַמָּא.

cannot perform the blessing."

Alright, that's not such a shock given the rabbis' understanding of *ko tivarchu*—but the Zohar also says the blessing cannot be recited:

עַמָּא לָא רַחֲמִין לֵיהּ

"if the people do not love the priest in return."[1] Wow!

In eulogy after eulogy, letter after letter, people spoke of my Abba's love for his people, and also their love for him. Perhaps it should come as no surprise, then, that Rabbi Wendy Zierler found the following in an article by my dad. He wrote: "When I was a boy, no Jewish ceremony had a greater impact upon me than the ritual of *duchanen*, which took place in my family's synagogue, as in all traditional synagogues in the Diaspora on the three pilgrimage festivals. As the priests would bless the people, a sense of *k'dushah*, of holiness and mystery, would pervade the room. I recall that ceremony at this moment because the priests, immediately prior to their recitation of the priestly benediction, would recite the words, 'Blessed are You, O Lord our God, Ruler of the Universe, who has sanctified us with the holiness of Aaron and commanded us *levarech et amo Yisra-el be-ahava*—to bless God's people Israel with love.'"[2] Clearly, that *b'racha* resonated with my Abba.

To this day, this is what the kohanim recite before lifting their hands in blessing.

אֲשֶׁר קִדְּשָׁנוּ בִּקְדֻשָּׁתוֹ שֶׁל אַהֲרֹן וְצִוָּנוּ לְבָרֵךְ אֶת עַמּוֹ יִשְׂרָאֵל בְּאַהֲבָה.

There are three commandments to love in the Torah: "love your neighbor as yourself;"[3] "love the stranger as yourself;"[4] and, "you shall love Adonai, your God."[5] These, however, are not preceded by *b'rachot*. Offering the priestly blessing is the only mitzvah preceded by a *b'racha* that demands *ahavah* as an essential component in its fulfillment.

My dad expressed his love openly: he loved colleagues, students, and friends; he loved Torah, the Jewish people, and Israel; and, of course, he especially loved his family. As a parent, as a rabbi, he provided me and so many others with a model for a kind of relationship that infused love into every action and word. So many of his students have recently taught and written about my Abba's love because, yes, my father loved his students.

In a post-Me-Too world, we might shudder at that. Thank goodness our professional codes of ethics are now more-and-more clearly delineating appropriate and inappropriate behavior. We know all too well the dangers of crossing boundaries. We know that love can be dangerous when abused—when people in power don't know how to give or receive love safely.

But should the risk of abuse mean we fear love altogether? *Bamidbar Rabbah* doesn't think so. Authoritative translators of the Zohar don't think so. And neither does Maimonides. In his Judeo-Arabic commentary on the teaching עֲשֵׂה לְךָ רַב, וּקְנֵה לְךָ חָבֵר, listen to how the Hebrew translation describes the third of three ways of being a *chaver*.[6]

חברים — שלושה מינים:
חבר תועלת
חבר נחת
הַמַּעֲלָה ואהוב

The first, *chaver to'elet*, is one of utility or benefit—between business partners or a king and an army. The second is *chaver nachat*—a relationship of pleasure or pride. Spouses in a marriage or someone that provides *bitachon*—security and confidence. The third is *ha'ma'alah ahuv*—the *beloved* that elevates.

הוא שתהיה תאות שניהם וכוונתם למטרה אחת, והיא: הטוב

A relationship of elevation is one in which the desire of both is for one thing: doing good.

וירצה כל אחד להעזר בחברו בהגיע הטוב ההוא לשניהם יחד

A relationship that elevates or uplifts, one where we are pushed farther than we think possible to create good—something bigger and better than each of us can achieve individually.

וזה הוא החבר אשר צוה לקנותו

This is the relationship that we are commanded to acquire.

והוא כחברות הרב לתלמיד והתלמיד לרב

And this is the relationship of a *rav* to a *talmid*, a *talmid* to a *rav*.

Maimonides is acknowledging the love that can exist between teacher and student, between colleagues and study partners, and he also goes further: he is saying this is the kind of connection we should want and pursue.

Hear the yearning for such nurturing intimacy in this metaphor offered by Rabbi Akiva, a teacher, to Rabbi Shimon, one of his students:

בְּנִי, יוֹתֵר מִמַּה שֶׁהָעֵגֶל רוֹצֶה לִינַק, פָּרָה רוֹצָה לְהָנִיק

"My son, more than the calf wants to nurse, the cow wants to give milk."[7]

The love that is described in all these examples is not romantic or sexual attraction, it is not physical affection, it is not simple acclaim or approval, and it is not unconditional acceptance. In fact, Rabbi Yossi bar Hannina taught, כָּל אַהֲבָה שֶׁאֵין עִמָּהּ תּוֹכָחָה אֵינָהּ אַהֲבָה "Any love without accountability is not love."[8]

In her book *All About Love*, writer and activist bell hooks quotes psychiatrist M. Scott Peck: "Love is the will to extend one's self for the purpose of nurturing one's own or another's spiritual growth..."⁹ How would my Abba have understood "spiritual growth?" I think he might have substituted the words "intellectual" and "moral." I can imagine him saying: Love is the will to extend one's self for the purpose of nurturing another's intellectual and moral growth.

I wish everyone could be uplifted by that kind of love.

Undoubtedly, some come here to HUC-JIR—consciously or unconsciously—seeking such love. And some become clergy or teachers with the hope of being loved by their students or congregants. Should we ignore our desire as teachers and students to give and receive such love? I'd like to simply say "no." That being said, our expectations should of course also be appropriate and realistic. We cannot expect to feel loved by *each* of our teachers or students.

עֲשֵׂה לְךָ רַב, וּקְנֵה לְךָ חָבֵר

We are only obliged to find one true *rav*, one true *chaver* or *ahuv*.

As *mamlekhet kohamim*, however, every time we channel *kedushato shel Aharon* and offer his blessing—whether as parents or teachers—may we feel love from those whom we bless, and bless them with our love.

I am grateful to my advisor, Rabbi Margaret Moers Wenig.

Notes

1. Zohar, Vol. III, 147b. Translation by Michael Berg.
2. David Ellenson, *Jewish Meaning in a World of Choice: Studies in Tradition and Modernity* (Jewish Publication Society, 2014), 84.
3. Leviticus 19:18
4. Leviticus 19:34
5. Deuteronomy 6:4
6. This entire text can be found in Maimonides's commentary on *Mishnah Avot* 1:6
7. *Pesachim* 112a— and often quoted by Dr. A. Stanley Dreyfus, as told by Rabbi Margaret Moers Wenig.
8. *Bereshit Rabbah* 54:3
9. M. Scott Peck, *The Road Less Travelled: A New Psychology of Love, Traditional Values, and Spiritual Growth* (Simon and Schuster, 2002).

General Articles
A Contemporary Controversy: Pope Pius and World War II

Rabbi Daniel Polish

Normally the act of canonizing someone, elevating them to the status of sainthood, is a procedural matter within the Catholic Church. Rarely are non-Catholics aware of, or attentive to, the process. By the very nature of the enterprise, it is unlikely that non-Catholics would involve themselves in it. Yet there has been a notable exception to this conventional decorum. In 2009, when Pope Benedict XVI issued a decree recognizing the candidacy for sainthood of one of his predecessors, there was a strong response from the Jewish community. Jewish individuals and organizations expressed outrage at the possibility that Pope Pius XII would be recognized as a saint.

Of course, this disagreement involved a fundamental difference in understanding the meaning of sainthood. For Catholics, sainthood involves the occurrence of miracles verified to have been enacted as a result of prayers for the intercession of the proposed saint. Jews seem to believe that the designation of saint involves the proposed saint's having lived an exemplary life—very much like the Jewish understanding of the role of the tzaddik, a supremely righteous person. And Jews were outspoken in their assertion that Pius XII had not lived an exemplary life. Jewish concerns involved the pontiff's discharge of his official role.

RABBI DANIEL POLISH (C '68) is Rabbi Emeritus of Congregation Shir Chadash of the Hudson Valley. He teaches in the Philosophy and Religion Department of Marist College. He is the co-author (with Rachel Fell McDermott) of the just-published *A Hindu-Jewish Conversation* (Lexington Books). He serves as representative of the CCAR on the executive board of IJCIC (the International Jewish Committee for Interreligious Consultations), the official Jewish interlocutor with the Vatican and other international religious bodies, and served as chair of that body from 2017 until 2019.

On March 2, 1939, Eugenio Maria Giuseppe Giovanni Pacelli was elected pope and took the papal name Pius XII. Prior to becoming pope, Pacelli had served as papal nuncio in Bavaria, from 1917 to 1929. After that posting, he was recalled to Rome and was appointed secretary of state in 1930. As nuncio in Bavaria, he undoubtedly had first-hand exposure to the rise of Nazi power and its attendant brutality. As secretary of state he must surely have had communication about Kristallnacht in November 1938. Yet we find no comment about these events in his public pronouncements; it is as if they occurred far from his area of responsibility or concern. It was his tenure as pope, however, that is at the core of the controversy that still swirls around his legacy.

Pius's pontificate coincided with the Second World War and the murder of six million Jews in the flames of the Shoah. Numerous world leaders were outspoken during the Shoah about what was transpiring. Many religious leaders, including the Catholic bishops of the United States, acquitted themselves honorably, and in some cases bravely, in denouncing the barbarity that was being enacted. Not so the pope. Pius himself was not otherwise given to passivity. He was outspoken in his feelings about communism—he issued encyclicals, gave speeches, and even made radio addresses about its evils. He seems not to have feared repercussions for challenging Stalin. In July 1943, as the allies bombed Rome in anticipation of their final triumph over Italian fascism, Pius dramatically expressed his outrage and his concern for the citizens of Rome by doing something popes rarely do: venturing out of the Vatican and going into the streets of the city. He extended himself to "be with" the people of Rome in the hour of their suffering. He seems not to have feared antagonizing Roosevelt or Churchill. Yet concerning the suffering and murder of multitudes of Jews, there has been great unclarity about his behavior, leading to deep division in assessing his legacy.

During the war Pius issued encyclicals denouncing the Nazi atrocities in Catholic Poland. He was outspoken against what he deemed to be Nazi offenses against the Catholic Church in Germany. He took action on behalf of Jewish converts to Catholicism—asserting that as Catholics, they deserved the concern of the Church. Yet about unbaptized Jews, there is no evidence of Pius taking any action or even speaking out about this moral catastrophe.

Not that there were no direct appeals to him on the subject; we are aware of many. Edith Stein, a Jewish convert to Catholicism who became a nun (and who was herself later beatified—not without a certain amount of controversy) wrote to him, imploring him to act on behalf of the Jews. So did Catholic religious figures in various countries, political leaders and diplomats of various nations, and of course Jewish leaders from all corners of the globe, including the chief rabbi of Palestine. The pleas went unanswered. Did they fall on deaf ears? Or was there some response hidden from public view?

Pius's apparent silence quickly became the subject of controversy. A decade after his death, perhaps as a response to his proposed canonization, his inaction was the subject of the *succes de scandale* "The Deputy: A Christian Tragedy," by the German playwright Rolf Hochhuth, which indicted the cold silence and indifference of the pope. In later years the British journalist John Cornwell excoriated him in a book, whose title encapsulated its assessment of Pius as *Hitler's Pope*. The American scholar David Kertzer returned repeatedly to the subject of Pius's culpability.

In response, other voices rose in Pius's defense. They argued that had the pope spoken up about the murder of Europe's Jews, he would only have exacerbated their plight. Some suggested that his defense of the Jews would have provoked atrocities against other minorities (as if Roma and gays were not already being murdered). It has been suggested that the pope's engagement on behalf of the Jews would have unleashed violence against Catholics in areas of German control. Numerous defenders of the pope have suggested that though he did not speak out publicly about the assault on Europe's Jews, he secretly took measures to assist them, including issuing instructions to various arms of the Church to shelter them. But the most forceful and frequent defense of the Pope was the claim that he simply did not have empirical evidence that the Shoah was taking place: he didn't act against the Shoah because he had no idea that it was happening.

It was in the midst of this protracted period of controversy and disputation, Jewish voices raised their argument against Pius's canonization. It seemed as if there were a confrontation between the "Anguish of Jews" (to use the title of Father Edward Flannery's scorching recounting of the Church's relations with the Jewish people) and the desire of the Catholic hierarchy to defend the reputation of one of their own.

For a long time, Jews and representatives of the Church contended over the actions of Pope Pius XII. Every meeting between representatives of the Jewish organizations and the Church that was held during this period included on its agenda the issues of Pius's canonization and the opening of the archives, as it was clear to all that no dispositive conclusion could be reached without access to the official documents of his pontificate. And those records continued to be sealed in the archives of Pius's papacy, not to be opened until a specified time after its conclusion. No resolution to the controversy seemed possible until access to the archives was obtained, and that access seemed to be continually postponed into the receding future.

Finally, in 1999, the gates of the archives began to be opened. The Vatican Commission on Religious Relations with the Jews established an entity it called the International Catholic-Jewish Historical Commission. Three Catholic scholars and three Jewish scholars would be granted access to the documents and charged with writing a report of their findings. The commission studied a significant amount of archival material and, in October 2000, released its initial findings, "The Vatican and the Holocaust." The findings focused on the questions that could be resolved only once fuller access to the archives would be made available. Its list of questions did not finally resolve the dispute, and the work of the commission thus concluded without even beginning to answer the very questions it had posed. The issue of what the pope knew remained elusive. The uncertainty was so gnawing that in 2009 Pope Benedict XVI promised a meeting of Jewish leaders that he would put the process of canonizing Pius on hold, as his seeming non-activity was subject to contradictory interpretations.

Until 2023. As the archives were finally opened up more fully, new information about Pius's pontificate became increasingly available—and the picture of those years came into fuller relief. In September 2023, two documents came to the public's attention. First, the Pontifical Biblical Institute of Rome disclosed that they had discovered in their own archives a list of the names of all 4,000 Jewish men, women, and children who had been hidden in various monasteries and convents in Italy, and thus saved from death. It has long been known that Jews were, indeed, hidden in Catholic monasteries and convents, but that fact is still worthy of celebration. These acts are a tribute to the greatness that is possible in the human spirit, and those responsible for undertaking these actions have been honored in the garden of the righteous among the nations at Yad Vashem, as testimony to the best that human beings are capable of. Even in *gei tzalmavet*, the valley of the shadow of death, there are human beings—in this case, Catholics—who rose to the heights of moral greatness. Jews and Catholics alike are right to celebrate them, and such heroics can serve as a bridge to reconciliation between the two communities. That said, it is not inconceivable that someone in the hierarchy of the Vatican may have ensured that the list of the Jews rescued by Catholics "happened" to find the light of day just before the second document was published, in order to serve as kind of a pre-emptive inoculation against the disclosure of that document—which was of a very different character.

Shortly after the disclosure of the list of rescued Jews, a second—and, frankly, more consequential—document was made public. An Italian newspaper published an article that disclosed the existence of a letter found in the Vatican archives from December 1942, which significantly changed the trajectory of the controversy about Pope Pius XII. In that letter, a German Jesuit, well connected in the Vatican, sent Pius's secretary specific information about the fact that 6,000 Jews and others were being gassed to death each day in German-conquered Poland. It is, of course, inconceivable that the secretary did not share this information with Pius himself. This document renders impossible the claim that the pope never spoke about the Shoah while it was happening or acted in any way to demonstrate concern for the imperiled Jews of Europe because he simply did not know what the Germans were doing. After the disclosure of this letter, Jews and Catholics must enter a different kind of conversation. What do we—both separately and together—make of the fact that Pius knew? He knew, and yet he did nothing.

"He knew, and yet he did nothing" echoes Eli Wiesel's chilling image in his novel *The Town Beyond the Wall*. Wiesel describes a man—representing every "good German"—who stands at his window and watches impassively as his Jewish neighbors are mercilessly rounded up, "watched and watched…and did nothing." Daniel Goldhagen has described the multitudes who are embodied in this man as "Hitler's willing executioners."[1] Such inaction must be condemned as complicity. And now we must wonder if we ought to say as much about the leader of the Catholic Church.

The list of Jews saved by Catholics stands in stark contrast to the to the shattering reality of Jews abandoned by the most consequential Catholic. At the very least, the juxtaposition of the actions of the many Catholics who resisted evil and the one who did not raises profound questions about aspects of Catholic theology.

All who labor in the vineyard of interfaith relations have been well-schooled about the inappropriateness of members of one tradition venturing an opinion about the theology of another. Indeed, among Jews, the Rav, Joseph Soloveitchik, admonished us not to engage in discussing theology at all during interfaith dialogue, out of the very concern that we would not want some aspect of our faith tradition to be challenged by our interlocutors. And yet, the implications of the situation at hand are so grave and so consequential that it is worth the risk of venturing into this territory.

How can we account for Pius's silence and seeming indifference to Jewish suffering? As Jews, our reflex is to assume and assert that the cause is antisemitism. But the fact is that the pope never displayed any virulent antisemitism. Certainly, his was not the racial antisemitism of the Nazis. Most probably he did harbor some measure of the antisemitism that was so much a part of Catholic teaching—what the Catholic theologian Rosemary Reuther called the "left hand of Christology": the accusation of theodicy. Perhaps on some level, conscious or not, the pope thought of the Jews as agents of deicide, and perhaps nothing more. So, one lesson from reflecting on Pope Pius is the reminder of the consequences of that malign doctrine. Paradoxically, at the same time we can also be heartened by the strides that the Church has made since Nostra Aetate was promulgated in the wake of the tragedy of the Shoah—and in response to its contribution to it. It is also a challenge: the reminder of how much the flame of the Church's new teaching must be tended and guarded—an obligation that falls on Catholics and Jews alike.

Yet it is possible to identify another source of the pope's reticence to rise to the protection of endangered Jews. There is an element of Catholic tradition that is difficult for Jews to comprehend because it has no counterpart in Jewish thought—or, for that matter, any tradition with which I am familiar: the institution of the Church itself is a significant aspect of the Catholic belief system. To be a believing Catholic is to venerate the Church. Pious Catholics see the Church as flawless and beyond reproach. It can do no wrong. The Church is to be shielded from blame, and its interests protected.

An example of this can be found at the advent of the new century and new millennium, when Pope John Paul II made apology to a number of groups, including the Jews. He addressed the long history of the Church's fraught relations with Jews and Judaism. That apology was skillfully crafted and made use of a very careful formulation. In his apology to the Jews, the pope asserted, "We are deeply saddened by the behavior of those who in the course of history have caused these children of yours to suffer, and asking your forgiveness we commit ourselves to genuine brotherhood with the people of the Covenant." In apologizing for "the behavior of those…" and for "some sons and daughters of the Church," John Paul II held the Church itself at a distance from the evils for which he was apologizing. Some interpret this apology as upholding the belief that while human members of the Church were capable of wickedness and culpable for perpetrating it, the Church itself could in no way be held accountable; the Church exists in a realm beyond human reproach.

These two documents that have so recently come to light offer an opportunity for a deepened dialogue. Engaging with both of them, we can say that while "sons and daughters of the Church" did indeed rise heroically to acts of great goodness, the Church itself—to the extent that the pope embodies the Church—was in fact complicit in not acting on behalf of Jews during the Shoah. And now, perhaps Jews and Catholics in dialogue can begin to talk about the culpability of the Church itself (and not merely some of its "sons and daughters") for the suffering it caused to Jews over the course of many long centuries.

If this view of the role of the Church was indeed the mindset of Pius XII, it is plausible that his silence and apparent indifference in the face of Jewish suffering was motivated not by a specific indifference to Jewish life but rather by a desire to protect the Church itself, to spare it from potential retaliation and danger. And if this was truly his motivation, then—even if others might imagine it was admirable of the pope to do what he had to do to defend the Church—he was in fact operating from a calculus that privileged institutional considerations over human lives. And such a calculus can easily result in great wickedness.

It is with no small measure of irony that we recognize that in recent years, that very perspective has ravaged the lives of pious Catholics and has inflicted grave harm on the sons and daughters of the Church itself. Can we not say that that same set of priorities that may have looked disinterestedly at the lives of the Jews of Europe most likely accounts for the tragically slow official response to the sex abuse scandals that have been roiling the Church for decades? Like the Jews of Europe, the young Catholics scarred by their experiences are the victims of the reflex to circle the wagons around the institution, to protect the Church itself even at tragic human cost to victims of grievous wrong.

As Jews and Catholics confront a calculus that places greater emphasis on the well-being of an institution over the lives of people, we can together conclude that in this regard, the pope is, sadly, not a singular phenomenon. Such prioritizing of institutions over people and over human well-being is a wickedness that is encountered so frequently in the world generally. Seeing the devastation that it wrought in the Shoah, understanding what we have learned from the failure of Pius XII and the Church, and recognizing the harm that this mindset continues to inflict in so many settings, Jews and Catholics must join together in labeling that mindset for the evil it is, raising collective recognition of it, and encouraging aspiration to a higher set of values for ourselves—and for all people.

It is possible that the most current revelations will succeed in bringing the long controversy over the Vatican and the Holocaust to a conclusion. We can move beyond uncertainty about the role of the pope. Now the two faith communities must struggle singly and together to grapple with the implications of the understanding that both must now share.

Certainly the new documents raise painful memories and associations for Jews. Undoubtedly they are painful, albeit in a different way, for Catholics as well. We are rightly concerned that the danger posed by the most recent revelation about Pius XII is that in raising memories of old hurts it can cause the two communities to withdraw from each other, finding solace in our separate enclaves. Some Jews may see Pope Pius XII's willful silence in the face of the Shoah and manifest indifference to Jewish well-being as representative of the essential character of the Church, and those with such a perspective may argue for the futility of any Jewish dialogue with the Church. But these recent disclosures can lead us to exactly the opposite conclusion: we can hope that, rather than distancing the two communities from one another, the two newly revealed documents might offer new opportunities for encounter and engagement. The fact is that they open profound new avenues for speaking with one another clearly and candidly. They certainly challenge us to search for deeper understanding of one another. And they inspire us to increase our efforts to build structures that enable members of both communities to attain ever greater heights of human decency and compassion. Out of our shared experience of pain or shame, we can join together in the work of moving all people beyond shallow values and narrow self-interest, laboring together to strengthen the human capacity for moral heroism.

Note

1. Daniel Goldhagen, *Hitler's Willing Executioners: Ordinary Germans and the Holocaust* (Alfred A. Knopf, 1996).

The Footnote—Reading Spinoza's *Ethics*: The End of Medieval Thought

Rabbi Paul Golomb

When Benedict Spinoza (1632–1677) finished writing his treatise *Ethics*, he planned to follow it with a work on politics.[1] *Politics* was only begun when Spinoza died. His overall intent was to follow Aristotle, who had composed similar books mapping a path from theory to praxis.

I would surmise that he had two more aims in mind. He was also following Maimonides. Rambam had composed his comprehensive philosophical discourse, *The Guide to the Perplexed*, as an explanation for the choices he made in compiling the *Mishneh Torah*. Spinoza's *Ethics/Politics* would serve as the philosophical grounding for his *Tractatus Politico-Theologica*, a work so radical and controversial that it had initially been published anonymously.

In addition, he employed his *Ethics*, I believe, as a response to Rene Descartes (1596–1650). Spinoza had earlier written a mostly approving analysis of the French rationalist, but he felt the need to establish his own schema. The *Ethics*, published posthumously, represented Spinoza's most mature expression of his philosophy.

Harry A. Wolfson, the eminent scholar of Jewish philosophy, opined that the entirety of (Western) medieval philosophy was bookended by two Jews: Philo and Spinoza.[2] Philo, writing at the beginning of the Common Era, was the first to blend in a coherent fashion the assertions of classic Greek philosophy with the Bible. In doing so, he established the hallmark of medieval thought: that of placing God at the heart of all metaphysics. In Wolfson's estimation, Spinoza represents the last expression of such a God-centered metaphysics.

RABBI PAUL GOLOMB (NY '75) is Senior Scholar at the Vassar Temple, Poughkeepsie, New York, and a former editor of *CCAR Journal: The Reform Jewish Quarterly*.

It might help to compare briefly Spinoza to Descartes. Although a generation older, Descartes straddles medieval and modern thought in a fashion that Spinoza did not. In accord with medieval thinking, Descartes's God cannot be perceived as distinct from both nature and the human psyche. Further, it is the epitome of perfection to which all else—including the angels—can only strive.

When he approached the question of certain knowledge of God, however, he executed a modern turn. Cosmological and teleological proofs of God were based on the axiomatic notion of an ordered world. Descartes rather constructed a new ontological argument that began with the human faculty of judgment. Thus, he posited the concept of the subjective self, the keystone of modern thinking.

Spinoza, on the other hand, wrote the *Ethics* from the standpoint of objective certainty. The treatise is organized as a set of propositions that are derived from axioms and definitions not subjected to investigation or evaluation; they just are. In this way, he turned away from the subjective self. Yet, Spinoza went as far as possible within the medieval project of putting God at the center.

Beginning with Aquinas and the scholastics and continuing through William of Occam, metaphysics as an explanation for all phenomena was being thinned out. With Spinoza, the metaphysics virtually disappeared altogether. A central feature of Spinoza's thought was the thoroughgoing skepticism of the Biblical God. Although hardly the first to question the truth claims of Scripture, his *Tractatus* was one of the most comprehensive efforts to undercut the religious foundations of Judaism and Christianity. While the entirety of Western medieval philosophy may be described as a systematic endeavor to formulate an expression of the will of the ineffable God within the context of rational thought, Spinoza posited that reason and God's will were one and the same.

The Ethics of *Ethics*

Spinoza did not abandon God. The central contention of the *Ethics* is that God is the entirety of all existence, and thus is the sum total of the immutable laws of nature. Further, he contended that human beings, wholly a part of God, operate fully in accord with those laws. Since the laws are immutable, God is incapable (not theoretically but ontologically) of asserting any sort of will that counter those laws, and neither can humans. We are therefore prisoners of illusions when we choose to think our wills are somehow distinct from the world. This illusion only serves to generate destructive passions within ourselves that tend to imprison us further, and deny us the opportunity to be fully human, fully free.

Hence, the focus of Spinoza's thesis is God and human freedom. Although titled "Ethics," the word "good" does not ever appear. What then is the good in the *Ethics*? How did Spinoza know what he claimed to know?

I believe that Spinoza wished to assert that the ultimate human good is freedom. There is the world and its immutable laws and nothing else. The world is also the vehicle for the sustenance of life. In this sense, the world can be labelled as good. (The Biblical appreciation of the world at the beginning of Genesis—that God pronounced it *tov m'od*—is, for Spinoza, true.) Human beings, however, perceive the world not as good, but as perfectible. Thus, their attempts at making the world a better place are not only folly; they actually cause pain. That pain can be relieved by accepting the world as it is: the manifestation of God, and intrinsically good. Human freedom is a radical act of acceptance; a freedom from illusion and pain.

The Footnote

How can one know that God is the world, and the world is all there is? A critical element of Spinoza's analysis is his epistemology. In the final section (Part V) of the *Ethics*, he predicates human understanding of the pantheistic and immutable God on a "third level" of knowing. This assertion of three levels, central to his overall thesis, is not described in the main body of his treatise, but rather in a footnote. In Part II, Spinoza sets forth a proposition defining what is to be meant by an adequate idea: that is, a thought that comports with unbiased perception. To this proposition Spinoza appends a footnote describing the levels of knowing. For all intents and purposes, he is burying this significant contention. Either, I would speculate, he considered his epistemology obvious and thus not necessary to be placed in the body of the treatise, or rather he tucked it away because it was not quite well-formed in his own mind. (I tend toward the latter.)

Regarding these epistemic levels, prior to knowing there is sheer perception. The first level is engaging in an organization within the mind so that the perception can be comprehended. Spinoza calls this level "opinion" or "imagination" (I believe a better term is "imaging.") It is then abstracted in order to allow certain inferences to be made from it. This second level is reason. Finally, there is a third tier which he labels intuition. This is the ability to comprehend a perception in the entirety of its context.

Spinoza concedes that the third level is elusive, and therefore gives an example of being able to determine the next number in a sequence without having to go through any mathematical calculations. One might also relate Spinoza's intuition to the recognition of a whole word in reading without the need to sound it out. Upon initial examination, this third level seems to be simply a faster version of the second.

In accord with the primary anti-metaphysical notion that the world is the totality of existence, every act of cognition is an act of analysis from the whole to the part. Perception, imaging, and reason provide everything that can be known (everything there is!), and no other mental faculty can add more. Yet, Spinoza insists on the significance of intuition. For him, perception allows a person to take in elements of the world. Imaging gives them names and relationships to one another. Reason permits abstraction, which allows one to posit with confidence things that cannot be physically perceived as they are too distant in space and time. Only intuition, however, brings all this perception, organization, and abstraction into a conceptual whole.

Hence, Spinoza proposes as *the highest endeavor of the mind, and the highest virtue, is to understand things by the third kind of knowledge* (Part V, Proposition 25). Left unasked and unexplored is the following: The physical world is acquired through perception, and the orderliness of that world is embedded in the laws of nature which are mentally constructed reason; from where does intuition arise? Spinoza provides no answer, at least none that I have discerned. Intuition just is, apparently. In a carefully constructed treatise that proceeds from commonly held definitions and axioms to proofs of propositions, corollaries, and lemmas, the unexplained existence of intuition is a stark omission.

Whither *Ethics*

Following Professor Wolfson, Spinoza represents the conclusion of a philosophic era. He, so to speak, shut the door on a project that attempted to resolve the claims of Scripture and the insights of Greek philosophy. Thus, Spinoza occupied an inflection point in which the project of modern thought could commence.

Although he did not abandon God, Spinoza's "theology" portended modern philosophical atheism. Thinkers from the Encyclopedists through Hume, Kant, Hegel, and into the twentieth century professed their difficulty with belief in a creative and commanding deity. John Wisdom (1904–1993) expressed the problem in Spinozist terms most succinctly in his Parable of the Invisible Gardener.[3] Two explorers come across a clearing in a thick forest. One explorer avers that the clearing suggests evidence of a gardener who tends the area; the other thinks the indication of order is simply a natural development. They wait for a gardener to show up. As no one appears, the first explorer provides excuses, ultimately asserting the gardener is simply undetectable. The other then exclaims: "What is the difference between your gardener and no gardener at all?" When Spinoza equated the totality of the natural universe with God, just what does positing the existence of a deity add to our understanding?

Among modern thinkers, Mordechai Kaplan (1881–1983) came close to promoting Spinoza's idea of God. Conventionally one counts among Kaplan's principal influences the cultural sensitivities of Solomon Schechter and Achad Haam, the development of the discipline of sociology, and American philosophical pragmatism. Spinoza nonetheless rises through those filters. For Kaplan, as for Spinoza, God does not reside outside of nature. There is no metaphysical object.

While Spinoza defines God as the totality of all existence, Kaplan narrows his definition of the deity to that which makes for redemption.[4] In this fashion, he makes explicit what Spinoza left as implicit: the world, through God, is indeed good. It is the human task to strive for that goodness. Kaplan thus replaces Spinoza's "freedom" with the more religiously weighted word "redemption." In Kaplan's conceptual universe, the Jew is a totality of a certain history, culture, and sociology: a civilization. With nothing outside of the world to manipulate it, it is a Jew's obligation—perhaps a better word is destiny—to fit properly within it. Some Jews might understand this project in wholly secular terms. Applying Kaplan's sociology, however, the secular becomes religious. Jewish objects, born out of history, are sacred; Jewish action, also born out of history and culture, is mitzvah. In the end, Kaplan has principally reworked Spinoza's *Ethics* into a Jewish religious text.

Stepping Over One's Shadow

Kaplan's theology is open to the criticism of burying the metaphysical in the physical. His God is One that does not command, but nonetheless compels. The universe is everything—good, wicked, and indifferent—and somehow within this everything, God points toward the good! How does this happen? Or is God indistinguishable (*a la* Wisdom) from human psychological and sociological pursuits of betterment?

One might find an answer in that provocative footnote. We turn to the Austrian philosopher Ludwig Wittgenstein (1889–1951). The relationship to Spinoza is rather obvious in the choice of title for his *Tractatus Logico-Philosophicus*.[5] Although the title intentionally mimics Spinoza's *Tractatus*, Wittgenstein was responding to *Ethics*. The commonality is announced in his first proposition: *The world is all that is the case* [*Tractatus* 1]. While this proposition essentially culminates Spinoza's thinking, it is, on the other hand, the beginning of Wittgenstein's. If, he is asking, the world is indeed all that is the case, how do we know that? It is, of course, the same question that Spinoza essentially set aside.

The faculty of intuition, particularly given Spinoza's elusive definition, is not quite of this world. Wittgenstein encapsulates this condition when he asserts: *nothing in the visual field allows you to infer that it is seen by an eye* [5.633]. Both the visual field and the eye are undoubtedly part of the material world, yet the ability to connect the two is a metaphysical act. As much as Spinoza wished to resist it, so is his faculty of intuition also metaphysical.

Wittgenstein moreover considered his *Tractatus* to be a treatise on ethics. This intent on his part has been consistently misunderstood, and for good reason. Just as it is hard to discern what is the ethic of Spinoza's *Ethics*, one is hard-pressed to articulate what sort of ethics is being presented in Wittgenstein's *Tractatus*. With regard to Spinoza, I, have already suggested that the "world" is God, and therefore is intrinsically good. Evil or wrongdoing arises principally from one's misplaced effort to improve the world, which is impossible. This conclusion, once more, is admittedly speculative but a reasonable surmise.

I think Wittgenstein roots his ethics as well in this "third level of knowledge," the knowledge that permits us to know that the visual field is being perceived by an eye. He labels it the "philosophical self," for which he asserts: *The philosophical self is not the human being, not the human body, or the human soul, with which psychology deals, but rather the metaphysical subject, the limit of the world—not a part of it* [5.641].

When, at the start, Wittgenstein states that the world is all that is the case (which he further defines as the totality of all facts), he is actually asserting that while it is "all that is the case," it is not everything! Indeed, what is most difficult to comprehend in Wittgenstein is his positing of the inexpressible. Since the world can be encompassed entirely in language, he non-felicitously poses that that which is outside of language is "nonsense." Non-sense, however, is not nonsense. He indicates as much when he writes: *What* can *be shown,* cannot *be said* [4.1212]. We all understand as much when we are trying to relate an incident we witnessed and are greeted with blank stares. Acknowledging the incomprehension, we conclude "you needed to have been there."

Spinoza's world was as limitless as God; Wittgenstein's is not. He need not find Good in the world, and he does not. He rather asserts: *The world of the happy man is different from that of the unhappy man* [6.43]. The facts of the world do not change—the world is the world, as per Spinoza—but the limit of the world does change. Then, Wittgenstein adds in a subtle but critical shift from Spinoza's pantheism: *How things are in the world is a matter of complete indifference for what is higher: God does not reveal himself in the world* [6.432]. It is as if Wittgenstein is admonishing Spinoza: Yes, the world is impervious to change, but human will, touched by God at its limit, is capable of remaking the world nonetheless.

Martin Heidegger observed that no one can step over one's own shadow. Spinoza could not see clearly the ramification of his employment of the third level of knowledge, an epistemology that requires acknowledgement of the subjective self. Spinoza did not reject the concept; rather he had no mechanism at hand in order to conceive it. He could only suggest it in that enigmatic footnote. Wittgenstein, armed with this modern insight, essentially jumps the shadow for Spinoza. His *Tractatus* is the *Ethics* that Spinoza might have written if he had the vocabulary.

Postscript: Spinoza the Jew

In 1989, I experienced one of the odder moments in my career when I spent five days discussing Spinoza with the late character actor Robert Loggia. We met on the first day of shooting on location for a movie in which my son had a small role. Loggia had just returned from filming in Israel, where crew members talked about the importance of Spinoza, and he wanted to learn more. What is important here is not how a veteran actor fills his time between scenes, but rather that Israelis in the late twentieth century acknowledged the significance of Spinoza.

Baruch Spinoza was indeed born into a Sephardic Jewish family and received an apparently good education in Hebrew Scripture and Rabbinic literature. After his older brother's death when he was seventeen, he began a slow but inexorable move away from Judaism. He dropped his Jewish studies and began to learn Latin; Baruch become Benedictus. By the age of twenty-three, he was so at odds with the Jewish community that he was placed in *cherem*, thus being cut off from both personal and commercial contact with Amsterdam's Jews.

In his *Tractatus*, he avoids any personal connection with either Jews or Judaism. Yet, in his critique of religion (Jewish and Christian), he does uphold a socio-political identification for the Jewish people. Whether he included himself or not, Spinoza essentially created the justification for the secular Jew. In proto-nationalist language, he established a Jewish national identity. In so doing, he provided the foundation for modern Zionism.

I find it most poignant that Ludwig Wittgenstein completed what Spinoza started. He was raised as a Catholic, and furthermore counted Leo Tolstoy's *The Gospel in Brief* as an important influence on his *Tractatus*. Yet, three of Wittgenstein's four grandparents were born Jews, and he evidenced both an awareness and an identification with his Jewishness.[6]

Wittgenstein, along with Edmund Husserl (1859–1938)—born a Jew and converted for pragmatic reasons to Lutheranism as a young man[7]—was among the most influential thinkers to pull nineteenth-century idealist philosophy into the twentieth century. Philo, Spinoza, Wittgenstein, Husserl; revolutionary philosophers. As Jews, they were on the societal margin of a gentile world. They were also on the margins of the Jewish world. (Philo, who fully identified with the Hellenistic Jewish community of Alexandria, nonetheless wrote only in Greek, and was therefore outside of the Hebrew-Aramaic community that became Rabbinic Judaism.) They dramatically moved forward the course of Western thought, and at the same time, expanded and problematized what it means to be a Jew.

Notes

1. General biographical information on Spinoza is widely available. For further reading see Steven Nadler, *Spinoza: A Life*, 2nd ed. (Cambridge University Press, 2020).
2. Wolfson in "This, then, is the new period in the history of philosophy, ushered in by Philo and ushered out by Spinoza." From *What's New in Philo* in **From Philo to Spinoza** (Behrman House, 1977) p. 37.
3. Wisdom delivered this parable in a paper entitled "Gods," in 1944. It most notably served as the basis for a symposium among Anthony Flew, R.M. Hare, and Basil Mitchell as "Theology and Falsification," published in Flew's *New Essays in Philosophical Theology* (SCM Press, 1961).
4. See Kaplan, *Judaism as a Civilization* (Schocken, 1957).
5. While the title was suggested by the philosopher G. E. Moore, Wittgenstein accepted it as a preference to other proposed titles. The *Tractatus* is the only work that Wittgenstein published as a fully complete text. His subsequent books were all compiled and organized by colleagues and students. For a comprehensive study of his life and work, see Ray Monk, *Wittgenstein: The Duty of Genius* (Penguin, 1991).
6. Hillary Putnam suggested that Wittgenstein was one-quarter Jewish in *Jewish Philosophy as a Guide to Life: Rosenzweig, Buber, Levinas, Wittgenstein* (Indiana University Press, 2008). For a direct examination of a Jewish Wittgenstein, see Ranjit Chatterjee, *Wittgenstein and Judaism: A Triumph of Concealment* (Peter Lang, 2005).
7. Husserl's connection to Spinoza is nowhere as direct as that Wittgenstein. Yet he shares with Spinoza an outsized influence on the course of systematic thought. For more on his life, see especially David Woodruff Smith, *Husserl*, 2nd ed. (Routledge, 2013). Further, one can discern the Jewish Husserl in his last major work, *The Crisis of European Science*.

The Truth Judge or the True Judge?

Daniel M. Berry and Rabbi Lori Cohen

Introduction

The blessing *baruch dayan ha-emet* (בָּרוּךְ דַּיָּן הָאֱמֶת) is included in a death announcement and it is recited when hearing of a death and also during the mourner's ritual of *k'riah* (tearing one's clothing, or a piece of ribbon). These days, *baruch dayan ha-emet* is often translated as "Blessed is the True Judge." However, in the earliest use of the blessing, it meant something that can be translated as "Blessed is the Truth Judge."[2] These two different translations of the blessing have significantly different meanings. This article discusses the two meanings, their implications, and their relations to Jewish theology about life, death, and transgression.

How to Translate and Understand the Phrase

These days, the phrase *dayan ha-emet* is often translated in Rabbinical sources, on the pulpit, and at funerals as "the True Judge."[3] However, in Modern Hebrew, "true judge" would be *dayan amiti* and "the True Judge" would be *ha-dayan ha-amiti*. In these phrases, *amiti* ("true") is an adjective. However, the phrase *dayan ha-emet* in Rabbinic Hebrew is a construct (*s'michut*) form made of two nouns, *dayan* ("judge") and *emet* ("truth"), plus the definite article *ha-* ("the"), which together mean "the Truth Judge."[4] Thus, in Modern Hebrew, *dayan ha-emet* is understood as "the Truth Judge," and not as "the True Judge."

DANIEL M. BERRY is professor of Computer Science and Software Engineering, University of Waterloo in Waterloo, Ontario, Canada.

RABBI LORI COHEN (C '00) is rabbi at Temple Kol Ami in Vaughan, Ontario, Canada.

The semantic difference between "the True Judge" and "the Truth Judge" is that a "true judge" is a judge who is worthy of the title "Judge," while a "truth judge," or a judge of the truth, *decides* what *is* the truth, perhaps by the judge's very actions. A truth judge can decide also if what someone is saying is the truth. This distinction in nuance is reflective of Modern Hebrew, which has an adjective form *amiti* that is derived from the noun *emet*—allowing two distinct formulations, with the different meanings.

History of the Blessing

In contrast with modern Hebrew, Biblical and Mishna Hebrew have few adjectives formed by adding *i* to a noun, as the *amiti* adjective is derived from the *emet* noun[5]. The earliest such adjective in the Tanach is *admoni* derived from *admon*, in Genesis 25:25, but *amiti* itself does not appear anywhere in the Tanach. Consequently, whenever an adjective would have been needed, a construct form with two nouns would have been used instead. That is, in Biblical or Rabbinical times, one wanting to say either "the True Judge" or "the Truth Judge" would say *dayan ha-emet* and would depend on context to express the intended meaning.

According to the Academy of the Hebrew Language in Israel, the earliest appearance of the word *amiti* is between 1100 and 1300 CE.[6] The earliest occurrence of the phrase *dayan ha-emet* appears to be in *Mishna Berachot* 9:2[7], which was edited in about 200 CE, long before the adjective *amiti* appeared in any Hebrew literary source. Thus, any occurrence of *dayan ha-emet* in the Mishna is ambiguous, and a reader needs to examine its context to understand the occurrence. This first occurrence says *v'al sh'muot raot omer baruch dayan ha-emet*, which therefore, means either "And for bad news, one says 'Blessed is the True Judge'" or "And for bad news, one says 'Blessed is the Truth Judge.'"

The first possibility does not fit, because in this situation, there is nothing and no one to judge. The bad news has already happened, there is no reason for a true judge to act in a judicial capacity, and to be blessed for doing so. The second possibility fits better. Evidently, God, the Decider of what is true, has decided that the bad news needed to happen. God is therefore the Truth Judge. We humans must reconcile ourselves to living with the reality of the bad news. We need to show that we accept it by blessing the one who caused it to happen, even if we feel sad about or are angry about the bad news. This early occurrence of *dayan ha-emet* clearly means "the Truth Judge" and not "the True Judge." A death is, of course, a prime example of bad news. So, *baruch dayan ha-emet* has come to be said immediately after learning of a death and at funerals.

God as Judge of Life and Death

Traditional Jewish sources have God judging our behavior annually, only when we are alive, on Rosh HaShanah, known also as *Yom HaDin*, the Day of Judgment. During the Ten Days of Repentance, from Rosh HaShanah through Yom Kippur, we have the opportunity to change our behavior in an attempt modify God's judgment before it is sealed at the end of Yom Kippur. Thus, there is no need to judge a person on the person's death, which occurs after the divine judgment rendered during the most recent Rosh HaShanah and sealed nine days later at the end of Yom Kippur.[8] Because death is not an occasion for judgment, there is little reason for the phrase *baruch dayan ha-emet* to mean "Blessed is the True Judge."

In fact, the word *dayan* occurs only rarely in *machzorim*, and never in the phrase *dayan ha-emet*. Among the *machzorim* at Sefaria, the sole occurrence that matches דין (*din* or *dayan*) is in *Hatarat Nedarim* ("Annullment of Vows"),[9] a legal formulation that stands outside of the liturgy itself, that was introduced in Ashkenazic communities as a mechanism for releasing people from their vows as they entered the High Holy Day period. The occurrence is in the text, *shim'u na rabotai, dayanim mumchim, kol neder …* ("Listen my masters, expert judges! Any vow …"). Here, *dayanim* refers to human *judges* and not to God, and is not part of the phrase *dayan ha-emet*.

In the CCAR Rosh HaShanah *machzor*,[10] neither of the two occurrences of דין (*din* or *dayan*) has the word *ha-emet* following it. They are in the *Untaneh Tokef* prayer:

1. *emet ki atah hu dayan u-mochiach v'yodei-a va-eid* ("It is true that you are judge, prover [prosecutor?], knower [jury?], and witness.")[11]
2. *v'yomru hineih yom haDin* ("And they will say 'Here is the Day of Judgment.'")

This prayer, in which God gives humans the opportunity to judge themselves, says also *v'chotam yad kol adam bo* ("the signature of each person is here") referring to *Sefer HaZichronot*, the Book of Memories. The prayer also mentions *v'chol ba-ei olam yaavrun l'fanecha ... v'tichtov et g'zar dinam* ("And all comers to the world will pass before You ... You will write their judgment decrees.") That is, judgment comes during a person's *lifetime*, during the Ten Days of Repentence, and not at the time of death.

The phrase *dayan ha-emet* never appears in the context of God's judging human beings on Rosh HaShanah; *dayan ha-emet* is not describing the True Judge, God's role on Rosh HaShanah, the Day of Judgment. The phrase *dayan ha-emet* is used *only* in response to hearing of a death or other bad news, when *dayan ha-emet* is describing the Truth Judge that has decided that the death or other bad news needed to happen.

Implications of the Different Understandings in Jewish Life

The phrase *baruch dayan ha-emet* typically occurs in a death announcement, for example, "Shahar, Z.L., died this morning after a long battle with cancer. *Baruch dayan ha-emet*. May Shahar's memory be a blessing." If *baruch dayan ha-emet* is taken to mean "blessed is the True Judge," the announcement implies that Shahar will somehow be judged by God, the True Judge. Why would Shahar be judged at the time of death? Such a judging implies the existence of an afterlife and some kind of reward for good behavior during life, for which each deceased must be judged upon death. However, Jewish theology is ambiguous and uncertain about what happens after death.[12] On the other hand, Christianity is certain of the existence of the afterlife, with its reward in heaven or punishment in hell for a deceased's behavior in life.[13] Therefore, the "True Judge" translation, in effect, accepts the doctrine of reward or punishment, which is far from certain in Judaism, but is certain in Christianity and is prevalent in the Christian culture that most diaspora Jews now live in.

In Judaism, each death reminds us that God's actions *are* the truth. There is no certain notion of saving Shahar's soul from eternal damnation in a fiery hell. Shahar lives on only in the memories of Shahar's survivors. Thus, Jews say "May Shahar's memory be a blessing" and not "May Shahar's soul rest in peace."[14] Therefore, understanding *baruch dayan ha-emet* as "Blessed is the Truth Judge," fits very well with Jewish theology. The blessing is saying that no matter how unjust or not right we humans might think Shahar's death is, it is the truth, because whatever God does, as the Truth Judge, is the truth. The blessing encourages Shahar's mourners to accept the reality of Shahar's death as reflecting God's great power, the power that is the truth, the power that is extolled in the Kaddish when we declare *yitgadal v'yitkadash sh'meih rabba* ("Enlarged and sanctified is the great name.")

The Mourner's Kaddish has nothing to do with death, the deceased, and even mourning. It is simply about God's great name, *sh'meih rabba*, which should be blessed *b'alma di v'ra chiruteih* ("throughout the world which God has created according to God's will.")[15] Creating the world "according to God's will"[16] is what causes the Creator to be the Truth Judge. Whatever the Creator creates *is* the truth. Understanding *baruch dayan ha-emet* as "Blessed is the True Judge" just does not fit with the meaning of the mourner's Kaddish.

Baruch dayan ha-emet is blessing the one God who establishes, by God's actions, what is the truth. In the wake of a death, reciting the blessing reminds us humans that no matter how unjust, unfair, painful, senseless, wasteful, etc., we might think the death is, no matter how we might not understand any purpose to the death, it is God's truth.[17]

Where Does the "True Judge" Understanding Originate?

Judaism has always been ambiguous about what happens after we humans die:

> Death forms the final chapter of life "in this world" and the opening page of life "in the world to come." In no way is death evil or unnatural, a penalty exacted for sin. True, death before one's time, understood in the oral Torah to be sixty years, is deemed "extirpation," that is, premature death, and under some circumstances is deemed penalty for sin.[18]

> Judaism is famously ambiguous about this matter. The immortality of the soul, the World to Come, and the resurrection of the dead all feature prominently in Jewish tradition, but exactly what these things are and how they relate to each other has always been vague.[19]

In particular, there is no clarity on what happens to one's soul between the body's death and the world to come, *olam ha-ba*, and the soul's resurrection when the Messiah comes in the far future.

The Tanach itself mentions only *she-ol*, meaning "the bowels of the earth." The word *she-ol* was used in the early Tanach to mean mainly the grave itself, particularly when one is sent to the grave early. Later, the term was used to describe the temporary place for each soul in between its body's death and its resurrection in the world to come.

The ideas of *Gan Eden* and *Gehinnom*, also called "heaven" and "hell" respectively, were developed later. However, it was never clear how hell was different from heaven[20] and to what extent the souls of sinners are confined to hell, because fundamentally, Mishnah Sanhedrin 10:1 assures us that *kol Yisrael yesh lahem chelek l'olam ha-ba* ("All Israel has a portion in the world to come.")[21] So, sin should have no bearing on any Jew's entry to the world to come. Given this assurance, a Jewish funeral ensures the burial of the deceased's body so that it can return, as commanded, to dust. The focus of the funeral then becomes to serve the needs of the mourners, whose role, going forward, is to remember the deceased and to thus be blessed. First and primary is the need for the mourners to accept the death as God's plan. Mourners say *baruch dayan ha-emet*, "Blessed is the Truth Judge," to remind themselves that regardless of what they may think of the death, it is God's truth. The mourners later recite the Mourner's Kaddish, acknowledging the greatness and holiness of the name of God who has just taken the life of their loved one.

Independently of the concern about death and funerals, the Torah proclaims in several places that a person's good behavior will be rewarded, and the person's bad behavior will be punished, all during the person's lifetime. For example, in Leviticus 26:3–43, God promises the Israelites that if they keep God's commandments, they will be prosperous and secure in their land. If, on the other hand, they ignore their covenant with God and violate the commandments, their land will not yield crops, their enemies will persecute them, and they will be exiled. These calamities are supposed to happen while they are living and not after they die.

It did not take long for Israelites to notice that what God promised did not happen.[22] As Vinson Cunningham said, "Why are some people caught and not others? Why do the 'least of these' keep catching hell while the richest and most powerful slide through life unaccosted and unaccountable, leaving God knows what in their wake?"[23] We believe that widespread thinking like this prompted Jewish religious leaders to introduce into the theology the idea that the deceased's soul, which leaves the deceased's body on death and just waits until the Messiah comes and initiates resurrection, at that time receiving the reward or punishment for the deceased's behavior during life. This would lead to the concepts of *Gan Eden*, heaven, and *Gehinnom*, hell, as the reward or punishment destinations for the deceased's soul.[24]

Once the concepts of heaven and hell have been introduced and there is a need for each deceased's life to be judged to determine the destination of the deceased's soul, the understanding of *dayan ha-emet* as "the True Judge" at least makes some sense, even though this sense depends on concepts that are not certain, that are debated, and that came into Judaism only in postbiblical, Rabbinical times. Now Jews can hope that the one who judges each deceased's life is a true judge. This hope would reinforce the understanding of *dayan ha-emet* as "the True Judge", even though this understanding is not the original, intended understanding.

Human Responsibility

This article has so far focused on one understanding of "Truth Judge," that is, as the *decider* of what *is* truth. So a death, decreed and enacted by God *is the truth*, even if we do not like it.

There is another, quite simple understanding of "Truth Judge" as one who decides if what someone is saying *is* the truth. This is the role of a human judge in a trial by judges. Whenever God is sitting in judgment of humans, e.g., at Rosh Hashanah, the humans being judged must give truthful accountings of their lives so far, because God cannot be deceived[25]. This understanding of *dayan ha-emet* puts the responsibility for facing truth and being truthful squarely into our human hands. We humans are responsible for accepting truth even if we perceive it as bad or we do not like it. We are responsible for being truthful, i.e., having integrity, and not just being honest.[26] Then God, *dayan ha-emet*, the Truth Judge, judges our truths.

Notes

1. The authors thank the reviewers for their comments, which sharpened our thinking and immensely improved the article. The authors thank August Adelman for her helpful information about *machzorim*, as well as Rabbi Rena Arshinoff and Yael David for their suggestions to improve the clarity of the article. They thank

also Michelle Kwitkin for ideas that helped make the article more concise.

2. It can be translated also as "the Judge of the Truth," which is considered equivalent to "Truth Judge" as used in this article, just as *ha-dayan shel ha-emet* is considered equivalent to *dayan ha-emet*.

3. For example, the *Tziduk HaDin* prayer contains the blessing *Baruch atah Adonai eloheinu melech ha-olam dayan ha-emet*, and the final phrase, *dayan ha-emet*, is often translated as "True Judge." See, for example: Reuven P. Bulka, *The RCA Lifecycle Madrikh* (Rabbinical Council of America, 1995); Chaim Binyamin Goldberg, *Mourning in Halachah* (Mesorah Publications, 1991); Hyman E. Goldin, *Hamadrikh: The Rabbi's Guide: A Manual of Jewish Religious Rituals, Ceremonials, and Customs* (Hebrew Publishing Company, 1939); Philip Birnbaum, *Daily Prayer Book* (Hebrew Publishing Company, 1949); and Zalman Goldstein, "The Jewish Burial," at www.chabad.org/library/article_cdo/aid/368092/jewish/The-Burial.htm. The phrase is much less frequently translated as "the Judge of the Truth". See, for example: Perry Raphael Rank and Gordon M. Freeman, eds. *Moreh Derekh: The Rabbinical Assembly Rabbi's Manual*, vol. 1 (Rabbinical Assembly, 1998).

4. The construct *dayan ha-emet* means, in Hebrew, *ha-dayan shel ha-emet*, just as the noun phrase "the Truth Judge" means, in English, "the Judge of the Truth." Moreover, *ha-dayan ha-amiti* is to *dayan ha-emet* as "the True Judge" is to "the Truth Judge," in terms of the relative placements of adjectives and nouns and of words with the same root.

5. David J. Kamhi, "The Gentilitial Adjective in Hebrew," *The Journal of the Royal Asiatic Society of Great Britain and Ireland* 1971, no. 1 (1971): 2–8.

6. The Academy of the Hebrew Language, "Hebrew–Hebrew Dictionary," (N.D.), https://hebrew-academy.org.il/מילון-עברי-עברי/

7. Sefaria.org, "Mishnah Berakhot 9.2," (N.D.), https://www.sefaria.org/Mishnah_Berakhot.9.2?lang=bi.

8. There are many opinions on this topic. Some say that the annual judgment on Rosh HaShanah is enough; others say that God judges a person at the time of death; still others say that God will judge all soon after the resurrection of the dead following the arrival of the Messiah. Finally, others say that only non-Jews will be judged. See "The last judgment" at https://en.wikipedia.org/wiki/Jewish_eschatology.

9. Sefaria.org, "Machzor Rosh Hashanah Ashkenaz, Annullment of Vows," (N.D.), https://www.sefaria.org/Machzor_Rosh_Hashanah_Ashkenaz%2C_Annullment_of_Vows?lang=bi.

10. Rabbis Edwin Goldberg, Janet Marder, Rabbi Sheldon Marder, and Leon Morris (eds.), *Mishkan HaNefesh: Machzor for the Days of Awe: Rosh HaShanah* (CCAR Press, 2016).

11. The authors' translations, not CCAR's.
12. "We really do not know, but if there is a life after this one, and a reward for what we do, then surely it will be dependent upon the kind of life we have lived. Therefore, let us strive to follow God's path for us as closely and as enthusiastically as possible, for then we surely will know all manner of rewards, especially the one of seeing a world that is a better place for our efforts." Rabbi Howard Jaffe, "In Judaism what is believed to happen to someone after they die? Is there some idea of an afterlife, or is that purely a Christian concept?" https://www.reformjudaism.org/learning/answers-jewish-questions/judaism-what-believed-happen-someone-after-they-die-there-some.
13. Vinson Cunningham, "How the Idea of Hell Has Shaped the Way We Think," *The New Yorker* (2019) https://www.newyorker.com/magazine/2019/01/21/how-the-idea-of-hell-has-shaped-the-way-we-think.
14. The typical Christian phrase "May Shahar's soul rest in peace" is possible only Shahar's soul ends up in heaven. The Jewish memorial prayer, *El Malei Rachamim*, includes the phrase *v'yanuachu b'shalom al mishkavam*, is sometimes mis-translated as "may they rest in peace," but a more accurate translation is "May they rest in peace in their resting-place", i.e., may their bodies be undisturbed.
15. The Aramaic original uses masculine gender here, literally, "which He created according to His will."
16. The Aramaic original uses masculine gender here, literally, "according to His will."
17. Understanding the phrase *dayan ha-emet* as "the True Judge" is at odds also with theological ideas that find expression in the *Tzidduk HaDin* prayer, in which the phrase also occurs. See the full discussion of this issue in Section 4 of an extended version of this article at https://cs.uwaterloo.ca/~dberry/FTP_SITE/tech.reports/BerryCohenTruthOrTrueJudge.pdf.
18. Jacob Neusner, *Death and the Afterlife* (Pilgrim Press, 2005), 30.
19. My Jewish Learning, "Is There a Jewish Afterlife?"; https://www.myjewishlearning.com/article/life-after-death/.
20. "There's a Jewish joke that says there's no Heaven or Hell: we all go to the same place when we die, where Moses and Rabbi Akiva give constant and everlasting classes on the Bible and the Talmud. For the righteous this is eternal bliss, while for the wicked this is eternal suffering." conveyed by Elon Gilad of haaretz.com
21. Sefaria.org, "Mishnah Sanhedrin 10:1," (N.D.), https://www.sefaria.org/Mishnah_Sanhedrin.10.1?lang=bi.
22. Madison S Fogle, "The purpose of Hell: control of communities through apocalyptic literature," College of Arts & Sciences Senior

Honors Theses, University of Louisville (2022) https://ir.library.louisville.edu/honors/292.

23. Vinson Cunningham, "How the Idea of Hell Has Shaped the Way We Think," *The New Yorker* (2019) https://www.newyorker.com/magazine/2019/01/21/how-the-idea-of-hell-has-shaped-the-way-we-think; Cunningham is paraphrasing Dorothy Day, *The Long Loneliness* (Harper Collins, 1952).

24. The Jewish concepts of heaven and hell, particularly of hell, is significantly different from those of Christianity, in which hell is a fiery place of eternal damnation. The idea that people's rewards come in their afterlives can be used for political ends, e.g., to keep the masses subjugated and accepting their lots in life. One perspective of Jewish hell is that one's own guilt leads to eventual repentance and transfer to heaven; see [My Jewish Learning, "Is There a Jewish Afterlife?," (N.D.), https://www.myjewishlearning.com/article/life-after-death/].

25. The Rabbinical Assembly, the United Synagogue of Conservative Judaism, *Etz Hayim: Torah and Commentary* (Jewish Publication Society, 2001).

26. There is a difference between truth and honesty. Lawyers must be honest, but they do not have to be truthful. Honesty and truthfulness are not the same thing. Being honest means not telling lies. Being truthful means actively making known the *full* truth of a matter. A criminal defense lawyer, for example, in zealously defending a client, has no obligation to actively present the truth. Counsel may not deliberately mislead the court, but has no obligation to tell the defendant's whole story [fs, Farnum Street, "The Difference Between Truth and Honesty: What Law School Teaches us About Insight, Logic, and Thinking," Farnum Street Articles, https://fs.blog/things-learned-law-school/.].

Jacob Schiff, the RPB, and My Retirement

Rabbi Alan Henkin[1]

In late 1916 Jacob Schiff's seventieth birthday was nearing, and Schiff, the noted businessman, financier, and philanthropist, was wondering how to commemorate the January 10 event. He decided upon donating $700,000 ($16,800,000 in 2023 dollars) to secular and Jewish causes. Among the beneficiaries of this largesse were the Jewish Theological Seminary, Yeshiva University, and a joint commission of the Union of American Hebrew Congregations (UAHC) and the Central Conference of American Rabbis (CCAR). Schiff wrote a check to the Reform institution for $100,000 "for the establishment of a fund to provide for pensioning superannuated rabbis," as reported in *The New York Times*.[2]

What prompted Schiff to make such a large donation—$2,398,000 in 2023 dollars—and why earmark it to such a specific cause?

"Retired Ministers of Our Faith"

At the CCAR's very first convention in 1891, the Conference memorialized in its original Constitution that one objective of the CCAR was "to prevent an unfortunate colleague or his family from becoming humiliated as objects of charity."[3] Half of each member's $5.00 dues was to be devoted to a relief fund. At the CCAR's third convention in August 1893 Rabbi Isaac Mayer Wise, the founder of the CCAR as well as the UAHC and Hebrew Union College, delivered his presidential address to the plenum reminding them that the first of the two goals of the CCAR was "to establish a fund for the support of aged and retired ministers of our faith."[4]

RABBI ALAN HENKIN (C '80) is the Placement Director Emeritus of the CCAR and Rabbi Emeritus of Congregation Beth Knesset Bamidbar in Lancaster, California. He is currently the Executive Vice President for Finance of the Pacific Association of Reform Rabbis (PARR).

How to pay for this fund? This brings us to another of Wise's major projects: the publication of a Union Prayer Book. The UPB would be sold to the congregations at no more than 12 percent above expenses: "[T]wo percent of this [12 percent will] go to the publication fund in the hands of that committee for publication expenses, and ten per cent to the fund for the support of retired ministers of our faith."[5] Despite the CCAR Constitution and Wise's plan to finance a relief fund, such a fund languished as merely a line item in the CCAR budget, only capitalized by donations from rabbis, congregations, and individual congregants, and not the UPB.

Finally in 1896 Wise, in a series of *ashamnus*, chided the Conference for its failure to create a relief fund in the way he had laid out three years earlier—namely, funded largely by the sale of the UPB. By 1899 the Indigent Ministers Relief Fund was operational, disbursing more than $1250 to needy rabbis.[6]

A typical report from the Committee was the one offered in 1914 by Rabbi Samuel Deinard (1873–1921), stating that the Committee has had "no financial care, worries nor responsibilities." The Committee disbursed two monthly "pensions" of $25 each to widows of deceased CCAR members for a total of $600. The Fund had received more money than it expended, enjoying a surplus of $26,015 ($799,000 in 2023 dollars).[7]

Despite the complacency of the Committee of the Relief Fund, something was amiss. When the CCAR adopted a new Constitution in 1906, Article II stated that one of the objects of the Conference was "to make provision for such worthy colleagues, as owing to advanced age or other cause, are prevented from following their calling."[8] In January of 1913 the president of the UAHC, J. Walter Freiberg (1858–1921), called for the creation of a joint CCAR-UAHC commission to consider a pension plan for "superannuated ministers." Freiberg, who held the UAHC presidency from 1911 until his death a decade later, was a Cincinnati businessman and philanthropist. "[T]he fact remains," he wrote, "that in most cases [of aged rabbis], such men have been discharged and thrown upon the world, with little or no chance of securing professional employment, or otherwise earning a livelihood."[9] He was no doubt aware of economic and social developments in the area of retirement.

Changes in the Understanding of Retirement

The joint CCAR-UAHC Special Commission on Superannuated Ministers Fund adumbrated some of those developments in their Report delivered in 1916.[10] The CCAR delegation was led by Joseph Stolz (1861–1941; Chicago, Illinois), who was a member of Hebrew Union College's second ordination class and served as president of the CCAR from 1905 to 1907.

The first change in the understanding of retirement was to see financial support not as charitable relief but as just earnings:

> [T]his fund is not a charity to be administered by the good will of some committee, but is the obligation which justice imposes upon every congregation and theological seminary to make adequate and dependable provision for the old age or disability of every rabbi and theological professor serving the cause of Judaism.[11]

The Commission cited "the moral claims" demanded by employees of church groups, railroads, governments, and others for "deferred compensation for services actually rendered." This is a reference to a change in attitude among Americans regarding aging.[12] With the rise of capitalism in nineteenth-century America, retirement served the interests of business, labor, and the professions by making room for younger workers, by transferring work from one generation to another, and by invigorating moribund organizations.[13] The elder workers who were moved out of employment had to be cared for, and fairness demanded a system to subsidize them in their unemployment. Pension plans among private sector employees began in early 1800s in industries such as railroads, banking, and public utilities. They then spread to employees of manufacturing firms later in the nineteenth and early twentieth centuries.[14]

The second development that the Commission Report noted was that church groups too had already started to offer retirement plans. For example, the Episcopal Church first resolved to create a pension program for its ministers in 1910. Its Church Pension Fund was incorporated in 1914, and by 1917 it held assets of $8,500,000.[15] The Methodist Church founded its retirement plan in 1796 (!), and the pension plan of the Methodist Episcopal Church (North), a forerunner of the United Methodist Church, began operations in 1908. By 1927 it had reserves of $20,000,000 (about $349,000,000 in 2023 dollars).[16] Indeed, by 1927, sixteen national churches "reported having a pension plan or a relief plan for aged ministers."[17]

Thirdly, in support of their advocacy for a rabbinic pension fund, the members of the Commission referred to "the extraordinary demands now made upon the Jews of our country for the relief of the war sufferers."[18] The Commission members were clearly following the fundraising efforts on behalf of the European and Palestinian Jewish victims of World War I. Jacob Schiff himself led one such effort in New York to successfully raise $5,000,000.[19] The Commissioners seemed to be arguing that if the Jews of America have awakened to their responsibility for Jews abroad, surely they must be awake to their responsibilities for Jews here in the U.S., especially retired rabbis.

The Commissioners' final argument for the creation of a retirement fund invoked the Biblical tradition of justice and compassion in such passages as Deuteronomy 16:20 (*tzedek tzedek tirdof*, "Justice, justice you shall pursue") and Numbers 8:24–26 (the "retirement" of the Levites): "Shall we presume that the Jew who in ancient times taught such tender care for the Levites and showed so much solicitude for old age will, in our day, give a deaf ear to the call for justice toward those who, with great material sacrifice, are giving themselves to the service of their religion?"[20] The 1916 Report also recommended that, among other things, the CCAR change the Commission's name to the Commission on Synagog Pension Funds.[21]

Uncited but in the background of Stolz's Report was the Progressive Era in American history.[22] When Theodore Roosevelt launched in 1912 a third-party challenge to his own Republican party, he called his effort the Progressive Party; popularly it was known as the Bull Moose Party. In the planks of the Progressive Party's platform was a genuine concern for the lives of impoverished working Americans and a need for a social safety net for them. Absent, however, was a direct call for a system of retirement pensions.[23] In other words, while the Progressive movement laid the foundations for the creation of a national retirement pension system, it left the funding of retirement to local groups such as labor unions, large corporations, and fraternal organizations.

Jacob Schiff's Donation

Stolz sent Schiff the 1916 Special Commission Report, raising with him the issue of pensions for rabbis and educators. While vacationing in Bar Harbor, Maine, Schiff wrote Stolz a supportive letter on August 11 of that year:

> Dear Rabbi Stolz:
>
> The Report of the Committee on Superannuated Minister Fund, which you have sent me, has had my careful attention...With the object it treats I am in entire sympathy, and I only regret that the fund sought has not already been long in existence. It is a standing reproach to American Israel that this should not be so.
>
> I shall be very willing to contribute something to the preliminary expense fund, and should be pleased to be advised how much it is thought is required to cover the preliminary expenses; and when the proper time comes, I should consider it a privilege to start the fund.
>
> Yours faithfully,
> Jacob H. Schiff[24]

On January 10, 1917, Schiff's birthday, he sent a check for $100,000 to Freiberg, the president of the UAHC. In his cover letter he told Freiberg that the money was "intended to inaugurate [the pension fund] in accordance with plans now being worked out by a Committee of the new A.H.C., of which the Rev. Dr. Joseph Stolz is the Chairman."[25] Actually Schiff had done some fundraising of his own for the Fund. He received contributions from some of American Jewry's most prominent members, including Julius Rosenwald ($250) and Louis Marshall ($250). B'nai Israel Congregation of Davenport, Iowa, sent in $5.00, and the communities of Erie, Pennsylvania, and Raleigh, North Carolina, raised a combined $448.15.[26] The Fund's seed money totaled $103,608.15 ($2,720,000 in 2023 dollars).

Stolz and other Commission members were overjoyed. Stolz called upon the Conference to thank Schiff. The UAHC agreed to handle the administrative expenses of the Fund and an actuary, Mr. S. H. Wolfe, was appointed as a consultant.[27] Though there was no pension plan yet in existence, the Commission set about gathering the actuarial information from the rabbis that was necessary for the plan's inception.

For the next two years the Commission on the Synagog Pension Fund plodded along, until it was combined with the Committee on the Relief Fund in 1919. True, its funds were growing through compound interest so that in 1920 the Commission reported assets of $115,017.88.[28] The Commission continued to gather demographic data on the American rabbinate and sent letters to congregations encouraging their moral and financial support of the Fund. But the members acknowledged the need to raise $100,000 a year to fully fund the pension.

The Reform Advocate, a Chicago-based Jewish newspaper published from 1891 to 1941, reported on a proposed plan in its June 5, 1920, issue. According to the *Reform Advocate,* the Fund would require $1,348,700 and would cover all congregational rabbis and professors at the seminaries.[29] The plan was described as calling for congregational contributions for their rabbis starting at 8 percent of the rabbi's salary. The percentage would increase as the rabbi aged.[30] Apparently this plan got very little traction.

The Passing of Jacob Schiff

Schiff died on September 25, 1920. His passing sent the Commission on the Synagog Pension Fund into turmoil. Though the Fund continued to grow through gifts and bequests, it was woefully short of the $1,250,000 that the actuary calculated to be necessary to launch the pension. The frustration of the Commission members was evident in their report:

> The longer the delay, the more expensive the plan will be. The more the matter is protracted, the more the congregations will lose interest in the project. The more we dilly-dally, the greater our injustice to the memory of Mr. Jacob H. Schiff, who felt keenly his disappointment over the delay in the execution of this project which was very dear to his heart.[31]

Though it seemed that a pension fund for rabbis would never come to pass, the CCAR Commission members were still sending out questionnaires to collect data for the actuary.

In 1920, the UAHC Executive Board removed Daniel P. Hays (1854–1923) as chair of the Commission and appointed Ludwig Vogelstein (1871–1934) in his stead. Vogelstein, a metal trader, was an ardent supporter of the Reform Movement in North America and around the world. His brother, Herman, was a rabbi and a leader of Liberal Judaism in Germany. Vogelstein firmly believed that supporting a pension plan that depended on raising $1,300,000 was a mistake. Vogelstein wrote the Executive Board a lengthy letter demonstrating the impracticality of this pension plan and urging instead an insurance-based plan.[32] The UAHC asked him to prepare such a plan to provide pensions for the rabbis. Vogelstein got to work devising a plan that would be "a decided departure from the original plan."[33] Indeed, in his 1921 report to the UAHC Executive Board, Vogelstein called the original plan "sheer recklessness."[34] The Executive Board gave Vogelstein permission to formulate a specific plan and bring it back to the Executive Board.[35] By 1924 the plan was ready to take to the CCAR.

Stolz again delivered the joint report of the combined Committee on Relief Fund and Commission on Synagog Pension Fund to the CCAR in 1924. In it, he referred to a Plan III proposed by Vogelstein.[36] This time a serious conversation ensued, chaired by CCAR president Abram Simon (1872–1938). Vogelstein had presented his Plan III to the Commission, hoping to get approval for it from the Conference. Ephraim Frisch (1880–1957) preferred the original plan, believing that raising $1,300,000 was possible. Others disagreed. In the end, Plan III was referred back to the Commission for a full formulation and presentation.[37]

The following year, 1925, saw Simon still in the president's chair. In his "Message of the President," he labeled the pension issue "a hanging fire."[38] He argued that with or without a pension fund for rabbis, the CCAR must provide relief for needy colleagues. Since the Synagog Pension Fund now had $143,000 in it, he suggested the obvious:

> I do not hesitate to declare that, in the failure to adopt a Pension System, this Fund ought to be place at the disposal of the Conference and merged with our Relief Fund…Unwilling therefore, to anticipate the result of Friday's discussion, I cannot make any recommendation. I am merely allowing myself the luxury of thinking out loud.[39]

Perhaps Jacob Schiff's $100,000 donation to seed a pension fund for "superannuated ministers" would be absorbed into another fund.

On Friday afternoon (!), October 23, 1925, Vogelstein described Plan III to the entire Conference. He began by referring back to Plan I, the original plan, which had envisioned providing every congregational rabbi (no matter movement affiliation) and every seminary professor (no matter the seminary) with a $2500 annual pension ($44,300 in 2023 dollars). This Plan required a corpus of $1,300,000 to generate the pensions, according to the actuary. But the problems with Plan I, according to Vogelstein, were insurmountable: (a) the UAHC would need decades to raise that amount; (b) the UAHC had to cover its own internal expenses; and (c) the UAHC also had financial commitments to Hebrew Union College. Plan I would be a financial failure.[40]

Plan II was offered in 1920. Initially it would have collected a pension premium starting with rabbis forty years old and younger. As these rabbis would age and continue funding their retirement at age sixty-eight, their eventual pension payment would increase. Over the course of thirty years, sometime in the mid-1950s, all the rabbis of the CCAR would be included. But the plan left out rabbis who were older than forty in 1925, because it would have been exorbitantly expensive to fund their retirement. How could the CCAR leave behind those older rabbis who were most in need of pension money, asked Vogelstein? Plan II would be a moral failure.[41]

Vogelstein next turned to Plan III, which was intended to meet the shortcomings of the previous plans. Here were its key features:

- If the rabbi was under age forty-five, he or his congregations would contribute about $800 per year to the plan. The UAHC would contribute nothing. Beginning at age sixty-eight the rabbi would receive up to $2500 in annual pension payments.
- If the rabbi was between ages forty-five and fifty-five, he or his congregation would contribute $800 per year. The UAHC would contribute an additional $800 per year so that the rabbi would have sufficient funds in the plan to receive $2500 in annual pension payments beginning at age 68.
- If the rabbi over 55, the UAHC would contribute $850 per year, and the rabbi, the congregation, and the rabbi's friends would make up the difference.

One virtue of the plan was that the UAHC would drop out from subsidizing it gradually over time. After twenty or thirty years the plan would self-supporting.[42]

"The thing for you to decide," Vogelstein told the rabbis in attendance, "a matter for which your committee did not wish to take responsibility is, do you want the Pension System?...[B]ut the question is—do you want any insurance at all?"[43] In other words, Vogelstein was saying, if you rabbis want a pension plan, this is what it must look like.

"[I]t was moved and carried that the Conference authorize Mr. Vogelstein to report to the Executive Committee of the Union that the Conference accepts Plan III and requests that a committee be appointed to work out the details."[44] A few days later Vogelstein let the UAHC Executive Board know that the CCAR had accepted the Plan III pension plan, and the Executive Board authorized him to assemble a "Committee of Ten" to draw up the plan in detail.[45]

The Aftermath

Stolz was delighted to deliver his Report at the June 1926 CCAR Convention. For one thing, he told the Conference that in January of 1926 the UAHC Executive Board approved both the plan in principle and the addition of $100,000 to the Pension Fund's $149,000 in order to implement Plan III:

> It now appears as if the long-cherished dream of a Synagog Pension Fund will soon become a reality through the good-will, generosity and high sense of duty toward the Jewish ministry evidenced by the Union of American Hebrew Congregations and it becomes the bounden obligation of the Conference to cooperate in the same spirit.[46]

He meant that the rabbis needed to fill out the insurance questionnaires for the final formulation of the plan.

In his report the following year, Stolz was still buoyed "that the dream of our founder for the establishment of a rabbinical pension fund is an established fact."[47] The UAHC was in negotiation with the Metropolitan Life Insurance Company, which proposed ways to educate congregations about the plan and encourage them to sign on to it. Metropolitan Life was pioneer in the field of retirement pensions, offering the first group annuity plan in 1921.[48]

Stolz was so sure of the success of Plan III and the completion of his work that he recommended that "this Commission be herewith discontinued and our by-laws be amended accordingly."[49] But not all the rabbis were as sanguine as Stolz. Ephraim Frisch expressed his concern that, despite the final formulation of the plan, it still depended on individual congregations making use of the plan.[50] His words would prove prophetic.

In January 1928 Mortimer Schiff, Jacob's son, gave the UAHC Executive Board permission for his father's $100,000 gift to be used for Vogelstein's Plan III.[51] Stolz, in his June 1929 report to the CCAR Convention, noted that the Relief Fund had $118,799. He also lamented the fact that for the pension plan to go forward, twenty-five congregations would have to adopt it; only three had done so.

> Delay is costly. Every year adds to the expense all around, and it is to the decided advantage of every congregation to enter upon the plan without procrastination. As the Rabbi advances in age, the cost of the premium is naturally increased to the congregation and the Rabbi.[52]

The problem of the pension had become so acute that in his presidential message H.G. Enelow (1877–1934) decried the UAHC's inability to devise a workable pension plan. He also condemned the late payout age of sixty-eight of the proposed insurance-based plan. He called for the creation of yet another CCAR committee to study the possibility of a group insurance plan.[53] No one knew that in four months the stock market would crash on Black Tuesday, October 29, touching off ten years of economic chaos.

In January 1931 a discouraged Vogelstein, now the chairman of the UAHC Board, told his Executive Committee:

> Our pension plan has not received the favorable reception which we had hoped for and has remained a dead letter to this day… Our member congregations do not seem to realize that the Union is ready to make a very substantial contribution towards the pension system.[54]

Later that year CCAR president David Lefkowitz (1875–1955) wondered aloud in his President's Message why congregations would not sign on to the insurance-based pension plan. One reason for the apathy was the cost of the premiums, especially for rabbis over forty-five years old.[55] The Committee on Group Insurance had discovered that New York law prohibited group policies for associations like the CCAR, though other states permitted the issuance such policies.[56]

By the next CCAR Convention in November 1932, the entire nation was hard pressed by the Depression, even those with retirement pensions. "As of 1932, only 15 percent of American workers were potentially covered under the plans, and perhaps 5 percent of those who need benefits were actually receiving any."[57] The rabbinate was no exception. The Committee on Relief had distributed more than $19,000 to rabbis and widows, more than double the amount disbursed in the previous year. Financially strapped congregations had reduced their rabbis' wages or dismissed them outright. The Executive Board of the UAHC voted to release the money that Jacob Schiff had donated fifteen years previously, now totaling $197,500, for the relief of impoverished rabbis.[58] The Committee on Group Insurance ascribed its failure to the fact that the members of the CCAR did not have a common employer: "[T]he conclusion was reached that by no manner of reckoning could any plan of Group Insurance be devised which might be made available to the members of our organization."[59] Thus the only plan remaining was Vogelstein's Plan III with its high premiums. The mood seemed bitter.

By 1933 and 1934, the members of the CCAR were feeling the full sting of the Depression. The Committee on Relief disbursed twice as much money in 1934 as they had in 1933. As Chairman Stolz reported, the Committee was able to afford this because in addition to the CCAR's own Relief Fund, the Committee had access to the newly created "Jacob Schiff Pension Fund for the Relief of both Reform and Orthodox Rabbis."[60] In addition, the CCAR was directing relief money to rabbis in Germany through the Joint Distribution Committee.

Enter Samuel Gup

By 1934 Samuel Gup had assumed the chair of the Committee on Group Insurance. Born in Mobile, Alabama in 1894, Gup received his ordination in 1918. He served Temple Israel of Columbus, Ohio, from 1932 to 1946—the years of our story. He had been deeply involved in CCAR leadership, chairing the Committee on Relief and serving as the Conference's corresponding secretary. In his Report of the Committee on Group Insurance, Gup informed the Conference that the obtaining a group annuity program did not seem possible. Nonetheless, he begged "leave for permission to further [the Committee's] investigation of this subject."[61]

When it became clear to Gup that a group insurance policy was impractical and illegal, he seized upon another strategy. Why not organize and subsidize a program of individual annuities? That is, working with an insurance company, CCAR could make available to its members an annuity program with an annual payout of $600 ($13,590 in 2023 dollars) at age sixty-five, with the Conference contributing $50 each year toward each member's premium.[62] Gup sent out explanatory letters to a sample of thirty-five members, ten of whom replied. Seven approved of the plan and offered to participate; three demurred over the cost of the premium.

Seven out of ten was good enough for Gup. Significantly, the word "group" was dropped from the name of his committee. He continued researching "old-age annuities" with the assistance of UAHC chairman Jacob Mack (1876 to 1942) and insurance experts and UAHC leaders David Bressler and Lee K. Frankel, Jr. Gup became increasingly convinced that an individualized retirement annuity program "presents the fundamentals of the most appealing and far-sighted plan."[63] Effusively grateful to his UAHC partners, Gup recommended the creation of a joint commission "to constitute and maintain a program designed to accomplish the objectives herein indicated."[64]

UAHC Board chairman Mack reminded the 35th Council that the Social Security Act of 1935 specifically omitted ministers of religion, on the assumption that their church bodies would cover them: "We have neglected this duty for too long…we must do for them what the government of the United States is demanding for all its citizens."[65] According to Gup, Mack encouraged the delegates to include in their congregational budgets provisions for the retirement of their rabbis.[66] Gup continued to pursue the proposal to offer individual retirement annuities to CCAR members, and so he set about compiling actuarial information and expressing optimism about the plan.

1937 also saw Joseph Stolz, now seventy-six years old, still in the chair of the Committee on Relief, a position he had held for more than two decades. He had retired from his Chicago congregation in 1929. On December 10, 1937, he fell entering his home and broke his hip, rendering him a "helpless invalid."[67] He never again took part in CCAR leadership, and he died on February 7, 1941, without seeing Jacob Schiff's money transformed into a retirement program for rabbis.

JACOB SCHIFF, THE RPB, AND MY RETIREMENT

Now sitting in the chair of the Committee on the Pension Fund, Gup's enthusiasm for an annuity-type retirement plan was boundless. He pleaded with his colleagues in 1938 to get on board with this concept. He noted that Jews donated millions of dollars annually to worthy causes. Hyperbolically he wrote, "Would that some of this golden stream irrigate our old age desert."[68] In a 1938 letter to the UAHC's Executive Committee, David Bressler (1879–1942), the co-chair of the Joint Committee on Old Age Pensions for Rabbis, stated the obvious: "No satisfactory pension plan can become operative without the terribly important factor of adequate money background."[69]

Gup opened his 1939 Report with the following statement: "Nothing has developed since making our last extended report to warrant the submission of another report at this particular time."[70] Nonetheless, he managed to write an additional page and a half, concluding with a pessimistic appraisal of the possibility of engaging American Jews in the issue of rabbinic retirement pensions in light of "the woes of disinherited Jewry."[71] In the following year's brief Report, he simply proposed that the CCAR create a new Conference Pension Fund to which it would contribute $10,000 annually in order to cover all the years of service of older rabbis.[72]

In June 1941, Gup reported that in the previous year the CCAR Board had voted to allocate $100,000 to launch a pension plan for its members. Part of the impetus for this allocation was to goad the UAHC leadership into matching it:

> It is apparent, however, that with the best of intentions, the Union can be of little help to us in this direction for some time to come. It is so absorbed [in] its own financial problems that it has little heart to undertake the responsibility of organizing a campaign to raise the large amount of money that we require for this purpose.[73]

In the subsequent discussion the frustration was palpable, and blame for the decades of failure of the pension plan careened between the CCAR, the UAHC, and the congregations. In the end, Gup prevailed. "It is my thought that a pension program can be expedited if we eliminate the Union altogether and have the congregation and the rabbi contribute jointly towards the payment of the premium," he wrote in the Committee Report.[74]

The entrance of the United States into World War II in December 1941 did not slow the indefatigable Samuel Gup. He had been meeting with representatives from several insurance companies and, most notably, consulting with Solomon Huebner (1882–1964), "the father of insurance education."[75] Gup presented to the Conference an annuity plan whose "premium cost is to be shared by the rabbi, the congregation, and the Union and Conference acting jointly."[76] Gup's plan called for every congregation to contribute 7 percent of the rabbi's salary to the annuity, and for every rabbi to contribute 3 percent. In addition, the UAHC and the CCAR would create a Synagog Pension Board that would annually contribute between 1 percent and 5 percent of the rabbi's salary, depending on the rabbi's age at the start of the plan. At age sixty-five the rabbi could expect a pension more than 50 percent of his lifetime average salary.

Furthermore, the CCAR and the UAHC had access to the joint pension fund (thank you, Jacob Schiff), which by now had about $200,000 in it. The two organizations could tap the pension fund for $10,000 a year and also jointly pledge $20,000 annually to the Synagog Pension Board for a total contribution of $30,000 for the proposed fund.[77] With that, Gup offered a lengthy resolution for the approval of his annuity-based plan, which was accepted by the plenum with the details left to the leaders of the CCAR and the UAHC to work out.[78]

A year later, 1943, Gup proposed a fully worked out plan. The highlights were:

- Use of insurance companies to manage and supervise the annuity plan;
- Premiums paid by the rabbi (3% of salary), the congregation (7%), and, in the case of older rabbis, the UAHC and the CCAR (from their pension funds);
- Age of retirement, i.e., the age at which the annuity payments start, at sixty-five;
- Life insurance as an add-on for the benefit of widows; and
- The creation of a centralized and permanent Synagog Pension Board to oversee and to promote the plan.[79]

In November Jacob Aronson (1887–1951), now the UAHC co-chair of the Joint Committee on Rabbinical Pensions, called the plan "salutary and wholesome" in his report to the UAHC's Administrative Committee.[80] With these reports, the stage was set to launch a retirement plan for CCAR members twenty-six years after Jacob Schiff's $100,000 donation.

Takeaways

1944 was the watershed year when Gup's extraordinary efforts came to fruition. As stated in the Committee's report, "The Conference and the Union have great cause for self-congratulations."[81] The report detailed the plan and the governing agency, now called the Rabbinical Pension Board (RPB), which was created by appointment of its members in January 1944. Moreover, the plan was explained in depth in Appendix J in the *Yearbook*.[82] The president of the CCAR, Solomon Freehof, who was also a member of the Committee, let the Convention know that "[w]e turned over almost the entire capital of our Relief and Subvention Fund (about $150,000) to the new Pension Fund."[83] This represented "a radical change…in the financial status of the Conference."[84]

At long last, after nearly three decades, Schiff's donation underwrote a rabbinical pension system. The Jewish Telegraphic Agency heralded the creation of the Rabbinical Pension Board, acknowledging Schiff's founding gift.[85] Isaac Mayer Wise did not live to see a pension plan; Joseph Stolz did not live to see a pension plan; Jacob Schiff did not live to see a pension plan. Samuel Gup, who got a plan over the goal line, died in 1955 at age sixty-one, too young to make use of his pension.

The UAHC and the CCAR had tried to institute numerous plans:

1. Isaac Meyer Wise's plan to fund pensions through the sale of the UPB I;
2. A retirement fund whose corpus would generate enough earnings to pay for all the pensions without invading the principal (Jacob Schiff's donation);
3. Pension premiums paid starting only with rabbis under age forty;
4. Vogelstein's plan with Metropolitan Life subsidized by the UAHC;
5. Group insurance;
6. Individualized annuity-based plan with life insurance feature;

All the plans had sounded good, but for financial, legal, or organizational reasons the UAHC and the CCAR had been unable to implement them. The two organizations had the best of intentions, but perhaps too many people, too many meetings, too much "expertise" and not enough capital prevented them from achieving the goal. The last one was only realized through the dogged efforts of Samuel Gup, whom very few rabbis could identify today.

The effort to establish a pension plan for rabbis harks back to an era of extraordinary comity and cooperation between the CCAR and the UAHC. In the pages of the CCAR *Yearbooks* and the *Proceedings* of the UAHC, there is little hint of distrust or dissatisfaction with rabbis or lay leaders. Quite the contrary, the rabbis seem genuinely grateful to UAHC leaders, and the UAHC leaders seem truly concerned for the well-being of retired rabbis.

Another striking feature of this effort is the sheer tenacity of the CCAR leaders in pursuit of this project. Literally from the founding of the CCAR in 1889 to 1944, fifty-five years, CCAR leaders explored different ways to create a pension system. Jacob Schiff's donation in 1917 supercharged the effort, but the amount was not enough to fund a plan. Despite many obstacles and failures, the resilient leaders of the CCAR kept at it through several different chairmen and committees. Moreover, they had to contend with two World Wars and the Great Depression. In the end, a rabbi known to few today delivered on a plan for which thousands of retired rabbis are beholden.

The creation of a pension system for CCAR rabbis can also be understood as a stage in the maturation of the Reform rabbinate. As the Reform rabbinate became increasingly professionalized, the CCAR emerged as the primary association for Reform rabbis. Over time, like any professional association, the CCAR developed eligibility standards and behavioral expectations for its members. It also sought to offer benefits such as annual conventions, educational opportunities, and collegial relationships. Eventually a placement system was created and financial incentives such as a pension program arose. The CCAR's pension plan came together around the same time as its placement system started to congeal.[286] The establishment of a pension plan, a placement system, and a code of ethics marks significant steps in the professionalization of the Reform rabbinate.

Thank you, Jacob Schiff, for the process that you set in motion that enabled me to retire.

Notes

1. I am deeply grateful to the early readers of this article: Rabbi Steven Fox, Susana Castillo, Robert Koppel, Michael Kimmel, Rabbi Beth Lieberman, and Rabbi Lance Sussman.
2. *New York Times*, January 16, 1917, p. 3.
3. *Year Book of the CCAR* 1 (1890–1891), 24.
4. "Presidential Address by Dr. I. M. Wise," *CCAR Yearbook* 3 (1893): 24. I am indebted to Noah Brockman of the Frances-Henry Library of HUC-JIR in Los Angeles for finding this document.
5. "Presidential Address," 27.
6. "Treasurer's Report," *Yearbook of the CCAR* 9 (1899): 28.
7. Samuel Deinard, Report of the Committee on the Relief Fund, *CCAR Yearbook* 24 (1914), 107–108. The word "pension" is a little confusing; these are not pensions in our modern sense of the word. These are allocations for which the rabbi had to apply and meet certain criteria. A committee then voted on the eligibility of the rabbi to receive this relief money. In this respect the fund appears to have functioned much like today's CCAR Hesed Fund.
8. *Year Book of the CCAR* 16 (1906): 17.
9. Walter Freiberg, "President's Message to the Twenty-Third Council," *Proceedings of the Union of American Hebrew Congregations*, 7 (1911–1915), 7082.
10. "Report of the Special Commission on Superannuated Ministers Fund," *CCAR Yearbook* 26 (1916): 47–50.
11. "Report of the Special Commission," 47–48.
12. William Graebner, *A History of Retirement* (Yale University Press, 1980), 10.
13. *History of Retirement*, 49.
14. Patrick W. Seburn, "Evolution of Employer-Provided Defined Benefit Pensions," *Monthly Labor Review* Vol. 114 No. 12 (December 1991): 17. Many thanks to Rabbi Lance Sussman for this article.
15. https://www.cpg.org/global/about-us/overview/our-history/. Today the CPG has assets of more than $17 billion (https://www.cpg.org/global/about-us/about-cpg/).
16. "Care of the Aged: Church Pension and Relief Plans," *Monthly Labor Review* 28.5 (1929): 92–109. http://www.jstor.org/stable/41813591. 100.
17. "Care of the Aged," 92.
18. "Report of Commission on Superannuated Ministers Fund," 48.

19. Jonathan Sarna, *American Judaism, A History* (Yale University Press, 2004), 208.
20. "Report of the Commission on Superannuated Rabbis Fund," 49.
21. "Report of the Commission on Superannuated Rabbis Fund," 49–50.
22. I am indebted to Rabbi Lance Sussman for this insight.
23. The federalization of a retirement pension system would await the passage of the 1935 Social Security Act.
24. Cyrus Adler, *Jacob H. Schiff: His Life and Letters*, vol. 2 (Doubleday Doran, 1928), 51–52. About Schiff vacationing in Bar Harbor, Daniel Schulman writes, "Each August the Schiff clan and their retinue of domestic help laboriously relocated from Sea Bright to Bar Harbor, Maine; even their horses made the journey...In Bar Harbor, Schiff enjoyed hiking the coastal trail and summiting the peaks of Mount Desert Island in what would become Acadia National Park." *The Money Kings: The Epic Story of the Jewish Immigrants Who Transformed Wall Street and Shaped Modern America* (Alfred Knopf, 2023), 256–57.
25. Jacob Schiff, letter dated January 10, 1917, American Jewish Archives (Cincinnati, Ohio), Union of Reform Judaism Records, MS-72, box A1-41, folder 8.
26. Jacob Schiff, letter dated January 10, 1917.
27. Wolfe (1874–1928) was a prominent actuary who published and lectured widely on actuary topics. He specialized in inheritance tax calculations, workers compensation, and reinsurance. He rose through the ranks of the Quartermaster Corps of the U.S. Army and President Warren Harding appointed him a Brigadier General. In 1926 he was stabbed by an irate relative whom he turned down for a loan. He died suddenly on January 1, 1928.
28. *CCAR Yearbook* 30 (1920): 30.
29. "Synagog Pension Fund," in *The Reform Advocate* 54.18 (June 5, 1920), 429.
30. "Synagog Pension Fund," 430.
31. *CCAR Yearbook* 31 (1921): 74.
32. "Report of the Sub-Committee on Synagog Pension Fund," *Proceedings of the Union of American Hebrew Congregations, 47th Annual Report (1919-1920)*, 8707–09.
33. *CCAR Yearbook* 32 (1922): 78.
34. "Report of the Sub-Committee on Synagog Pension Fund," *Proceedings of the Union of American Hebrew Congregations," 48th Annual Report (1920–1921)*, 8953.
35. "Report of the Sub-Committee on Synagog Pension Fund," *Proceedings...48th Annual Report*, 8960.
36. *CCAR Yearbook* 34 (1924): 98.

37. *CCAR Yearbook* 34 (1924): 110–12.
38. "Message of the President," *CCAR Yearbook* 35 (1925): 236.
39. "Message of the President," 236–37.
40. "Plans for Pension Fund," *CCAR Yearbook* 35 (1925): 358–59.
41. "Plans for Pension Fund," 359–60.
42. "Plans for Pension Fund," 360–62.
43. "Plans for Pension Fund," 362.
44. "Discussion of Pension Plan," *CCAR Yearbook* 35 (1925): 185.
45. "Report of the Synagog Pension Fund Commission," *Proceedings of the Union of American Hebrew Congregations, 52nd Annual Report (1924-1925)*, 9913–14.
46. "Report of the Committee of Relief Fund and Commission on Synagog Pension Fund," *CCAR Yearbook* 36 (1926): 117.
47. "Report of the Committee on Relief Fund and Commission on Synagog Pension Fund," *CCAR Yearbook* 37 (1927): 133.
48. Seburn, "Evolution of Pensions," 18.
49. Seburn, "Evolution of Pensions," 18.
50. Seburn, "Evolution of Pensions," 133–34.
51. "Proceedings of the Executive Board—January 1928," *Proceedings of the Union of American Hebrew Congregations* 11 (1926–1930): 22.
52. "Report of the Committee on Relief," *CCAR Yearbook* 39 (1929): 97.
53. "President's Message," *CCAR Yearbook* 39 (1929): 195–96.
54. Ludwig Vogelstein, "Address of the Chairman of the Executive Committee—January 19, 1931," *Proceedings of the Union of American Hebrew Congregations* 12 (1931–1935):189.
55. "President's Message," *CCAR Yearbook* 41 (1931): 200.
56. "Report of the Committee on Group Insurance," *CCAR Yearbook* 41 (1931):130–35.
57. Graebner, *A History of Retirement*, 133.
58. "Report of the Committee on Relief," *CCAR Yearbook* 42 (1932): 91–93.
59. "Report of the Committee on Group Insurance," *CCAR Yearbook* 42 (1932): 136–7.
60. "Report of the Committee on Relief," *CCAR Yearbook* 43 (1933): 96.
61. "Report of the Committee on Group Insurance," *CCAR Yearbook* 44 (1934): 68
62. "Report of the Committee on Group Insurance," *CCAR Yearbook* 45 (1935): 90–91.
63. "Report of the Committee on Insurance," *CCAR Yearbook* 46 (1936): 86.
64. "Report of the Committee on Insurance," *CCAR Yearbook* 46 (1936): 86.

65. Jacob Mack, "The Address of the Chairman—1937," *Proceedings of the 35th Council of the Union of American Hebrew Congregations*, in the Proceedings of the Union of American Hebrew Congregations Vol. XII (1936–1943): 183. Clergy were also omitted because Social Security contributions were considered a tax, and churches were tax exempt. Amendments to the Act in 1954, 1967, and 1972 made clergy participation permissible.
66. "Report of the Committee on Insurance," *CCAR Yearbook* 47 (1937): 82–83.
67. Tobias Schanfarber, "Joseph Stolz," *American Jewish Yearbook* 43 (1941–1942): 442; ajcarchives.org/portal/Yearbooks/en-US/Record/View/Index/6.
68. "Report of the Committee of the Pension Fund," *CCAR Yearbook* 48 (1938): 151.
69. David Bressler, "Appendix IL Report of the Committee on Rabbinical Pensions—June 1938," *Proceedings of the Executive Board of the Union of American Hebrew Congregations* in the Proceedings of the Union of American Hebrew Congregations Vol. XIII (1936–1943): 46.
70. "Report of the Committee on Pension Fund," *CCAR Yearbook* 49 (1939): 178.
71. "Report of the Committee on Pension Fund," *CCAR Yearbook* 49 (1939): 179.
72. "Report of the Committee on Pensions," *CCAR Yearbook* 50 (1940): 178–79.
73. "Report of the Committee on Pension Fund," *CCAR Yearbook* 51(1941): 179–80.
74. "Report of the Committee on Pension Fund," *CCAR Yearbook* 51(1941): 180.
75. "Report of the Committee on Pension Plan," *CCAR Yearbook* 52 (1942): 188–89. In 1942 Huebner was Professor of Insurance and Commerce at the Wharton School and Dean of the American College of Underwriters. He was the author of many volumes on insurance and retired from teaching in 1953. See https://en.wikipedia.org/wiki/Solomon_S._Huebner.
76. "Report of the Committee on Pension Plan," *CCAR Yearbook* 52 (1942): 189.
77. "Report of the Committee on Pension Plan," *CCAR Yearbook* 52 (1942): 192.
78. "Report of the Committee on Pension Plan," *CCAR Yearbook* 52 (1942): 197.
79. "Report of the Committee on Pension Plan," *CCAR Yearbook* 52 (1943): 87–91.
80. Jacob Aronson, "Appendix A: Report of the Joint Committee on Rabbinical Pensions—November 1943," in *Proceedings of the*

       Executive Board of the Union of American Hebrew Congregations in Proceedings of the Union of American Hebrew Congregations 13 (1936–1943): 23.
81. "Report of the Committee on Pension Plan," *CCAR Yearbook* 54 (1944): 122.
82. "Appendix J," *CCAR Yearbook* 54 (1944): 278–85.
83. "Report of the President," *CCAR Yearbook* 54 (1944): 23.
84. "Report of the President," *CCAR Yearbook* 54 (1944): 23.
85. "Pension Plan for Rabbis Established by Union of American Hebrew Congregations," *Jewish Telegraphic Agency Daily Bulletin* Vol. XI No. 47 (February 27, 1944): 4.
86. Alan Henkin, "The Unholy Scramble for Pulpits: A History of the Reform Rabbinical Placement (Part 1): 1893–1961," *CCAR Journal* 61.4 (Fall 2014): 107–32.

CCAR RESPONSUM 5784.1
Photographic Images on Tombstones

Sh'eilah

My congregation has recently re-established its cemetery committee and we have been working on formulating policies. The question has come up about just what is permitted on tombstones in the way of images or pictures. It was mentioned that there is a Russian practice of having images of the deceased on the tombstone, and that at least some Russian Jews have brought the practice with them to the US. We don't currently have any Russian Jews in the congregation, but we want to be as inclusive as possible in our policies. (Rabbi Renni Altman, Vassar Temple, Poughkeepsie, NY)

T'shuvah

This *sh'eilah*[1] is about halachah and *minhag* (custom) and the relationship between them. It is not enough to consider what the halachah says with regard to photographic images on tombstones. There is also the question of the variation in practice among different Jewish communities. We Jews are deeply attached to customs that have little grounding in law; how should we reconcile commitments to very different customs? To what extent should a congregation with an established *minhag* be open to other *minhagim*, and under what circumstances?

I. Halachah: tombstones and imagery

Although the Torah's first mention of a burial practice is Abraham purchasing the cave of Machpelah in order to bury his wife Sarah, the Torah also references the practice of burying the dead in the earth and erecting a marker, both to mark the location and to remember the person buried there. This ritual is first recorded at the death of the matriarch Rachel: "Thus Rachel died. She was buried on the road to Ephrath—now Bethlehem. Over her grave

Jacob set up a pillar (*matzeivah*); it is the pillar at Rachel's grave to this day" (Genesis 35:19–20). The term *matzeivah*, from the root for "standing in place," is the classic Hebrew term still in use for grave markers today.

The Jews of the Land of Israel practiced both cave burial and earth burial from ancient times well into the first millennium. Archaeological findings attest to elaborate inscriptions on the sarcophagi or grave markers of those who could afford them, although some early rabbis expressed strong sentiment against such elaborate displays.[2] For example, R. Shimon ben Gamliel said: "One does not erect *n'fashot* [grave markers] to the righteous, for their words are their memorial,"[3] a sentiment repeated by Maimonides even as he describes what had become the norm by his time:

> They dig pits in the earth and make a burial chamber in the side of the pit and bury him in it face up. Then they replace the earth and the stones (*avanim*) upon him. And they should bury him in a wooden coffin. And those that accompany him say to him, "Go in peace," as it is said, "You shall go to your fathers in peace" (Genesis 15:15). And they mark off the entire cemetery [so that *kohanim* will not accidentally tread on graves] and they build a marker (*nefesh*) on the grave. But we do not build markers on the graves of the righteous, for their words are their memorials.[4]

What is inscribed on the *matzeivah* varies widely. In many traditional Jewish communities in the United States, it is still the custom to raise up a large marker that contains "an elaborate tribute to the virtues of the occupant of the grave," as Rabbi Isaac Klein described it.[5] In other communities, markers are more modest, smaller and lower to the ground. They often include the name of the deceased in English and Hebrew, the dates of birth and death, perhaps a symbol indicating that the deceased claimed descent from priestly (hands in prayer) or Levitical (ewer from Temple service) lineage, and sometimes a line of prose or poetry describing positive traits of the deceased.

While many rabbinic authorities praised simplicity, the people did not always agree. As the *Encyclopedia Judaica* states:

> A desire for originality allied to an emphasis on tradition is characteristic of the tombstones in Jewish cemeteries. Here the anonymous Jewish craftsman succeeded perhaps better than in most

other fields of art in establishing an individual style. There are few branches of Jewish art which are distinguished by such richness of decoration, and by such a variety of symbolism, as tombstone art. Thus a study of Jewish tombstones is a rich source of material for the study of Jewish art from ancient times to the present. The artistic and traditional development of the tombstone and of its individual style is based on two factors: (a) the desire for perpetuation; (b) artistic expression and the participation of the various branches of the plastic arts in its creation. Hence the great value of the tombstone not only lies in the study of epitaphs, but also in its ornamentation.[6]

It further notes that early modern Ashkenazic headstones were often quite elaborate, with carvings indicating not only *kohen* or *levi* status, but also praiseworthy qualities (a pair of lit candles for a pious woman), an individual's name (e.g., a deer for someone named Naftali Hirsch), or even their trade (e.g., scissors for a barber). The artistry went beyond even these.

All the religious and philosophical ideas connected with death, the phenomenon of death itself, man's mortality, his ways on earth and his relationship with God and eternity, were given artistic expression in stone. Sometimes death was depicted as a flickering flame, as a shipwrecked vessel, an overturned and extinguished lamp, or a flock without a shepherd. The fear of death was sometimes symbolized by fledglings nestling under their mother's wing. Heraldic designs were also used on tombstones, particularly in Eastern Europe. They took the form of a pair of lions, deer or even sea-horses holding the crowns of the Torah. Other animals also appeared occasionally, such as bears, hares, squirrels and ravens—the raven being the harbinger of disaster.[7]

Nevertheless, there were limits to what sort of images were acceptable. In the *Shulchan Aruch* (1575), R. Yosef Karo likened imagery to idolatry and prohibited certain images, especially human ones, on tombstones:

It is prohibited to form figures of the divine heavenly realm such as the four faces (of the prophetic vision) together and similarly the figures of *ofanim*, and *seraphim*, and the ministering angels. And similarly [this prohibition includes] the figure of a human being itself (i.e., in its entirety)…When was this stated? When they are images that protrude (such as three-dimensional images).

However, flat or engraved images like those woven onto a garment or those formed on a wall with dyes (murals) are permitted. The form of the sun, moon, and stars are prohibited whether they protrude or are flat or engraved. But if they are for the purposes of learning—to understand and to teach all are permitted, even protruding [images].

Isserles: And there are those that permit these figures if they are publicly owned[8] as then there is no suspicion about their use.[9]

Thus Karo prohibits protruding human figures, but not two-dimensional ones or engraved ones, while Isserles opens a possible door to them. Nevertheless, the authors of the encyclopedia article point out, Ashkenazic tombstones rarely, if ever, included human figures at all.

The question of what sorts of images were permitted on Jewish grave markers became a matter of controversy in the nineteenth century as acculturated Jews in western and central Europe adopted the aesthetics of the societies among whom they lived. This in turn aroused the ire of Rabbi Moses Sofer (1762–1839) of Pressburg (Bratislava), known as the Chatam Sofer, a leading voice in the defense of traditional values and practices. Asked about a Jewish tombstone with a "protruding human figure" on it,[10] he castigated the practice as unacceptable. Even though, he acknowledged, the *Shulchan Aruch* allowed such practices in public, nevertheless, he stated, it was "an unseemly thing." Furthermore, people come to graves to pray, and it would be improper to pray in front of a human image. If they could not persuade the family to remove it, or to deface it, no one should pray at that grave. Finally, it is problematic, he argued, because it is a gentile custom.[11] They are accustomed to putting the image they worship on all of their structures; we should not appear to imitate them by putting a human image on a grave.

Rabbi Naftali Brawer, a contemporary Orthodox rabbi, surmises that the Chatam Sofer would not have approved even of photos on tombstones. "He does not…refer to pictures (it would have been paintings in his time as photography didn't really exist before the 1830s)…[but] it is more than likely that his opposition would extend to photos as well. Rabbi Sofer was a harsh critic of Jewish acculturation to non-Jewish modern trends and this, more than anything, may have driven his reaction to this modish practice."[12]

In this instance, as in many others, the Chatam Sofer's complete resistance to any perceived imitation of gentile ways led to the emergence of a more restrictive view of what "tradition" regarded as acceptable. Thus, a certain Rabbi Menachem Posner feels free, in a responsum on a Chabad website, to cite his responsum as categorical proof that one may not put a photograph on a tombstone: "So, what about a photograph: would Rabbi Sofer have allowed it? While the issue of a graven image may not apply, the issue of placing a human image in a place of worship most certainly would. *And for this reason, it is not Jewish practice to have photos placed on headstones* [emphasis added]."[13]

However, the modern Orthodox authority Rabbi Yekutiel Yehudah Greenwald of Columbus took issue with the Chatam Sofer's restrictive attitude toward imagery specifically in regard to photographs, in his masterwork *Kol Bo al Aveilut* (Comprehensive Guide to Mourning),[14] choosing instead to rely strictly on the *Shulchan Aruch*. He emphasizes that *only* protruding images are prohibited, not photographs or similar two-dimensional images. Referring to the nineteenth-century fashion of adorning a headstone with the portrait of the deceased person printed on paper and placed under glass, he rules: "There is no prohibition except for a full three-dimensional form. All the more so in cases like this where it is not sunk in or three-dimensional but merely painted, [it is permissible] according to the *Tosafot*."[15] His only restriction is that the image should not have legs, i.e., should not be a complete human image. Greenwald further cites a precedent from none other than Rabbi Abraham Sofer (1815–1871), the son of the Chatam Sofer, approving for synagogue use a *Shiviti*[16] with a portrait of Sir Moses Montefiore. The younger Sofer stated that there was no prohibition unless the image included a full likeness of the person. Greenwald then adds the proviso that in a synagogue, the image should be "above the height of a man, so that it would not be looked upon at the time of *t'filah*" and take one's thoughts away from prayer (and *not* because it might be construed as idolatry).

Greenwald notes additionally that the Maharam Schick (R. Moses b. Joseph Schick, 1807–1879), a student of the Chatam Sofer, prohibited images on tombstones, but refuses to extrapolate from there to a ban on photographs:

> I saw that [an unidentified rabbi] prohibited placing images on tombstones on the strength of what Maharam Schick wrote (YD

120): "It is certainly incumbent upon us to preserve every Jewish custom, including the custom not to permit placing images of the dead on tombstones." But in fact, Maharam Schick only prohibited protruding images there, and with regard to photographs, he did not say anything explicit, either in the question or in the response, and we cannot assume what was in his heart. Therefore we find no grounds anywhere to prohibit photographs, and therefore we must not spark conflicts by claiming such a prohibition comes from Maharam Schick.[17]

From this discussion it is clear that a photograph or other two-dimensional image of the deceased's face and upper body (or, for that matter, an incised image) on a tombstone is not a violation of halachah. It is not a prohibited three-dimensional protruding image, nor a prohibited complete human image, nor is it possibly going to be mistaken for an idolatrous image. And if it conforms to those three requirements, it cannot *ipso facto* be regarded as a prohibited imitation of gentile customs. There is, therefore, no objection in halachah to photographs on tombstones.

II. *Minhag* (custom) and acculturation

Why, then, has this question arisen? It is because of the power of *minhag*. As we are often reminded by the halachic literature itself, *Minhag Yisrael Torah hu*, "Jewish custom has the force of law."[18] American Jews have generally not placed photos on tombstones because it was not the normative custom of the great wave of immigrants who arrived between 1881 and 1924. We also note that American Jews generally do not include floral wreaths at funerals, regarding it as a "gentile practice;"[19] but anyone who has seen a Jewish funeral in Israel knows that it is commonly done there.

Similarly, there are Jews for whom photos on tombstones is a normative custom, and in recent years they have immigrated to the US in larger and larger numbers. Russian, Georgian, and Bukharan Jews whose families lived in the Soviet Union commonly erect elaborate tombstones with photographs of the deceased, following the custom of their place of origin. In 2013, the *Forward* published a story on the proliferation of photos on elaborate tombstones of Jews at Brooklyn's Washington Cemetery. Author Josh Nathan-Kazis dated the origin of the practice to the 1950s when the Bukharan Jews were still living in central Asia. "'All over the

Soviet Union the cemeteries have pictures on the headstones. It's a totally Soviet thing,' said Leonard Petlakh, executive director of the Kings Bay Y in Brooklyn, in response to a reporter's question."[20] Significantly, however, after that article appeared, Jewish Heritage Europe published large, detailed photos of several such gravestones in Sharhorod, Ukraine, noting that the practice actually predates the Soviet era: "Starting in the latter part of the 19th century, long before laser technology came in, it was common practice in many countries to attach enamel photographs of the deceased on headstones."[21] Such depictions of the faces of the deceased are also well-attested among Jews in central Europe, including Prague's newer Jewish cemetery in the Vinohrady neighborhood.[22] These examples make it clear that this question is not a matter of halachah, but of *minhag hamakom*, "local custom."

During the great wave of immigration to the US, Jews from different locations in the Old World often organized synagogues around shared liturgical practices, which reflected either ideological or geographical commonalities.[23] However, after the Second World War, as native-born American Jews moved out of the immigrant neighborhoods, those older identifying customs lost their significance, especially in Conservative and Reform synagogues.

To be sure, people tend to like doing things "as we always have done them," even if it is not strictly accurate. It does not take more than a generation or two to establish a practice that is seen as "the way we have always done it here."[24] That can be especially true for anything involving death or burial, matters about which people are often surprisingly conservative. But given the absence of halachic basis for prohibiting photographs, and the reality that it is strictly a matter of custom (and perhaps personal taste), it behooves us to be flexible. The photos themselves may be a practice that will disappear as the newest immigrants nativize. As Leonard Petlakh observed regarding the practice: "We're all products of the culture. It will not be definitely there in the next generation."[25]

III. Conclusion

Sometime ago, this committee was asked about the propriety of adding a QR code to a tombstone, a practice that allows others to access more detailed information about the deceased than what can be included on a tombstone. In our affirmative response, we cited Rabbi Greenwald's comments on the changing nature of tombstone inscriptions: "The story [Yekutiel Greenwald] tells is of a *minhag* that has developed over the centuries in accordance with changing tastes. Each Jewish community in each generation has determined its own standards for what is proper and improper to inscribe upon a tombstone."[26]

We conclude that the same holds true for photographs or incised images on tombstones, within the halachic parameters of representation of human images. Prohibitions of such images have no foundation in halachah, but only in *minhag hamakom*. In this particular case we encourage the community to be inclusive with regard to the customs of fellow Jews.

The CCAR Responsa Committee

Rabbi Carey Brown
Rabbi Phil Cohen
Rabbi Joan S. Friedman, chair
Rabbi Ben Gurin
Rabbi Suzie Jacobson
Rabbi Audrey Korotkin
Rabbi Amy Scheinerman
Rabbi Brian Stoller
Rabbi Micah Streiffer
Rabbi David Vaisberg
Rabbi Michael Walden
Rabbi Dvora Weisberg
Rabbi Jeremy Weisblatt

Notes

1. Credit for the primary work on this responsum goes to Rabbi Audrey Korotkin.
2. For a fuller account of the evolution of Jewish practice with regard to grave markers see Ze'ev Yeivin and David Davidovitch, "Tombs and Tombstones," in *Encyclopaedia Judaica*, 2nd ed., edited by Michael Berenbaum and Fred Skolnik (Macmillan Reference USA, 2007), vol. 20, 32–37.
3. *B'reishit Rabbah* 82:10; Jerusalem Talmud, *Shekalim* 2:7, 47a.
4. *Mishneh Torah, Hilkhot Evel* 4:4.
5. Isaac Klein, *A Guide to Jewish Religious Practice* (Jewish Theological Seminary of America, 1979), 296.

6. "Tombs and Tombstones," 35.
7. "Tombs and Tombstones," 37.
8. A Jew who would set up such an image in private would immediately be suspected of doing so for worship, i.e., of following Christian or other non-Jewish practices. But that suspicion would not apply to someone who erects an image in public.
9. *Shulchan Aruch, Yoreh Dei-ah* 141:4.
10. *Sh'eilot U-T'shuvot, Chatam Sofer* 6:4.
11. The Torah passage *You shall not copy the practices of the land of Egypt where you dwelt, or of the land of Canaan where I am taking you; nor shall you observe their laws* (Leviticus 18:3) is understood by the tradition as a negative commandment, prohibiting imitating gentile ways, especially in religious practice.
12. https://www.thejc.com/judaism/all/can-i-incorporate-a-photograph-into-a-gravestone-1.519170.
13. "Can We Put a Photo on the Tombstone?" https://www.chabad.org/library/article_cdo/aid/1222460/jewish/Can-We-Put-a-Photo-on-the-Tombstone.htm.
14. Yekutiel Yehuda Greenwald (1889–1955), *Kol Bo al Aveilut* (Philip Feldheim, Inc., 1973 [original publication 1947–1952]), 380, n. 1.
15. *Tosafot* to *Bavli Yoma* 54a, in which the rabbis discussed the fact that when the Temple stood, the people were shown the *k'ruvim* joined together on the Holy Ark as long as they were already inserted into their containers and thus posed no risk of worshiping idols. He also offers multiple prooftexts here froma a range of later Ashkenazic authorities that also forbid only full three-dimensional forms.
16. A *Shiviti* is a plaque or marker inscribed with Psalm 16:8, "I set (*shiviti*) Adonai before my eyes at all times," hung in a synagogue or home to mark the eastern wall.
17. Greenwald, *Kol Bo*, 380, n. 1.
18. *Magen Avraham* 307:16 and many other sources.
19. As Isaac Klein writes: "The use of flowers at funerals—myrtles, to be exact—is mentioned in the Talmud (Babylonian Talmud, B'rachot. 53a, Bava Kama 16b; *Shulchan Aruch, Orach Chayim* 526:4), but is discouraged in current practice, both from a desire to keep funerals simple and in opposition to the introduction of alien and pagan customs." Klein, *Guide*, 280.
20. Josh Nathan-Kazis, "Ornate Gravestones Tell Stories of Soviet Lives," *Forward*, January 20, 2013; https://forward.com/news/169454/ornate-gravestones-tell-stories-of-soviet-lives/.

    The custom is also found in Iran. In May 2023, in western Iran, officials ordered the removal of a gravestone depicting the image of a woman without a hijab, deemed inappropriate as well as illegal. According to one journalistic account: "Last year, Iran started policing the compulsory Islamic dress code—or hijab—on tombstones in the country's largest cemetery, located in the southern part of the capital Tehran. The cemetery removed scores of gravestones which had pictures of deceased women without veils." The director of the Behesht-e Zahra cemetery, Saeed Ghazanfari, had stated that the procedure will continue in the future "in accordance with the opinion of [religious] scholars until all the gravestones with such pictures are removed." See https://www.iranintl.com/en/202304297680.

21. https://jewish-heritage-europe.eu/2013/01/20/portraits-on-jewish-gravestones-laser-and-photo/.
22. Seen by Rabbi Joan Friedman when she was living in Prague in 1988.
23. For example, many US cities had or still have synagogues named *Anshei Sfard*. This does not mean that the founders were Sephardic Jews, but that they used the Sephardic rite favored by the Chasidim. Note also the "First Roumanian-American Congregation" established on the Lower East Side in 1860 and the "Meserich Synagogue" founded there in 1888 by immigrants from that Polish city. There are many more such examples.
24. Rabbi Audrey Korotkin observes, for example, that at Mount Sinai Cemetery in Altoona, Pennsylvania, families have typically erected large headstones with last names on them and, after death, dedicated a small footstone that sits flat and low to the ground with the deceased's English and Hebrew names and dates of birth and death, and community members expect that others will conform to that model.
25. "Ornate Gravestones," *Forward*.
26. 5773.4: Quick Response Codes Embedded in Tombstone, https://www.ccarnet.org/ccar-responsa/qr-codes-embedded-tombstone/.

True Forgiveness: A Responsum and Two Case Studies

Rabbi Marc J. Rosenstein[1]

Intrigued by Hannah Arendt's statement that the "role of forgiveness in the realm of human affairs" was discovered by Jesus of Nazareth,[2] I began to search Jewish classical and modern texts for insights on interpersonal forgiveness. It turns out that forgiveness is not so simple, standing at the interface of performance and intention. In this essay I examine a modern responsum and then explore its implications in two classical texts, Jacob's reconciliation with Esau, and Rabbi Eleazar and the ugly man.

Rabbi Haim David Halevi

Rabbi Haim David Halevi (1924–1998) succeeded Rabbi Ovadiah Yosef in 1973 as Sephardic Chief Rabbi of Tel Aviv. In 1984, just before Yom Kippur, he received this question:

> There is a man who for over a year has been troubling me greatly, including slandering me, and despite all my efforts to reconcile with him I have not been successful, and he continues to persecute me. What will be the verdict on the coming Yom Kippur eve? Must I forgive him? Is there an obligation to forgive him if he does not seek my forgiveness? And if I am sure that after Yom Kippur he will continue to persecute me, am I obligated to forgive him even so? And I fear that even if by law I am obligated to forgive him, I will not be able; even if I forgive him in my words, in my heart I will not be able to do so.[3]

Rabbi Halevi's answer to his query is organized around four general questions that arise in any consideration of forgiveness.

RABBI MARC J. ROSENSTEIN (NY '75) has lived in Moshav Shorashim, in the Galilee, since 1990. He directed the Israel Rabbinic Program at HUC-JIR from 2009 until 2015. His most recent book is *Contested Utopia: Jewish Dreams and Israeli Realities* (Jewish Publication Society, 2021).

Is forgiving conditional on apology/repentance by the offender, or is it unilateral and unconditional?

Rabbi Halevi adduces Rambam's highly influential treatment of repentance in the *Mishneh Torah*:

> Interpersonal sins are not forgiven until one pays one's fellow what is owed to them and satisfies them. And even if one repaid them the money owed, one must satisfy them, asking for forgiveness. And even if the damage was only verbal (i.e., not material) one must seek reconciliation and beg them for forgiveness… From this, how can one seek reconciliation if one does not promise never to harm or trouble the victim any more? This is very simple.[4]

Moreover, Halevi argues, even if the questioner wishes to qualify as a *chasid*, he is only obligated to forgive an offender who shows a change of heart and behavior, apologizing and committing to ceasing their hurtful behavior.

Are there some offenses that are unforgivable?

Rabbi Halevi emphasizes that slander is a special category: "Where forgiveness is difficult, especially as long as you continue to suffer from this slander—it…is clear that you are not obligated to forgive them, for slander is not the same as other sins…Those who heard the slander will not necessarily hear the apology, so that the damage is not undone; it is only a measure of [extreme] humility to forgive. But if…you are able to conquer your anger and sorrow, and forgive them, may you be blessed."

Who benefits from forgiveness: the victim, the offender, or the community?

Rabbi Halevi here offers two different conceptions of forgiving. On the one hand, he suggests:

> Perhaps you suspect that after Yom Kippur they will return to their evil way, and thus you want to withhold forgiveness from them in order to protect yourself. If this is your intention, you are surely permitted…If you think that your stubbornness will succeed in preventing them from returning to their sin, it may be worthwhile to refuse.

Granting forgiveness is a coin in the realm of social interactions; Halevi suggests that granting or refusing forgiveness can be seen as a means for encouraging behavioral change, and may be done out of rational considerations of personal and social benefit. On the other hand, there is a longer view that sees forgiving as a manifestation of a moral disposition or character trait, which is inherently good regardless of short-term utilitarian considerations: "However, if [regardless of] your refusal they will in any case continue to persecute you, then you haven't gained anything, and better you should forgive them, for 'one who passes over sins—their sins will be passed over.'[4] May heaven have mercy on you and save you from their hand." There may be reasons not to forgive in a specific case, but one should aspire to be a forgiving person—a status that has implications for one's relationship to God

Can a change of heart really be legally mandated?

Here, Rabbi Halevi gets to the "heart" of the matter of forgiveness, exploring whether there can be any positive value to forgiveness that is spoken without a change of heart. He concludes:

> The Holy Blessed One forgives with absolute and complete forgiveness, and the sin is as if it had never been...[God's] forgiveness uproots and erases the sin completely. But a person cannot forgive [like this], for the residue of the sin will remain forever in the heart, at least in the first period after the reconciliation. A person can "bear sin" in the sense of bearing with their fellow's sin, acting, in practice, as if the sinner's sin never was; and perhaps, over time that residue will be cleansed from the heart completely; it all depends on the person and their qualities.

> Therefore, if this man comes to request forgiveness, and promises to cease from troubling you, and you are convinced of his sincerity, then your aspiration to piety and humility would lead you to forgive him and to overlook your pain and start a new page in your relationship with him, even though every time you see him you will remember, and the memory will trouble you and arouse painful feelings—and thus uncomfortable feelings towards him. Don't worry, you (like all human beings) can only "bear sin" (not erase it); more than that you cannot be obligated to do.

Three major conclusions emerge from Halevi's responsum:

1. The questioner is seeking halachic guidance: What does the law require of me? In this context, Halevi answers that while there is an obligation to forgive in certain circumstances (when the offender apologizes and seeks reconciliation), there are also limitations: if the offender continues to offend, and/or if the offense is slander, then there is no such obligation to forgive.
2. This leads Halevi to emphasize that while there may be situations in which the act of forgiving is not obligatory or even desirable, still, one should aspire—and make an effort—to be a forgiving person. Forgivingness should be an aspirational component of Jewish identity, even if in particular cases it is not put into practice.
3. The difficulty of achieving the ideal of a true change of heart, genuine forgiveness, should not deter us from trying. Indeed, performative forgiveness may be a stage in the process of genuine forgiveness: Saying "I forgive you" to an offender when we're not sure we really mean it can be a crucial stage in a process leading to a re-setting of our relationship, so that ultimately, we really do mean it.

Jacob and Esau

The episode of the stolen blessing concludes with Rebekah sending Jacob off to Laban in Haran, "until your brother's anger against you subsides—and he forgets what you have done to him." (Genesis 27:45). Vengeance is in the offing and temporary distancing is called for; it seems that forgetting is the expectation. Does Rebekah expect Esau to forget this injury just because the passing of time dulls the pain of such offenses—or does she foresee that Esau will achieve sufficient power and prosperity, even with his inferior blessing, that he will no longer have any objective reason to resent Jacob's trickery? This question lingers as the "temporary distancing" extends to twenty years. And then Jacob, the wealthy head of a large clan, returns home—passing the territory where Esau, too, has prospered. The night before their meeting, Jacob, "greatly frightened" (Genesis 32:8), prays: "Deliver me, I pray, from the hand of my brother, from the hand of Esau; else, I fear, he may come and strike me down, mothers and children alike" (32:12). He then has a mysterious encounter with a presence that might be understood to represent his own regrets or fears; in any case, he makes elaborate preparations to appease Esau and to defend himself.

Esau may or may not have forgotten past offenses— but Jacob remembers all too well. We read:

> Looking up, Jacob saw Esau coming, accompanied by four hundred men. He divided the children among Leah, Rachel, and the two maids, putting the maids and their children first, Leah and her children next, and Rachel and Joseph last. He himself went on ahead and bowed low to the ground seven times until he was near his brother. Esau ran to greet him. He embraced him and, falling on his neck, he kissed him; and they wept. (Genesis 33:1–4)

Here we have a story of reconciliation after a painful rift caused by Jacob's wronging of Esau. But what stands behind that reconciliation is unclear. We know that Jacob fears his brother's vengeance; but we don't know if he feels remorse. Perhaps he believes that his usurping Esau's birthright and blessing was God's will, and that he need feel no regret. But of course, Esau cannot be expected to understand or acquiesce to that divinely ordained usurpation. On the other hand, they are brothers—and one would hope that Jacob, despite his chosenness, might feel some compassion for Esau's hurt and humiliation, and seek to mend their relationship. Restitution may not be possible, but generous symbolic gifts and humble apology might help.

Indeed, it may be that Esau—seeing how life has gone, having had time to think about their relationship, and seeing Jacob's conciliatory behavior—makes the decision to forgive him. Or has he just "moved on," forgetting (as Rebekah foresaw)—or seeing the offense, in perspective, as trivial—an old slight that, in the end, does not seem to have impaired his life's trajectory to wealth and power? Maybe the twins laugh together, remembering their shared resentment of Rebekah's intervention, realizing that they both were manipulated. Or perhaps, seeing Jacob bowing and scraping before him, the power dynamic reversed, Esau feels vindicated and empowered and thus released from his old anger. Or maybe in their unrecorded first words at this fraught meeting Jacob did in fact express heartfelt remorse for his past deeds, offering material restitution, to which Esau perhaps responded with relief and acceptance, and assured Jacob of his forgiveness. The text, alas, does not tell us what was in their hearts. If there was forgiveness, the Bible does not make it explicit.

The questions we are left with by this episode expand and deepen the ones we encountered in Rabbi Halevi's responsum, in particular by clarifying alternatives to heart-felt forgiveness. These include:

4. Forgetting.
5. Re-understanding. Perhaps if Jacob and Esau had a calm conversation about what really happened two decades ago—how Jacob was innocently manipulated by their mother—Esau's anger and Jacob's guilt would be defused.
6. Condoning. Esau was inherently (!) cruel, the mythical ancestor of a bitter enemy; Jacob was right to treat him as he did; ostensible reconciliation was simply a matter of political expediency, for the moment and for future generations. Forgiving is not relevant.
7. Performance. Maybe Jacob felt no remorse and Esau was still angry, but both realized that the best way forward for them and their clans would be to act as if the past had been set aside—"as if" repentance and forgiveness, for the sake of practical reconciliation and an end to the threat of violence.

Rabbi Eleazar and the Ugly Man

We find another perspective on forgiving, repentance, and forgivingness in the well-known Talmudic *aggadah* of Rabbi Eleazar and the ugly man.[6] The great Torah scholar—intoxicated by his own knowledge and elite status, high on his donkey—encounters an "ugly man" on the road, and shockingly reveals a streak of cruel insensitivity, calling out, "Hey, empty one! Are all the folks from your town as ugly as you?" He thus casually and gratuitously causes pain and humiliation to a fellow human being. Slander and public humiliation are often compared to bloodshed in rabbinic sources, so while this may seem to be a trivial episode of street-level name-calling, the stakes are high—especially given that the offender is a respected Torah scholar. Indeed, it is hard to understand what motivated Rabbi Eleazar to act this way. Apparently, even great rabbis have momentary lapses (like the rest of us), and have to deal with undoing that which should not have been done, or unsaying that which should not have been said.

The victim's sarcastic reprimand—"OK, if you're so close to God, why don't you go tell God how ugly God's creations are?"—knocks poor Rabbi Eleazar right off his high horse (donkey). The ugly man may not be beautiful, but his ability to articulate the beauty of the Torah, for the moment at least, exceeds that of Rabbi Eleazar. Rabbi Eleazar sobers up quickly, and instantly transitions from riding high to groveling before the man. Note that the victim does not respond with a counter-insult or with violence, or with rage, but rather he addresses the rabbi in terms of what he must know to be the rabbi's own beliefs, the values that he and the rabbi are supposed to share. It works. The rabbi demonstrates shame and contrition, begging for forgiveness. (But what about restitution or setting things right? How does one undo such an insult?)

As the story continues, it becomes clear that being a lowly victim with a sharp wit doesn't necessarily endow one with the virtue of forgivingness, and the ugly man seems intent on revenge, not reconciliation. He rejects Rabbi Eleazar's pleas for forgiveness throughout the three-mile journey to town, and he then attempts to exact a fair revenge by publicly humiliating the rabbi. Indeed, there seems to be a degree of "measure for measure" in his actions: the rabbi shamed him by his insult, and the man shames the offender by bringing the rabbi's moral lapse to the attention of the rabbi's whole community. Finally, accepting the people as character witnesses—or perhaps just buckling under social pressure—the victim announces his forgiveness. In the confrontation at the town gate, only the townspeople and the offended man speak. The rabbi is silent, not confirming the story, nor expressing remorse or apology, nor defending himself. Is he too mortified to speak? Does he see himself as above the fray? Does he see no possibility of dialogue with such an angry man? Note that the man never says "I forgive you" to Rabbi Eleazar; his expression of forgiveness is only public, phrased in the third person, and expressed grudgingly, "For *you* I hereby forgive him, but only if he will no longer behave this way." "For you..."—because you people insist.

Perhaps, indeed, the interaction between the two men should be seen as reflecting a larger social reality. The rabbi is respected and powerful, an honored figure in his town. The victim is doubly an outsider—both as esthetically atypical, and as a non-resident of the town. While morally he may seem to have the higher ground, he is in fact powerless in the social dynamic. Eager to rehabilitate their rabbi's reputation, the people do not reprove the rabbi or encourage him to make some kind of reparation to the injured man; rather, they press the ugly man to forgive Rabbi Eleazar, to put an end to this awkward unpleasantness. The victim is the "problem," not the offender.

The lean narrative leaves us wondering: Is the rabbi truly repentant? Is his apology sufficient? Has he really changed his ways? Does the man genuinely forgive Rabbi Eleazar? In any case, it seems clear that the story does not end with true reconciliation. So this simple story turns out to be not so simple, leaving us with a number of questions:

1. Can the obligation of interpersonal forgiveness be fulfilled by means of a public proclamation (I forgive *him*, for *you*)? What is the relationship between direct interpersonal reconciliation and symbolic public acts?
2. Are there acts that are difficult or impossible to forgive? Or are their situations where, on the surface, forgiveness may seem warranted, but a better understanding of the victim's whole story may lead us to realize that it may be too much to expect forgiveness?
3. How do class, status, and power disparities between offender and victim influence the possibility and process of forgiving? Is it different for a weak victim to forgive a powerful perpetrator, from the reverse situation, when the victim is powerful and the offender occupies a weak social position? Can forgiveness be "purified" of such considerations?

This text is one among many suggesting that the virtue of forgivingness is an important Jewish value. However, like the other texts we have examined, it implies that the act of genuine forgiving is often difficult to define and problematic to prescribe, and can even be hard to recognize when we see it.

Concluding Reflection

The difficulty of doing—or even recognizing—true forgiveness is perhaps an echo of the *keva-kavanah* dilemma: insisting that true forgiveness be heartfelt seems in line with the position that we should pray only when we can do so with authentic intent. Routine performance seems inauthentic. But what if what we feel is, to some extent at least, determined by what we do? Everyone—but especially the rabbi, as model and teacher—is challenged by this dilemma. We are required to live at the fuzzy interface, performing as if we really mean it, aspiring, striving, praying(!) to really mean what we perform.

Notes

1. In 2021 I corresponded briefly with David Ellenson about the responsum discussed here. David described it as characteristic of Rabbi Halevi's "sensitivity, scholarship, and insight." Since those are characteristics that we students of David associate with *him*, it seems appropriate to dedicate this essay to his memory.
2. Hannah Arendt, *The Human Condition*, (University of Chicago Press, 1958), 238.
3. Rabbi Haim David Halevi, *Responsa Aseh Lecha Rav*, Tel Aviv, 1976–89, part 6, no. 42.
4. *Hilchot T'shuvah* 2:9.
5. Babylonian Talmud, *Rosh HaShanah* 17a.
6. Found in Babylonian Talmud, *Taanit* 20a–b and *Avot D'Rabbi Natan* A 41. In some versions, the protagonist is Rabbi Shimon ben Eleazar.

Responding to Moral Injury: The Healing Power of Jewish Texts, Teachings and Practices

Rabbi Kim S. Geringer and Rabbi Nancy H. Wiener

This is the second article in a two-part series, the first published in the CCAR Journal Spring/Summer 2024 issue.

The Spiritual Wound of Moral Injury

Moral injury is the harm resulting from perpetrating, failing to prevent, bearing witness to, learning about, or being the recipient of acts that transgress deeply held moral beliefs and expectations. Moral injury results from an act or acts of transgression that severely and abruptly contradict an individual's previously held

---

RABBI KIM S. GERINGER, MSW (NY '99) is a member of the faculty at HUC-JIR/New York where she teaches courses on interpersonal and family systems theory, clergy formation, moral injury, and fieldwork supervision. She served as a congregational rabbi for fifteen years and on the staff of the URJ's Department of Worship, Music, and Religious Living. Her publications include "Insights into Moral Injury and Soul Repair from Classical Jewish Texts," *Journal of Pastoral Psychology* (2018) and Chapter 5 in *Military Moral Injury and Spiritual Care: A Resource for Religious Leaders and Professional Caregiver* (Chalice 2019). She currently serves on the Advisory Board of the Soul Repair Center. Prior to becoming a rabbi, she worked as a psychotherapist. A recipient of trauma debriefing training and an EMT, she has also worked with families of 9/11 victims, witnesses to workplace violence, and earthquake survivors in Haiti.

RABBI NANCY H. WIENER, DMIN, BCC (NY '90) is founding Director of the Jacob and Hilda Blaustein Center for Pastoral Counseling, and the Dr. Paul and Trudy Steinberg Distinguished Professor in Human Relations at HUC-JIR/New York. Her publications include: "Insights into Moral Injury and Soul Repair from Classical Jewish Texts," *Journal of Pastoral Psychology* (2018) and Chapter 5 in *Military Moral Injury and Spiritual Care: A Resource for Religious Leaders and Professional Caregiver* (Chalice 2019); and *Maps and Meaning: Levitical Models for Contemporary Care* (Fortress 2014). She is a board member of both Neshama: National Association of Jewish Chaplains and The Soul Repair Center at Brite Divinity School, as well as a past co-chair of T'ruah: The Rabbinic Call for Human Rights.

personal or shared expectations about the rules or code of ethical conduct. Moral injury is a trauma of moral conscience, when harm cannot be corrected, and empathy results only in pain and self-condemnation. Those suffering from moral injury may feel a crisis of moral selfhood, perhaps seeing themselves as unworthy of forgiveness by God and uncertain about life's ultimate meaning and purpose. This profound sense of loss—of the self they had known prior to experiencing moral injury, of deeply held convictions and values, of community and of a relationship with God, for example—carries no visible scars and, until recently, had remained largely unnamed and unnoticed. It is a form of what psychologist Pauline Boss has titled "ambiguous loss." As Boss notes:

> The inability to resolve such ambiguous losses is due to the outside situation, not to internal personality defects. And the outside force that freezes the grief is the uncertainty and ambiguity of the loss.[1]

Some of those suffering from moral injury adopt a coping strategy that results in a bifurcated sense of self. They view themselves before, during, and after their moral injury experience through two distinct categories, "me" and "not-me," needing to separate themselves from parts too painful or shameful to acknowledge. While perhaps initially helpful in the short term, this leads to a sense of self that is fractured. Jewish tradition has always understood that one's ability to survive and thrive depends on nurturing the parts of oneself that are intact while simultaneously honoring and carrying those parts that are broken. The powerful and evocative image from the Jerusalem Talmud (*Shekalim* 6:1) of the two arks that traveled with the people through the desert, one containing an intact set of commandments and the other holding the broken set, can guide rabbis' work as they seek to offer care to the morally injured.

The process of healing from moral injury is often referred to as soul repair, and it requires a multi-disciplinary and multi-modality approach including psychological, spiritual, traditional, and complementary medical approaches. Generally, no single approach alone is successful, but combinations of practices are. Religious leaders have a unique role to play in helping individuals heal from moral injury when they utilize spiritual language, concepts, and rituals.[2] The resources available to Jewish clergy span the ages, from ancient to contemporary, and encompass genres from uniquely Jewish to non-Jewish and approaches from the philosophical to the scientific.

Safe Space and Community

For those suffering from moral injury, shame, a sense of worthlessness, chaos, or loss of meaning can lead to self-imposed isolation and, in the most extreme of cases, to suicide. Fear of encountering harsh judgment that mirrors the sufferer's own sense of moral breach may result in their avoiding contact with once-trusted family, friends, or social and religious groups; the resulting despair goes to the heart of their perception of themselves as a human being. This is, as Cassell wrote in his classic work, a "severe distress that threatens the intactness of a person…it continues until the threat of disintegration has passed or until the integrity of the person can be restored by some other manner."[3] The presence of safe spaces can facilitate the type of healing experience essential in the wake of moral injury. Reducing isolation is critical. Group settings in which individuals can be with others like themselves, who also identify as perpetrators, recipients, or witnesses to moral injury, can help ease their sense that no one can understand the moral dilemma they faced, relate to the choices they made or the forces that were at play, or feel the loss of integrity they have experienced.

Arei Miklat (In a Modern Context)

In the desert, as the land is being divided among the tribes, God instructs the Israelites to establish *arei miklat* ("cities of refuge") for unintentional killers (Numbers 35:1–24 and Deuteronomy 19:1–10, 4:41–42.). Having caused the death of another, the unintentional manslayers were forever changed. They ceased being the people they had been, and their actions also changed their relationship to the kin of their victim and to the community at large. In addition to their feelings about the inadvertent killing, they feared for their own lives at the hands of family members bound for revenge. In recognition of these circumstances, the Israelite community at large was tasked with protecting inadvertent killers. As a collective, the community was responsible for maintaining, always, six cities of refuge. Each medium-sized city of refuge was required to have its own Levites, inhabitants with a range of professions, and a dependable source of water. Each was to be a weapon-free zone, lest avengers entered its gates, and there were to be clearly marked signs between population centers indicating the route to the nearest city of refuge. All of this provided unintentional killers the opportunity to reestablish themselves anew, in safety, with the social and religious supports necessary to facilitate their return to community and God. The local inhabitants served as protectors and witnesses, shielding unintentional manslayers from harm, and witnessing their transformation into contributing members of the community. The Levites who lived in these cities guaranteed that their spiritual needs would be recognized and addressed. In *Mishnah Makot* 2:5 we read, "And the court would provide the unintentional manslayers fleeing to a city of refuge with two Torah scholars, due to the concern that perhaps the blood redeemer, i.e., a relative of the murder victim seeking [revenge]..." would exact revenge en route. These Torah scholars thus served two purposes: they could positively influence the unintentional manslayer; moreover, they could serve as protection on the journey to a city of refuge, since marauders or avengers would not likely attack revered members of the community.

Today, this ancient system can serve as a model for clergy, congregations, and social service organizations, and it can inform social justice efforts as well. There are limitless ways and places to create safe spaces for individuals to reflect on who they are in their unabashed humanity, what they have done and experienced, and who they would like to become. They can be provided with opportunities to explore their relationship with God (however understood) and to Jewish community and Judaism. Contemporary *arei miklat* can offer such individuals another chance to create a meaningful life.

Kahal: Being in Relationship and Community

Sacred relationship is central to Jewish life. Beginning with Abraham and continuing through God's active engagement with the people Israel as a collective, God and Jews have always been in relationship with each other. The power of the Talmudic dictum—*O chevruta o m'tuta*, "either companionship or death"—can be seen in the ways Jews have gathered over the millennia to pray, study, support communal institutions, celebrate, and mourn. This ethos, countercultural to the American emphasis on individualism, is the *sine qua non* of building, establishing, and maintaining community.[4] While our Jewish communal institutions often stress programs, Rabbi Dr. Lawrence Hoffman has taught: "People may come for program, but they stay for relationship."[5] Ultimately, as Dr. Ron Wolfson writes, "It's all about relationships."[6]

For the morally injured, shame drives isolation, a state out of which healing is unlikely to emerge. In a very real sense, those suffering from moral injury need to be invited to reengage with community and actively welcomed back in, since they may feel that they are unworthy of a community's embrace. Like Abraham welcoming the three visitors in *parashat Vayeira* (Genesis 18:2–5), Jewish community must actively "run out" to greet those who might not approach our tents, demonstrating—in word and deed—our open hearts and generosity of spirit. We must recognize their "godliness," even when it may be hidden (especially from them). As we think of how to prepare our communities to be places of holy relationships, we must look beyond the design/program model (think Exodus 36–39's focus on the details of the *mishkan*) and consider how best to provide opportunities for real meeting. Everyone in our communities should have an opportunity to spread their wings and look at others face to face, like the *k'ruvim* in the *mishkan* (Exodus 37:9). Our communal institutions will truly be spaces for healing when relationships are centered, stories are shared and received with compassion, and we hear our individual narratives as inextricably bound to each other.

Looking Back to Look Forward

Sharing Stories

Narrative medicine has demonstrated the importance of narrative humility and narrative ethics as well as the importance of story for both teller and listener.[7] Through personal story, the disparate pieces of lived experience can cohere, and the storyteller can reconnect with old meanings or find new ones. The surfacing of memories can profoundly disrupt the worlds of individual perpetrators and recipients and their families many years later.[8] Confronting those memories and the emotions they evoke can be an important first step toward healing for moral injury recipient, perpetrator, and witness alike.[9]

Meaning Making and Midrash

This process of reworking disparate pieces of one's story is what Jews have always done through the process of creating midrash. Like narrative medicine,[10] midrash is the art of working with a person's story to make meaning, promote healing, and effect change. Since humans organize their individual "worlds" through the stories they tell about themselves and others, working with story is a powerful tool in "remaking" worlds that have become broken. The experience of the storyteller is validated, and the capacity for self-reflection and creativity of the caregiver is enhanced. Similarly, Arthur Frank, in his book *The Wounded Storyteller*, wrote, "The act of telling is a dual reaffirmation. Relationships with others are reaffirmed, and the self is reaffirmed" (vii).

Every person has a unique spiritual orienting system consisting of values, beliefs, and practices.[11] Making midrash from—that is, expanding—a story can be the beginning of a creative process that enhances the exploration of values, beliefs, and coping strategies. As medical professionals work with a person's body, spiritual healers work with a person's soul—and the key to the soul is story. Rami Shapiro notes that midrash-based healing rests on four assumptions: that storytelling is at the heart of what it is to be human; that spiritual healing arises from the act of finding new meaning in one's story; that finding new meaning is the work of the spiritual healer; and that the means for finding and sharing that new meaning is the art of midrash.[12] Family and cultural systems of meaning must be plumbed for their impact on a person's story as well. Midrash recognizes that while the facts of personal stories cannot be changed, new understandings of those stories and of oneself can emerge. Ideally, the meanings one makes from life's stories will be both life-giving and life-sustaining.

Imagine working with a person who has witnessed an act that breached their moral code, and then afterward remained silent. Exploring the story of Esther and Mordechai, for instance, might lead the sufferer to a new understanding of the internal and external messages that informed their decision to remain silent, as well to consider what internal or external shifts might allow them to raise their voice in the future. Or consider studying the prophets as witnesses transformed into upstanders and whistleblowers.[13] By revisiting these texts with someone engaged in the process of soul repair, spiritual healers might contribute to the individual feeling empowered to act on what they are seeing and give voice to the possibility of change. Or, from the Jewish legal tradition, imagine studying different Maimonidean texts to promote healing from moral injury: "The Epistle on Martyrdom" to examine issues of acting under duress; *Hilchot Rotzei-ach* to consider how all deaths at the hand of another cannot be treated the same; *Hilchot T'shuvah* to look at the nexus of *din* and *rachamim* and to identify the ultimate goals of *t'shuvah*.

Given the breadth and depth of the Jewish halachic and literary traditions, the possibilities are limitless. We can help those suffering from moral injury to "name the role of society as a whole in a moral injury"[14] and to see their actions in a broader context, acknowledging what they did while also recognizing the ways in which social, circumstantial, or political factors contributed or were complicit. We can listen to hear if someone is able to own what they were responsible for and, also, if they are able to discern the responsibility of others. Ultimately, these initial steps can lead to a process of *t'shuvah* that can open them up to a new chapter in their lives.

Ritual

Many support groups for those suffering from moral injury ritualize the opening and closing of group sessions, as well as the ways in which contributions to conversations are made. The regularity and predictability of these ritualized gatherings diminish participants' anxiety. Rituals facilitate acknowledgement of woundedness and play a pivotal role in supporting individuals' reintegration into their families and communities. Rituals can create "alternative worlds to the one the injured lives in every day, 'worlds' in which they can experience forgiveness and hope and express sorrow and joy, anger and protest while creating a new reality of wholeness and integrity."[15] Rituals, liberal Jews know, are not set in stone; every ritual emerges in response to a historical, communal, or spiritual need and continues to evolve as needed over time. A particular ritual comes to be because, in the words of Vanessa Ochs, "Something has changed, something is missing, or something needs marking or remembering."[16] Moral injury—however derived and however received—evokes a heightened sense of something missing or something profound having changed, and that absence or change cries out for ritual enactments of transformation.

Jews have long recognized the transformative power of water. Water is at the same time gentle and powerful. It is the medium of birth and it also can be a savage force of death. Water breaks apart, cleanses, transforms, and disperses that which is no longer needed or wanted. Those working with the morally injured might consider repurposing two of Judaism's oldest water-based rituals, *mikveh* and *Tashlich*.

Mikveh. In traditional usage, *mikveh* effects a transition from one status to another. Removal of clothing, jewelry, makeup, and other barriers to the water ensures that no part of the body is untouched physically and spiritually by the passage between states of being. Following in the footsteps of ritual "pioneers" of recent decades, one might use *mikveh* to mark and celebrate the significant life transitions that accompany soul repair. As Rabbi Miriam C. Berkowitz explains, "Although the healing ceremonies [utilizing *mikveh*] do not provide a magical cure or instant fix—they cannot replace therapy, time, and other long-term healing efforts—they can provide a turning point, a focus on other thoughts and symbols besides pain and victimization. They can help people to feel they are taking active roles in their recovery."[17] Spiritual healers can work with those suffering from moral injury to create *mikveh*-related rituals to facilitate their journey to healing.

Tashlich. *Tashlich* is based on the last verse of the Book of Micah: "And You will cast into the depths of the sea all their sins" (7:19). The ritual is the embodied experience of shedding undesired parts of oneself using crumbs of bread to represent sin and regret. The ancient ritual reaffirms one's ability to repent, God's readiness to forgive, and the possibility of a renewed and deepened relationship between the individual and God. For those suffering from moral injury, having the opportunity to proclaim their resolution to return to a self in harmony with God can be very powerful, as can the reminder also of God's desire to re-embrace those who repent. By engaging in bodily actions along with words, the desired transition can be affected. Though traditionally performed on Rosh Hashanah afternoon, a *Tashlich*-like rite can easily be recast and recontextualized as a symbolic casting off of both sins and their life-constricting sequelae of guilt, shame, self-recrimination, and isolation from self, community, and God.

Changing One's Name

Another time-honored ritual tradition for witnessing and honoring internal transformations is the adoption of a new name. Stories in Genesis teach that such an internal transformation can be accompanied by a change of name (Genesis 16:5, 15; 32:29). Enacting a symbolic representation of a change in status (desired or already experienced) was creatively utilized by the twentieth-century Hebrew poet Reuven Grossman. After his son died in the Israel War of Independence, Grossman changed his own name to Avinoam.[18] Like the patriarch Jacob, Grossman's name change reflected the pain and struggle that he would carry with him for the remainder of his life.

In postbiblical Jewish communities, name changes were often offered to a seriously ill person to outwit the Angel of Death. For those suffering from moral injury, whose downward spiral is often life-limiting, a sort of living death, symbolically reclaiming their lives through the adoption of a new name can offer a potent opportunity for healing. Imagine the power and potential of offering those suffering from moral injury the opportunity to see themselves continuing in a chain of tradition dating back to the Bible, in which they adopt a name that reflects a new understanding of themselves in the world and allows them to move into the future more whole.

Learning from the Experience of the *M'tzora*

Like the *m'tzora-im* described in painstaking detail in Leviticus 13 and 14, those suffering from moral injury bear afflictions that may not be visible to the naked eye, and the severity of their experience may become apparent only over time. The ability to return to one's community and a full life depends on a variety of factors, many of which cannot be tied to a fixed timetable. Because their wounds are invisible, sufferers may need to name them aloud, so others will know they are there. Indeed, their receiving care and comfort depends on their ability to name and identify their wounds to others. Undetectable yet very real moral injuries can be a source of shame and pain for those who suffer from them, and a source of anxiety for their families and community. In Leviticus, the *m'tzora-im* had a roadmap for the journey from diagnosis to full recovery. This helped them anticipate the future with the reassurance that there was a path to recovery and a return to life. Today, those suffering from moral injury often lack these tools and assurances. The challenge for spiritual caregivers is to be like the ancient priests, unstintingly and consistently carrying the message that no matter the duration of their sojourn outside the camp, sufferers can return to God and community.[19]

Learning from the Trajectory of the Israelite Warriors

Deuteronomy 20 and Numbers 31 describe the procedures to be employed when sending warriors off to and receiving them back from war. These texts model ways to accompany those who are aware of morally fraught situations before they enter them. Like the priests and the military leaders in Deuteronomy 20, spiritual healers can begin by helping individuals to name the threats that exist and the things that give their life meaning. These will be essential tools for them to consciously and thoughtfully identify and hone, prior to going into morally fraught situations.

In the Numbers text, troops returning from battle were to be met symbolically by the entire community with greetings from its religious and political leaders outside the camp (Numbers 31:19–20). There, Moses was to speak clearly about how living and dying on battlefields changed all of them. The *tum'ah*, the invisible miasma that indicated an imbalance in the world's order,[20] would permeate their bodies, clothing, weapons, and spoils of war. All were required to go through a physical and spiritual transition, replete with cleansing rituals and prescribed waiting periods, before reentering the camp and rejoining the community in the rhythms of daily life. Spiritual caregivers can use these texts as a model for supporting community members following a moral injury-producing experience. Like the ancient warriors, such individuals will need time to assess the inner and outer effects (wounds and scars) that they now bear. Before moving forward, their relationship to the world, to the instruments with which they engaged in "battle," and with others around them will all need to be considered in the new light of having survived a crucible experience.

The potentially devastating effects of unacknowledged moral injuries, for both individuals and those who encounter them, have been extensively discussed in moral injury literature. The Biblical text clearly recognizes the peril for warriors were their changed status to go unacknowledged upon reentry to community. The absence of ritual to manage the transition and rid them of *tum'ah* could result in their transmitting their *tum'ah* to the community, rendering the entire encampment unfit for God's presence. The rabbis of the Mishnah, Talmud, and codes also explored the damage wrought on individuals and communities by unaddressed sources of *tum'ah*. They discussed a process of transmission in which an *av ha-tum'ah*, an original source, then transmits its altered state to others, who in turn continue to pass it along.[21] In a contemporary context, this unintentional transmission may appear in classrooms and boardrooms, at family dinner tables and community gatherings, when one person's unaddressed moral injuries go on to affect the emotional, psychological, and spiritual experiences of others. The injury and its accompanying disequilibrium cause disorientation in others who may have no personal experience of the source of the original injury, but nonetheless suffer second-, third- or fourth-hand from it.[22]

Memorials and Lamentation

Moral injury may be experienced both individually and communally, and both individuals and communities may benefit from opportunities to publicly acknowledge wrongdoing, grief, and loss. Communal ritual practices are extremely important for individuals who would otherwise have to bear alone the consequences of actions they had been asked to assume on behalf of the community-at-large but for which they were not solely responsible.[23] Larry Kent Graham notes: "Corporate ritual processes such as lamentation and memorialization also help the body politic itself to mourn its losses, share its anguish, confront its failings, honor or modify its values, and reinvest its hopes in a transformed future."[24]

In the wake of tragedy, examples of communal mourning abound. The now regular and spontaneous creation of street corner "shrines" such as "Hostages Square" in Tel Aviv and formal memorials, such as those to the Shoah or 9/11, in both small towns and major cities, pay tribute to the missing and the dead. These memorials and shrines enable communities to translate feeling into action by confessing collective responsibility for actions both taken and omitted, calling for accountability, and providing a central location for remembrance, conscience, and action. A memorial or shrine offers a locus for the modality of expression known as lamentation. Kathleen O'Conner, Kadie Billman, and Daniel L. Migliore have identified the central purpose of lamentation as the personal and communal way to truthfully express the sorrows of the world and to register protest, complaint, and anger at those responsible for them, thus rendering the affliction bearable and opening a way toward healing.[25] Creating a public memorial as a representation of one's moral injury is one of many options that can be offered by the spiritual caregiver.

Reconsidering *Tachanun and Vidui*

Rachel Adler aptly describes the emotional and spiritual state of many who suffer from moral injury: "In severe torment, the sufferer is utterly isolated, unable to experience relatedness, unable to defend her values from a torturer's insistence that she betray them…unable to attend to her surroundings, unable to speak—for language is displaced by gasps, moans and screams." How does the tormented "re-enter the realm of language and speak the unspeakable? The doorway…is lament."[26]

A first component of spiritual care for those suffering from moral injury is the creation of safe space in which "lament"—naming, confessing, and acknowledging one's brokenness—can take place. The *Tachanun and Vidui* prayers can help the morally injured articulate their brokenness, guilt, loss, shame, rage, and despair as a first step in healing. Morally injured individuals can join their own voices to ancient words of the Jewish tradition, drawing on their strength and finding ways to articulate their own laments as they embark on the often long and tortured path to integration and wholeness. Lament can be "a way to truthfully express the sorrow of the world that has come upon them…[an] immersion into the truth of one's affliction [so that] paradoxically, that affliction becomes bearable and the way is opened toward healing."[27] Making a place for lament can allow those suffering from moral injury to express regrets and fears while revealing buried or as yet unexpressed hopes for the future. The emotional arcs of *Tachanun* and

Vidui provide a template for an individual to engage in confession, while being reminded of the promise (however distant or unattainable it may feel in the moment) of divine forgiveness.

Tikkun Olam

Judaism has always emphasized the power of engaging in *tzedakah* and the importance of contributing to *tikkun olam*. Contemporary moral injury literature highlights, in its own language, the ways in which these profound Jewish insights contribute to soul repair. When plagued by guilt and self-recrimination, or a conviction that they are unworthy of participating in the social sphere (often for fear of the harm they will inflict), moral injury sufferers may be helped by opportunities for pro-social engagement—responsibility-oriented actions that engage "qualities such as generosity, kindness, and altruism."[28] Engagement in pro-social actions can remind the morally injured that they still have the capacity to contribute to the betterment of the world; such actions may, incidentally, also aid in their own healing. Pro-social actions have been undertaken by veterans of the Vietnam War who have returned to Vietnam to contribute to its rebuilding, and ex-military officers who have publicly allied themselves with indigenous peoples at the Standing Rock Reservation on the border between North and South Dakota.

The Jewish belief in human beings as partners with God in *tikkun olam* can be a powerful reminder for those suffering from moral injury that their own actions and contributions to the world need not remain defined solely by deeds related to their injury; they can still contribute to the world's betterment. All forms of *g'milut chasadim* and *tzedakah*, Judaism's own forms of pro-social activities, can bolster this more positive self-perception.

As the midrash in *Avot D'Rabbi Natan* 11 teaches:

> One says, "Woe to us! The Temple where we atoned for our sins has been destroyed." The other responds, "My son, don't see it as a bad thing for you, since we have another form of atonement which is comparable—that is, acts of lovingkindness. As it says in Hosea 6:6, 'It is lovingkindness I desire, not sacrifice.'" And he said, "A world of lovingkindness will be established." And God is described as saying, "Dearer to me is the kindness that you provide for each other than all the sacrifices you sacrificed completely before me...."

The need to reengage with the world and restore balance is eternal. The means to achieve it are beyond number.

In Conclusion

While our non-Jewish colleagues sometimes struggle to understand our lack of dogma and absence of catechism and systematic theology, these seeming "lacks" can actually be a wellspring of healing potential for those suffering from moral injury. We have all spent time with individuals struggling to articulate for themselves their relationship with God and what it means to be a Jew. The theological crisis often precipitated by moral injury is but one manifestation of the deep, existential questions that bring people to spiritual caregivers every day. As those caregivers listen to the lament over the God a sufferer no longer believes in, they can help these individuals grieve what has been lost and explore possible alternative understandings that may resonate more profoundly with who they now are. If we have, indeed, created a safe space for them to reveal their pain, doubts, and despair, we, along with other healing professionals, can lead them through a process of rebuilding that reflects their lived experiences and can sustain them on their journeys to reintegration. Soul repair is a slow, painful, and imperfect process. No one can predict its path, and no single approach alone is likely to be successful. However, one element—attention to the spiritual dimensions of moral injury—is universally recognized as an essential part of soul repair. And that is our area of specialization.

Notes

1. Pauline Boss, Ambiguous Loss: Learning to Live with Unresolved Grief (Harvard University Press, 1999), 10.
2. Boss, Ambiguous Loss, 10.
3. Eric Cassell, "The Nature of Suffering and the Goals of Medicine," The New England Journal of Medicine 306, 11 (March 18, 1982): 639–45.
4. Richard Address, Seekers of Meaning: Baby Boomers, Judaism, and the Pursuit of Healthy Aging (URJ Press 2012), 25.
5. Private correspondence.
6. Ron Wolfson, Relational Judaism: Using the Power of Relationships to Transform Jewish Communities (Jewish Lights, 2013), 2.
7. Arthur W. Frank, The Wounded Storyteller: Body, Illness, and Ethics (University of Chicago Press, 1997), 57.

8. http://www.conscienceinwar.org
9. Brett T. Litz, et al, "Moral Injury and Moral Repair in War Veterans: A Preliminary Model and Intervention Strategy," Clinical Psychology Review 29.8 (December 2009): 701.
10. For more information about "narrative medicine," see, for example, the website of Columbia University Medical Center Program in Narrative Medicine, www.narrativemedicine.org.
11. Carrie Doehring, "Military Moral Injury: An Evidence-based and Intercultural Approach to Spiritual Care," in Military Moral Injury and Spiritual Care, eds. Ramsay and Doehring (Chalice Press, 2019), 20.
12. Rami M. Shapiro, "Our Stories, Our Selves: The Jewish Chaplain as Midrashic Healer," Jewish Spiritual Care 6.1 (Winter 2003): 5.
13. The Reverend Doctor John C. Lenz, Jr., "The Bystander in the Bible," Utah Law Review: Vol. (2017): No. 4, Article 3.
14. Rita Nakashima Brock and G. Lettini, Soul Repair: Recovering from Moral Injury after War (Beacon Press 2012), 112.
15. Nancy J. Ramsay, "Moral Injury as Loss and Grief with Attention to Ritual," Pastoral Psychology (2018): 115.
16. Vanessa Ochs, "The Courage to Reinvent Jewish Ritual," Contact (Winter 2010): 5.
17. Miriam C. Berkowitz, "Creative Lifecycle Rituals," Contact (Winter 2012).
18. Avirama Golan, "My Soul Has Been Taken," Haartez (September 3, 2010), https://www.haaretz.com/life/books/2010-09-03/ty-article/my-soul-has-been-taken/0000017f-df1d-df7c-a5ff-df7ff30a0000.
19. For further discussion of the m'tzora-im and parallels with contemporary care, see Nancy H Wiener and Jo Hirschmann, Maps and Meaning: Levitical Models for Contemporary Care (Fortress, 2014).
20. Wiener and Hirschmann, Maps and Meaning, 43.
21. For a brief explanation of this phenomenon see Steinsaltz, The Talmud: A Reference Guide, (Jerusalem, 1988; Random House, 1989), 157.
22. Brock and Lettini, Soul Repair, 52, 130.
23. Larry Kent Graham, personal communication.
24. Larry Kent Graham, "The Healing Power of Public Lamentation," paper presented at Pathways to Hope Conference Soul Repair Center Kansas City, Kansas, October 30, 2015 (revised for distribution December 29, 2015), 2.
25. Kathleen M. O'Connor, Lamentations and the Tears of the World (Maryknoll, 2002), 3, 96.

26. Rachel Adler, "For These I Weep: A Theology of Lament," The Chronicle 68 (2006): 16.
27. Larry Kent, "Religious Response to Disaster," unpublished manuscript (2015), 8.
28. Cynda Hylton Rushton, Moral Resilience: Transforming Moral Suffering (Oxford University Press, 2018), 161.

When Sons Disappoint: The Consequences of Filial Failure in the *Tanach*

Rabbi Barry L. Schwartz

What do Cain, Ham, Ishmael, Esau, Jacob, Reuben, Simeon, Levi, Judah, Er, Onan, Nadab, Abihu, Hophni, Phinehas, Joel, Abijah, Jonathan, Amnon, Absalom, Adonijah, and Solomon have in common? They are all guilty, according to Scripture, of filial failure: the inability to live up to their parents' expectations.

The consequences of such failure are always significant and often severe. They damage not only family, but community. This is especially true when the fathers are leaders and their sons are expected to follow in their footsteps, as in the clan, the priesthood, or the monarchy.

Yet the phenomenon of filial failure, familiar even in our own day when the children of leaders or celebrities go astray (think the British royal family!), not to mention in our own families, is curiously understudied. Perhaps this is because sibling rivalry is the key family dynamic that receives the most attention in biblical commentary. Jonathan Sacks, for example, spoke for many when he wrote, "Freud thought the great symbol of conflict was Laius and Oedipus, the tension between fathers and sons. Bereishit thinks otherwise. The root of human conflict is sibling rivalry..."[1]

But Freud was at least partially right. Father-son rivalry is also at the root of human conflict. And millennia before modern psychotherapy, the Torah understood a key truth about the intimate connection between the two: *Sibling rivalry has less to do with direct conflict between brothers or sisters than with competition for their*

RABBI BARRY L. SCHWARTZ (NY '85) is director emeritus of The Jewish Publication Society and rabbi of Congregation Adas Emuno in Leonia, New Jersey. He is the author, most recently, of *Open Judaism: A Guide for Believers, Atheists, and Agnostics* (2023), and *Biblical Israel: A Family History* (forthcoming).

parents' attention.[2] From the sons of Adam to the sons of David this dynamic rings true.

Filial failure is often so painful that we prefer to overlook or minimize it in our Scriptures and in our lives. Who wants to admit to being disappointed if not downright dejected by their children, never mind addressing it openly? Who wants to confront the role we as parents may play in the phenomena? We understandably shy away from talking about when our kids fall short.

Yet there are so many stories of sons disappointing fathers that it behooves us to try to understand this family dynamic. What are the root causes of filial failure? How should we respond? What responsibility do parents bear when young adult or fully adult children act out? To what extent does parental absenteeism or parental favoritism exacerbate the problem or exonerate the misbehavior? By examining the long list of biblical boys behaving badly, we hope to answer these questions—or at least shed some light on an uncomfortable subject.

We focus on sons for two reasons. First, because there is a dearth of parent-daughter accounts in the *Tanach*. The few mentions that exist are scattered snippets rather than full renderings. While we cannot wish away the biblical bias, we can make our contemporary discussion more inclusive. Many of the Torah's insights about sons apply to daughters as well. Second, because the stakes are greater with sons. Simply put, young adult males present the greatest threat of conflict and violence to society. Men make up an astounding 93 percent of those imprisoned in our country.[3] Young men between the ages of 18 and 24 represent 10 percent of the general population but 20 percent of the prison population.

The *Tanach* grapples with the problem through both lore and law. Before investigating the many aggadic examples in the *Tanach*, we should also acknowledge the significance of this issue in the (in)famous halachic case of the Torah. Known rabbinically as the *ben sorer u-moreh* ("the wayward and rebellious son"), we read:

> If a man has a wayward and defiant son, who does not heed his father or mother and does not obey them even after they discipline him, his father and mother shall take him and bring him out to the elders of his town at the public place of his community. They shall say to the elders of his town, "This son of ours is disloyal and defiant; he does not heed us. He is a glutton and a

drunkard." Thereupon the people of his town shall stone him to death. Thus you shall sweep out evil from your midst; all Israel will hear and be afraid" (Deuteronomy 21:18–21).

As Jeffrey Tigay comments, "Filial insubordination is a grave offense because respect and obedience toward parents is regarded as the cornerstone of all order and authority, especially in a tribal, patriarchal society like ancient Israel."[4] Even if, as many sages and modern scholars suggest, the death penalty was more a warning than a reality, the seriousness of the subject is evident. The Torah passage brings the elders into the picture, underscoring the repercussions beyond the aggrieved party. Filial failure rends apart family and community in such tragic ways that "all Israel" must be warned.

Cain

In the first story of filial failure, the biological parents are curiously missing in action. The Torah never relates to Adam and Eve as parents. Their reaction to the shocking act of fratricide is nowhere to be found. But the Torah offers a possible motive for the murder—namely, jealousy: "GOD paid heed to Abel and his offering, but to Cain and his offering GOD paid no heed. Cain was much distressed and his face fell" (Genesis 4:4–5).

God is very much the *parentis in loco* here. Does God step in for absent, distracted, clueless parents? And why does the Divine seemingly play favorites? The question is important because the issue of favoritism arises in Genesis time and again.

Whatever the answer, God senses that an emotionally distraught Cain will lash out and warns him that "Sin couches at the door; its urge is toward you, yet you can be its master" (4:6). When this warning goes unheeded and the vile deed is done, God exclaims, in a burst of parent-like heartbreak and anger, "What have you done? The voice of your brother's blood cries out to Me from the ground! Therefore, you shall be more cursed than the ground, which opened it mouth to receive your brother's blood from your hand. If you till the soil, it shall no longer yield it strength to you. You shall become a ceaseless wanderer on earth" (4:10–12).

Cain compounds his sin by appearing to be largely unrepentant. Having famously replied to God's first query about Abel's whereabouts, "I do not know. Am I my brother's keeper?" (4:9), he not only fails another opportunity to apologize but plays the victim:

"My punishment is too great to bear! Since You have banished me…anyone who meets me may kill me!" (4:13–14). The argument apparently has some merit; God does not decree that Cain should die, and puts a mark of protection on Cain. Nevertheless, "Cain left God's presence" (4:16).

Like his parents, Cain experiences banishment, wandering, and exile, both physical and spiritual. Like them, he will eventually settle down, marry, and bear children. However, his progeny, although chronicled in Genesis, are ultimately doomed. The saving remnant of humanity, Noah's line, will go through another son born to Adam and Eve, named Seth.

From a God's-eye perspective, Cain's grievous failure must, and is, requited. He has shed innocent blood. He is "Exhibit A" in the human propensity toward violence. He may survive, but his descendants will not. The sins of one generation will be visited on subsequent generations. Though we may protest the fairness of that, the precedent now established will plague humanity in general, and the people of Israel in particular.

Ham

When Noah came out of the ark, he planted vineyards, had too much to drink, and uncovered himself. His son Ham "saw his father's nakedness" (Genesis 9:22). Whatever that may have meant (Rabbinic sources range from immodesty and disrespect to much, much worse), it was not good. Noah is enraged, cussing his son by damning his grandson: "Cursed be Canaan; the lowest of slaves shall he be to his brothers" (9:25). Besides the obvious polemic against Israel's nemesis, the Canaanites, we again see the sins of sons being visited on their progeny. The covenanted people, Abraham's line, will go through another son, named Shem. Ham's descendants will be subjugated. Once more, from a God's-eye view there is no escaping punishment for misdeed. The perpetrator may go on with their life, but somewhere down the line their descendants will pay the price.

Ishmael

The eldest son of Abraham is a curious case of filial failure. Ishmael is born of Sarah's maidservant, Hagar, at Sarah's instigation no less. But no sooner does Hagar become pregnant than her mistress becomes jealous and is full of regret. Sarah mistreats Hagar, who runs away, only to return at God's bidding.

Ishmael is clearly loved by his father. When God makes a lofty promise that Sarah will conceive a child who will bear the covenant, Abraham can only think of his oldest: "Oh that Ishamel might live by Your favor!" (17:17).

Young Ishmael fails not in the sight of his father, but his step-mother. One day after her own son Isaac is weaned, Sarah spies Ishmael "playing" (the word itself a play on Isaac's name in Hebrew, Yitzchak). The plain meaning seems to be innocent enough: playing is what kids do. The Rabbis speculate, however, that something more nefarious was happening: that Ishmael was mocking Isaac, or worse, abusing him. Sarah demands that mother and son be cast out, "for the son of that slave-woman shall not share in the inheritance with my son Isaac" (21:10). Though "the matter distressed Abraham greatly, for it concerned a son of his" (21:11), he accedes to his wife's demand after God reassures him that Ishmael too will be the father of a nation.

Ishmael may have God's sympathy, and ours. He failure is no fault of his own, unless you accept the rather far-fetched Rabbinic interpretation. Even though he is circumcised into the covenant Ishmael, will not be the covenant bearer. God does not renounce Ishmael; his line is recorded, yet the innocent lad and his mother pay the heavy price of exile. Even unintentional and undeserved filial failure has its consequences.

Ishmael's tale is problematic and enigmatic, and scrutiny of the parents is warranted. What kind of father is Abraham? What kind of step-mother is Sarah? For that matter, what kind of surrogate parent is God? The mystery of it all is why the first words of Melville's *Moby Dick*, "Call me Ishmael," have been deemed one of the greatest opening lines in all of literature.

Esau and Jacob

Both twin sons of Isaac and Rebekah prove to be a disappointment to their parents, in different ways.

In a rare admission of blatant parental favoritism that will only heighten the acrimony, the Torah states that "Isaac favored Esau because he had a taste for game, but Rebekah favored Jacob" (Genesis 25:27). We may surmise that Jacob was starved for his father's attention and affection—and this is a prescription for trouble. Remote parenting, especially from fathers, does not bode well.

When Jacob swindles the birthright from Esau, it may have been more of a swipe against father than brother. But if Isaac is upset or attempts to take any action, we're not party to it. The text simply says, "Thus did Esau spurn the birthright" (25:34). Both parents are dismayed when Esau twice marries Hittite women, the narrator noting that "they were a source of bitterness to Isaac and Rebekah" (26:35). Later Rebekah says to her husband, in one of the most acerbic exchanges in the *Tanach*, "I am disgusted with my life because of the Hittite women. If Jacob marries a Hittite woman like these, from among the native women, what good will life be to me?" (27:46).

Esau is again deceived by his brother (in cahoots with their mother) and loses his father's blessing. In a strikingly poignant scene Esau discovers the deception and "he burst into wild and bitter sobbing, and said to his father, 'Bless me too, Father!…First he [Jacob] took away my birthright and now he has taken away my blessing! Have you not reserved a blessing for me?" (27:34, 36). When Isaac demurs, Esau piteously continues, "'Have you but one blessing, Father? Bless me too, Father!' And Esau wept aloud" (27:38). It's all rather heartbreaking; the narrator seems not without sympathy for the hapless hunter.

We're also informed that "Esau realized that the Canaanite women displeased his father Isaac" (28:8) and set out to make amends. In a surprising twist he locates his estranged uncle Ishmael and marries his daughter Mahalath. But it seems to be too little, too late, and rather odd: the spurned eldest of one generation turning to the spurned eldest of the previous generation, both having been denied the status of covenant-bearer. Many years later Esau will magnanimously reconcile with his brother (although Jacob will go his separate way after their meeting). Like his uncle, Esau will father a nation; indeed an entire chapter carefully chronicles his line (Genesis 36). Alas, that nation—Edom—will become an adversary of Israel, and one branch, Amalek, the arch-enemy. Esau's reputation, and that of his progeny, will fare even worse in the Rabbinic mind, when Edom is equated with Rome.[5]

For his part, Jacob—the flawed but chosen one—pays for his failures too. Isaac laments to Esau that "Your brother came with guile and took away your blessing" (27:35), and the deceiver will face deception time and again in his life. Like his ancestors, he will face exile and estrangement. He will describe his days as "few and hard" when he meets Pharaoh (47:9). Bearing the covenant is no guarantee of happiness or avoidance of tragedy. To the contrary, failure of character has its consequences, immediate and/or long-term. If necessary, YHVH will mete out punishment to Israel collectively or individually to any of its covenant bearers.

Reuben, Simeon, and Levi

Jacob had reason to be particularly disillusioned with Reuben, his eldest. In a single verse the Torah reports that "Reuben went and lay with Bilhah, his father's concubine [given to Rachel]; and Israel found out" (35:22). Jacob would never forget the transgression, and on his deathbed he rebukes Reuben, saying: "Unstable as water; you will excel no longer; for when you mounted your father's bed, you brought disgrace-my couch he mounted!" (49:4).

Could it be that Reuben saw that his mother, Leah, was unloved and mistreated by his father, and this was his way of getting back? Earlier, Reuben had (wittingly or unwittingly) contributed to the dissension between Leah and his aunt Rachel. He finds some mandrakes (widely consider to be a fertility enhancement) which he brings to his mother. When Rachel finds out, she asks for a few, to which Leah caustically replies, "Was it enough for you to take away my husband, that you should also take my son's mandrakes?" (30:15). In the end, Leah's shares the mandrakes when Rachel promises that Jacob will sleep with Leah that night. Leah openly admits to Jacob that "I have hired you with my son's mandrakes" (30:16).

Given his status as firstborn, Reuben should have saved Joseph from his brothers. Indeed, "When Reuben heard it, he did try, saying, 'Let us not take his life'" (37:2). Reuben convinced his brothers to cast Joseph in a pit, but he failed to keep him safe when his brothers decided to sell Joseph into slavery. Reuben then participates in the ruse of convincing his father that a wild animal devoured Joseph.

Nor do Jacob's second and third born sons, Simeon and Levi, distinguish themselves. To the contrary, they are rough, violent men involved in an episode that causes considerable consternation to their father. When their sister Dinah is raped by Shechem, son of the local chieftain Hamor, Jacob attempts to deal with the situation by arranging for his daughter to be married to Shechem. Jacob's sons, "speaking with guile" (34:13), inform Hamor and Shechem that their sister could only be given to a circumcised man from a clan that practices the same. Father and son and village agree, and when they are recovering from the procedure, Simeon and Levi attack and kill all the males. The other sons plunder the town, taking the women and children and cattle as captives and booty.

Jacob is outraged, though perhaps more for political than moral reasons. He angrily reprimands Simeon and Levi, "You have brought trouble on me, making me odious among the inhabitants of the land…so that if they unite against me and attack me, I and my house will destroyed" (34:30). The sons in turn issue a stunning rebuke to their father: "Should our sister be treated like a whore?" (30:31). On his deathbed Jacob will again accost his sons, letting loose this diatribe: "Simeon and Levi are a pair; their weapons are tool of lawlessness. Let not my person be included in their council; let not my being be counted in their assembly. For when angry they slay men; and when pleased they maim oxen. Cursed be their anger so fierce; and their wrath so relentless. I will divide them in Jacob; scatter them in Israel" (49:3–7).

Between the shameful concubine matter, the horrific Shechem incident, and the dreadful Joseph affair, to say that the sons of Jacob disappointed their father is a gross understatement.

Judah, Er, and Onan

A bizarre incident involving another son, and two of his ill-fated grandsons, only adds to Jacob's already hefty heartache. Like Reuben, Judah may deserve some credit for convincing his brothers not to immediately kill Joseph, when he says, "What do we gain by killing our brother and covering up his blood!? Come, let us sell him to the Ishmaelites, but let us not do away with him ourselves" (37:28). But selling a brother into slavery is a terrible deed in and of itself, and Judah too is party to the deception of their father.

Judah marries a Canaanite women named Shua, who bears him three sons. The eldest, Er, marries Tamar, but commits an unspecified sin "displeasing to GOD" and dies. Judah asks his second son, Onan, to perform the duty of a sibling according to the levirate law and take the widow Tamar as a wife. "But Onan, knowing that the seed would not count as his, let it go to waste whenever he joined with his brother's wife, so as not to provide offspring for his brother. What he did was displeasing to God, who took his life also" (38:9–10).

Judah decided to shelter his young third son, Shelah, from Tamar, fearing that he too might die. In doing so, he is acting contrary to levirate law. Tamar, taking matters into her own hands, disguises herself as a prostitute and sleeps with Judah. The eldest of the twins she bears, Perez, will ironically father the line that produces King David and his dynasty!

But Jacob must have seen the Judah affair as just another instance of one of his sons failing as a brother and now as a father. He tragically saw two of his grandsons pay for their sins with their lives. Judah too must have been despondent over the loss of Er and Onan. Then he was humiliated and humbled by his daughter-in-law.

Much later, in his moving appeal to Joseph (Genesis 44), which precipitates the reuniting and reconciliation of estranged brothers, Judah seems to have at least partially redeemed himself in the eyes of his father. On his deathbed Jacob predicts the royal future of the Judahite clan 49:8–11). But the overall harshness and pessimism of Jacob's last testament to his twelve sons indicates that the specter of filial failure has reached deep into the family of Jacob/Israel. The failures of the sons of Israel will continue to haunt the family as it evolves into the people of Israel.

Nadab and Abihu

We often forget that Moses had two sons. According to Exodus, Gershom and Eliezer were not failures, but rather non-entities. Besides their names, we know nothing about them. In fact, when the Book of Numbers lists "the line of Aaron and Moses" the four sons of Aaron are mentioned, but not the sons of Moses. The text goes on to say, "But Nadab and Abihu died by the will of God, when they offered alien fire before God in the wilderness of Sinai, and they left no sons" (3:4). The elder two sons of Aaron committed a grievous sin. Their punishment was so severe that they paid with their lives, and their line was cut off.

Just what was "alien fire" and why was this so egregious? The narrative in Leviticus is enigmatic, saying only that "God had not enjoined" the alien fire, and that the sons died "at the instance of

God" (10:1–2). The sages seek to fill in the textual ellipses, with some Rabbinic commentators faulting the sons for hubris; others for drunkenness; yet others for outright idolatry.

In the immediate aftermath of the tragedy Moses makes a comment that seems to suggest that Nadab and Abihu's status as sons of his brother Aaron, the high priest, made them all the more culpable: "This is what God meant by saying: Through those near to Me I show Myself holy, and gain glory before all the people" (10:3). In response, "Aaron was silent." Moses does not come across as compassionate here; to the contrary, his point seems harsh and judgmental, even if true. He is issuing a warning, but these are his nephews, and his grieving brother is right before him. Aaron is mute with grief. Might this also be his silent protest? Yes, his sons had done something wrong, publicly erring as well. Yet did the punishment fit the crime?

Hophni and Phinehas; Joel and Abijah

Another case of extreme filial failure also involves two sons of an important priest: Eli, who serves with his sons at Shiloh. He is the one who hears Hannah praying for a son, at first mistakenly thinking she is drunk. He will also serve a mentor for the young Samuel, who comes to live with him. The Book of Samuel makes clear, however, that his sons are nothing like their father: "Now Eli's sons were scoundrels; they paid no heed to God" (1:12). After describing the ruse by which they extorted people bringing sacrifices, the text adds, "The sin of the young men against God was very great, for the men treated God's offerings impiously" (1:17).

The story goes on to include a rare example of a father rebuking his wayward sons: "Now Eli was very old. When he heard all that his sons were doing to all Israel, and how they lay with the women who performed at the entrance to the Tent of Meeting, he said to them, 'Why do you do such things? I get evil reports about you from the people on all hands. Don't my sons. It is no favorable report I hear the people of God spreading about. If someone sins against another person, God may grant a pardon; but if someone offends against GOD, who can obtain a pardon?" (1:22–25).

The continuation of the story is tragic and troubling. "But they ignored their father's plea; for God was resolved that they should die" (1:25). A messenger of God faults not only the sons, but Eli as well, apparently for allowing them to misbehave for so long and not rebuking them strongly enough. Then the agent announces that "this shall be a sign for you: the fate of your two sons Hophni and Phinehas- they shall both die on the same day" (1:34). Indeed, they both fall on the battlefield, and the Ark of God is captured. When old Eli hears the terrible news, he falls backward off his seat, breaks his neck, and dies.

A coda to the catastrophic story mentions that the wife of Phinehas, when she hears the news about her husband and father-in-law, immediately goes into labor, and has a son before dying in childbirth. Just before expiring, "She names the boy Ichabod, meaning 'The glory has departed from Israel'"(4:21). God had promised that Eli's priestly line would suffer but not perish. And so it was.

Throughout this story, the writer contrasts the wicked sons with the righteous Samuel: "Young Samuel meanwhile grew up in the service of God" (2:21). Even though "In those days the word of God was rare; prophecy was not widespread" (3:1), God famously calls out to Samuel while he is yet a boy. As a result, "Samuel grew up and God was with him—not leaving any of his predication unfulfilled. All Israel, from Dan to Beer-sheba, knew that Samuel was trustworthy as a prophet of God" (3:19–20).

It was logical to assume that Samuel, who was priest, prophet, and judge, might be succeeded by his own sons. Indeed, when he grows old Samuel appoints his first-born, Joel, and his second-born, Abijah, as judges. But the text reports: "But his sons did not follow in his ways; they were bent on gain, they accepted bribes, and they subverted justice" (8:3). This time, the consequences of sons disappointing will be not just personally distressing to a father, but politically enormous for the people: "All the elders of Israel assembled and came to Samuel at Ramah, and they said to him, 'You have grown old, and your sons have not followed your ways. Therefore appoint a king for us, to govern us like all other nations'" (8:4). Samuel takes the news hard, and so does God. Samuel's protest to the people occupies the entire twelfth chapter of the Book of Samuel. Yet God instructs the prophet to accede to the people's demand, even though "it is Me they have rejected to rule over them" (8:7).

The failures of Eli's and Samuel's sons have left a void and set in motion a radical change in ancient Israel. The Bible's ambivalent attitude toward kingship is on full display as Samuel warns the people of the abuses of power that will inevitably follow the monarchy. Even the glory of David and his dynasty will be dimmed by scandal. More often than not, this will result from one of two phenomena: the failure of sons to live up to the good example of their fathers, or the failure of sons to distance themselves from the bad example of their fathers.

Jonathan

The lives of Saul and David, the first and second kings of Israel, were deeply intertwined. As the elder Saul grew increasingly paranoid about the young David, he tried to enlist his son Jonathan in his campaign against the upstart whom he saw as a threat to his rule. We read in 1 Samuel that "Saul urged his son Jonathan and all his courtiers to kill David. But Saul's son Jonathan was very fond of David…" (19:1). Jonathan actively protects David on several occasions, greatly adding to his father's distress. After the final incident, Saul explodes at his son, "You son of a perverse, rebellious women; I know that you side with the son of Jesse—to your shame and to the shame of your mother's nakedness!" (20:20).

In a rare instance, 1 Samuel also gives us an example of a daughter disappointing her father. Saul's daughter, Michal, is married off to David by her father, in the hope that, in Saul's own words, "I will give her to him, and she can serve as a snare for him…" (18:21). But Michal, like her brother, is smitten by David and risks her life for him. In a vivid scene she dresses up a household idol to look like David in bed. When her father discovers the ruse he bitterly complains, "Why did you play that trick on me and let my enemy get away safely?" (19:17).

One might write off Saul's accusations against his son and daughter, never mind his murderous intent toward his son-in-law, as the result of his deteriorating mental health. But history has repeatedly shown us potentates who see their own flesh and blood, or those who marry into the family, as rivals to their power. Is this animosity toward one's own kin part of the corruption of power? Are there greater Freudian insecurities at play here? These parent-child hostilities are not confined to fathers who hold high positions of political power. Parents often demand unwavering fealty. The question of when and to what extent children should obey, and when they should not, is challenging.

WHEN SONS DISAPPOINT

Amnon, Absalom, Adonijah, Solomon

It is said that the great and mighty King David could control a kingdom but not his own household. Indeed, after his grievous sin of adultery with Batsheva and the killing of Uriah, the prophet Nathan ominously warns in 2 Samuel that "the sword shall never depart from your house" (12:10). David will never have a moment's rest from family turmoil perpetrated by his sons.

First, his son Amnon rapes his half-sister Tamar. While we are not told of David's reaction, when Tamar's full brother Absalom finds out he is full of rage but bides his time for the moment of revenge. This comes two years later at a sheep-shearing festival when Absalom arranges to have Amnon killed. The text tells us that "David and all his courtiers wept bitterly" (13:36), Absalom fled the country and David "mourned over his son a long time" (13:27), but then, curiously, David "was pining way for Absalom, for [the king] had gotten over Amnon's death" (13:39).

Absalom was apparently the king's favorite, but he too will fail miserably and tragically in the sight of his father. Several years after returning from exile, he proclaims himself king in Hebron, armed with several hundred men. David, acknowledging the threat but reluctant to force a confrontation, flees from Jerusalem. Absalom arrives at the capital and then proceeds to sleep with his father's concubines, based on an advisor who says, "Have intercourse with your father's concubines, whom he left to mind the palace, and when all Israel hears that you have dared the wrath of your father, all who support you will be encouraged" (16:21). The dastardly act had actually been predicted by Nathan, who had said when he was chastising David, "Thus said GOD, I will make a calamity rise against you from within your very own house; I will take your wives and give them to another man before your very eyes and he shall sleep with your wives under this very sun. You acted in secret, but I will make this happen in the sight of all Israel and in broad daylight" (12:11–12).

Even after this, David still seems to have a soft spot for Absalom. When he directs his commander Joab to fight the insurgency he adds, "Deal gently with my boy Absalom, for my sake" (18:5). But when Joab is brought to Absalom, who is caught in a thicket, he drives three darts into his chest. When messengers reach the king, he twice asks, "Is my boy Absalom safe?" (18:29, 32). Upon hearing the truth, "The king was shaken. He went up to the upper chamber of the gateway and wept, moaning these words as he went, My son Absalom! O my son, my son Absalom! If only I had died instead of you! O Absalom, my son, my son!" (19:1).

Filial failure often causes anger to parents. It also causes heartbreak. And sometimes both at the same time.

David's travails would not end with the deaths of Amnon and Absalom. Yet another son, Adonijah, would rise up against his father, near the end of David's life. 1 Kings intriguingly notes, "His father had never scolded him: 'Why did you do that?'; he was the one born after Absalom and, like him, was very handsome" (1:6). Although this is not the first time an editorial gloss appears pointing out the failure of a father to properly rebuke his sons (remember Eli), it is rare. Here David appears to be falling short again, due to the loss of two previous sons.

At this sensitive juncture the prophet Nathan makes a reappearance to urge Batsheba to elevate her own son. Together they intercede with David and the frail, aging monarch proclaims Solomon the king. Adonijah seeks amnesty and refuge, which Solomon grants conditionally: "If he behaves worthily not a hair of his head shall fall to the ground; but if he is caught in any offense, he shall die" (1:51). After David dies, Adonijah approaches Batsheba requesting that David's concubine Abishag be given to him as a wife. Solomon is outraged, responding to his mother, "Why request Abishag the Shunammite for Adonijah? Request the kingship for him!" (2:22). The new king orders his older brother executed.

David did not live to see this latest chapter in his family's tragedy. One wonders if his broken heart could have survived another death of a son at the hand of a brother. Nor did David live to see either the glory of Solomon's reign, or its decline. For while Solomon is celebrated for his wisdom and riches, 1·Kings paints a different picture of his latter days: "In his old age, his wives turned away Solomon's heart after other gods…Solomon did what was displeasing to GOD, and did not remain loyal to GOD like his father David…and GOD was angry with Solomon…." (11:4, 6, 9). Once again, punishment will come down the line, for God says, "I will tear the kingdom away from you…not in your lifetime; I will tear it away from your son" (11:11–12).

The sword of discord never did depart from the House of David. Rehoboam, the aforementioned son of Solomon, "did what was displeasing to GOD, provoking more outrage than their ancestors had by the sins they committed" (14:22). His son Abijam "continued in all the sins that his father before him had committed" (15:3). Generation after generation, with few exceptions, sons do "what was displeasing to GOD." The expression serves as a trope of filial failure.

Final Filial Thoughts

Neither does the sword of domestic discord departs from our homes. The stories from long ago are all too familiar to us. While Scripture rarely delves into emotional motivations for the misbehavior it describes, enough hints and recurring themes in its multitude of disparate stories serve as cautionary lessons.

Clearly, parents have a role in their children's acting out. From the first tale of Cain and Abel, through Jacob and Esau to the sons of David, we observe that parental favoritism leads to jealousy and resentment. Parents may be blind to this favoritism, and children may find it impossibly difficult to articulate. Sibling rivalry is so often the unfortunate byproduct of parental favoritism. The flip side of parental favoritism is parental absenteeism, especially in the eyes of the child who feels scorned. The perceived deprivation that results from a physically or emotionally remote parent can lead to a desperate yearning for parental affection and approval on the part of the alienated child. Of course, parents can be absent or remote for other reasons, from basic personality make-up to professional demands. Unrealistic expectations of children by parents, or of parents by children, can and do exacerbate the situation. So too does overly judgmental criticism by either side of the other. The causation for the abundance of filial failure, and the blame that often goes with it, cannot then be exclusively laid at the feet of either parents or children.

Modern psychology seeks to uncover the motivations for endemic familial conflict. Freud famously theorized that sons are in competition with their fathers from an early age. Psychoanalytic analysis through the lens of his Oedipus theory is illuminating. One researcher has dubbed Absalom as the "Hebraic Oedipus." More than a few scholars have delved into the striking parallels between certain Biblical and Greek stories with strong father-son rivalries, especially those of Isaac, Moses, and David.[6]

More recent work has concentrated on the socialization of boys into the "pecking order" of modern society, which leads them to cultivating traits of masculinity that include "aggressiveness, assertiveness, dominance, and forcefulness."[7] To this we may add the poor communication skills that often characterize young men when it relates to the expressing of complex emotions. When we combine these biological, psychological, and sociological challenges, a toxic brew results that fuels the endemic persistence of filial failure.

Yet, even if the *Tanach* skews to the dark side of human nature, we know from our experience that many healthy and loving father-son relationships do exist. In the face of so many challenges, how does the positive prevail? More than anything, the presence of a loving parent will often help alleviate the conflict; the absence of loving parent will only exacerbate it.

We ought to add that for those who feel trapped today in failing filial relationships, the intervention of family therapists and other trained mental health professionals is an important resource not be overlooked. The abundance of cautionary tales from our tradition, and from our lived family experiences, should prompt us, as leaders in the community, to redouble our efforts to break the generational patterns of filial failure. Then we will be one step closer to that blessed day that the prophet Malachi envisioned, when Elijah,[8] with our help, "shall reconcile parents to their children and children to their parents" (3:24).

Notes

Biblical citations are from The JPS TANAKH: Gender-Sensitive Edition (2023).

1. Jonathan Sacks, "Covenant and Conversation: Sibling Rivalry" (Mikketz, 5771, 5784), https://rabbisacks.org/covenant-conversation/mikketz/sibling-rivalry/.
2. I am indebted for the formulation of this insight to Naomi Rosenblatt (with Joshua Horwitz), *Wrestling with Angels* (Delacorte Press, 1995), 56.
3. Federal Bureau of Prisons, "Inmate Gender" (as of January 6, 2024). https://www.bop.gov/about/statistics/statistics_inmate_gender.jsp.
4. Jeffrey Tigay, *The JPS Torah Commentary: Deuteronomy* (Jewish Publication Society, 1996), 196.

5. For the convoluted but fascinating linkage between Edom and Rome see Malka Simkovich, "Esau the Ancestor of Rome," https://www.thetorah.com/article/esau-the-ancestor-of-rome.
6. See Sam Himelfarb, "A Psychoanalytic Reading of the Father-Son Relationship in the Bible" (Princeton University unpublished thesis, April 2022). A good overview of existing literature on this subject can be found in Paul Cantz, "Toward a Biblical Psychoanalysis" in *Mental Health, Religion and Culture* 15.8 (October 2012): 779–97. One of the first books to explore this was Erich Wellish, *Isaac and Oedipus* (Routledge, 1954).
7. John G. Cottone, "Fathers and Sons: Masculinity, Men, and Relationships" in *Psychology Today* (June 18, 2023); https://www.psychologytoday.com/us/blog/the-cube/202206/fathers-and-sons-masculinity-men-and-relationships.
8. On the problematics of Elijah being the harbinger of father-son reconciliation, see Wendy Zierler, "Can Elijah Reconcile Fathers and Sons?" (April 13, 2016); https://www.thetorah.com/article/can-elijah-reconcile-fathers-and-sons.

Book Reviews

A Life of Psalms in Jewish Late Antiquity by Dr. A.J. Berkovitz (University of Pennsylvania Press, 2023), 274 pp.

Whether appended to prayers for the safety of soldiers, gifted in full as an illegibly small talisman, or sung joyfully in services, psalms appear everywhere in contemporary Jewish life. I must admit, I have taken the healing potential of psalm recitation, the preponderance of psalms in liturgy, and the very notion of a canonized Psalter for granted—that is, until now.

A. J. Berkovitz's *A Life of Psalms in Jewish Late Antiquity* encourages a celebration of the historical context of the foundations of "the Psalms['] pride of place within the practices of liturgy, piety, and magic" (3). This erudite book is an outgrowth of Berkovitz's dissertation at Princeton University. In its final form, *A Life of Psalms* fulfills Berkovitz's stated aim to "capture the vitality of the Psalter" in Jewish late antiquity, which he porously periodizes as the "late second century—mid-seventh century" (8, 4). Berkovitz, currently a faculty member of the Hebrew Union College-Jewish Institute of Religion, utilizes amulets, inscriptions, Christian texts, and other archaeological documents as evidence for his arguments. Yet, the Rabbinic canon stands as his most ample source for exploring the life of psalms in their physical and oral forms in late antiquity. Drawing on convergent fields like book history, Rabbinics, comparative religion, archaeology, and more, Berkovitz joins the ranks of scholars who study psalms, books in general, and the Bible specifically. He builds on their work by asking new questions, chief among them: "How did Jews encounter the Psalms?"—a question that sets exegesis in a secondary role and privileges the quotidian (11).

In his first chapter, Berkovitz describes the experience of "Holding the Scrolls of Psalms." The *pièce de résistance* of this section appears early, as a table estimating the "conjectured length of various psalters" including Qumran manuscripts and the Leningrad Codex (20). In a page-long footnote, Berkovitz enumerates the lengthy process he endured to extrapolate the number of columns a Psalms manuscript may have contained based on the number of characters in the Masoretic text (164). Relying on other scholars' measurements of extant psalters, Berkovitz estimates the total length of various psalters from late antiquity between approximately 45 and 128 feet! As such, he speculates that "ancient Jews seldom interacted with a complete Hebrew Psalter written on a single scroll" (20). Not only does this conclusion help explain the practical "convenience" of dividing the Psalter into five units, but it also highlights Berkovitz's commitment to imagining the vitality of the past (19).

Berkovitz further explores the variables that could influence the various lengths of these psalters, including "forms of versification," spacing, line division, and "several layout options" all preserved in ancient psalm scrolls (20). Further, in examining the littering of "ambiguous hallelujahs" throughout the Psalter, Berkovitz takes readers on a journey into Talmudic texts in which sages argue about whether "hallelujah" begins or ends a psalm (41). Berkovitz writes that the Rabbinic debate is not merely a matter of opinion but "likely revolves around writing and laying out a Psalm scroll" and "perhaps the scrolls most accessible to the [sages] shaped their respective opinions" (42). This novel conclusion remains crucial for future scholarship. How many other Rabbinic disagreements may be attributed to access to different manuscripts of Biblical texts?

In his second chapter, Berkovitz explores the various modes of reading a material Psalter in late antiquity. In his attempt to describe readers outside the Rabbinic ideal, Berkovitz explores the Psalter's role in reading for leisure, to "inculcate ethics," to cause one to act, and for scholarship (51–60). Importantly, each of his prooftexts for these variant forms of reading Scripture stem from Rabbinic literature. Thus, though Berkovitz exposes non-exegetical reading of psalms, the evidence he leans on inevitably colors each experience through Rabbinic ideals.

In examining the singing of psalms in his third chapter, Berkovitz unearths the foundations of an issue a prayerful Jewish individual may easily take for granted: daily psalmody. After the destruction of the Jerusalem cult, it was not a given that the Rabbis would incorporate daily recitation of psalms into the rubric of prayer. "In fact," Berkovitz writes, "the earliest rabbis never discuss the place of Psalms in their own daily liturgy" (77, 79). Yet, in the intervening centuries, "fitful and nonlinear development of daily psalmody" progressed (83). In another eye-opening observation, Berkovitz shares at least one of these Rabbinic "fits" in examining *Ashrei*. He cites the sole Talmudic mention of this liturgical piece, which contains all of Psalm 145 but begins with words from Psalm 84. The Rabbinic inquiry arises regarding an exegetical question about Psalm 145 but refers to the entire liturgical piece with its incipit, *ashrei*, from Psalm 84. As a result, Berkovitz concludes that "a unit of daily liturgy…was sufficiently well-known to be cited" in this fashion (86). Berkovitz's examination of *Ashrei* is an exemplar of his work in the entire monograph, throughout which he provides an attention to detail and fresh conclusions that open new lines of inquiry into this canonical Jewish text.

As part of his impressive work, Berkovitz introduces an entirely distinct purpose of the Psalter: it served not merely for reading, but also for piety and magic. In examining the potency of psalms, Berkovitz explores Christian monastic recitation. In a lengthy section about these practices, Berkovitz seems to forget the "Jewish" moniker in the title of his work. Regardless, he introduces a crucial concept that does bridge the religious gap, namely that "the book of Psalms surrounds those who recite its words with a shield" (115). In the Jewish sphere, the words of the Psalter itself transmit piety (115). Rabbinic texts encourage the repetitive recitation of psalm verses that encourage "trust and faith in God" (126). Further, psalms, in their protective capacity, arise in magic—an example of "non-rabbinic ancient Jewish Psalm piety" (137). In examining amulets and magical bowls, as well as intentional recitation of psalms at midnight or on one's deathbed, Berkovitz highlights the protective power of psalmody. Though this final content-rich chapter is Berkovitz's weakest in terms of bringing vitality to non-Rabbinic explorations of Jewish interactions with psalms, he still deepens the "soundscape reverberating with Psalms" of the ancient world (137).

In his final chapter, Berkovitz acknowledges his limitations and suggests prospects for future works. He expertly evokes late ancient Jewish psalmody and its manifest occurrences. In so many ways, Berkovitz left me hungry for more; hinting at titillating morsels of future projects and footnotes to exciting scholarly debate. On almost every page, Berkovitz accomplishes his goal of setting aside exegesis and searching for the "counterintuitive history" of the Psalter (151). His biggest blind spot in examining "the important non-scholarly ways in which Jews interacted with the Psalms" is, in my opinion, the near universal absence of women in this counterintuitive history (151). He mentions, yes, that the "wealthy readers of Scripture clearly included Jewish women" and he briefly compares their literacy to their Christian counterparts (71–72). He also nods to further reading on "female readers in Late Antiquity" in a few footnotes (190, 202). Yet, the primary content remains wanting for a deeper dive into women's interactions with the Psalter. Knowing the limits of extant data and the large absence of women in Rabbinic literature as a whole, I wish that Berkovitz had gone deeper in examining non-Rabbinic and non-synagogal psalmody in late antiquity. In asking questions such as who had the opportunity to memorize psalms for bedtime piety or who sought protection from demons in the home, Berkovitz could have introduced more women to his analysis. In describing psalmody outside of the Rabbinic male elite, Berkovitz still relies heavily on the data left by that class.

Ultimately, Berkovitz paints a brilliant picture of *A Life of Psalms in Jewish Late Antiquity*, as his title promises. The ideal audience of this book extends beyond Biblical scholars already working in the field, and includes anyone with a passing interest in archaeology. Moreover, certainly anyone who interacts with the psalms—whether as scripture, liturgy, or poetry; from settings ranging from sickbeds to pews—may find something interesting at least, and spiritually compelling at most, within the pages of this book. For me, the echoes of this book will continue to reverberate, like the psalms themselves, as I continue to encounter them with this new historical understanding. Simply put, A. J. Berkovitz has given me one of the best gifts an author can give to a reader: a new framework with which to understand my world.

EDEN GLASER is a rabbinical student at HUC-JIR on her hometown campus in Los Angeles and will receive ordination in the spring of 2025. In addition to her scholarly interests in translation and text, she enjoys cooking, live comedy, and spending time with family.

BOOK REVIEWS

Judaism Is About Love: Recovering the Heart of Jewish Life
by Rabbi Shai Held
(Farrar, Straus and Giroux, 2024), 560 pp.

Upon opening *Judaism Is About Love* for the first time, I was moved to see a blurb from our teacher Rabbi David Ellenson, z"l, who died before the book was actually published. He calls this work Rabbi Shai Held's "theological magnum opus," and I couldn't agree more. In the weeks I spent reading the book, I could already sense the transformational impact the work is having, both on my understanding of Judaism and on my work as a rabbi and educator. I felt alternatingly challenged, guided, comforted, and inspired by Held's writing, and I expect other readers will feel the same.

I was excited for the opportunity to review *Judaism Is About Love*, given my existing appreciation for Rabbi Shai Held's teachings. For a number of years, I've listened to his *shiurim* and read his essays published by the Hadar Institute, where he serves as president and dean. His two-volume collection of weekly *divrei Torah*, *The Heart of Torah* (2017), is a well-used set on my bookshelf, and his works in theology and philosophy are powerful resources for thoughtful Jewish learners.

What sets *Judaism Is About Love* apart, though, is its comprehensiveness; the book seemingly touches nearly every aspect of Jewish life, showing how love suffuses each one. By "love," Held means both an affective experience of emotional connection *and* a dispositional orientation that persists even in the absence of emotion in a given moment. Both aspects are at play in his discussions of human worth, interpersonal relationships, ethical behavior, and theological concepts. Depending on which chapter one opens, one can find passages that speak to the importance of parents providing a loving environment for their children, to the tension between universal human dignity and the existence of those who cause harm, and to the necessity of chosenness as a concept in Judaism. Each, and more, is described as an expression of God's love for us, our love for God, or humans' love for one another.

One element of Held's writing that I appreciated most is his realistic descriptions of what we can expect of ourselves. He frequently reminds readers that the ideals he posits are, in fact, ideals. No human can ever be perfectly loving, in every moment or situation, but that does not excuse us from trying. Held notes that, in many of our sacred texts, even God—whose capacity for love far outclasses our own—struggles with how God's love is expressed. I find this idea comforting.

Held also grapples with a question many students raise in response to learning the *Shema*: What does it mean to be told, "You shall love *Adonai* your God" (Deuteronomy 6:5)? How can love be commanded? Held offers guidance on this topic by focusing readers' attention on commanded behaviors, but not *only* on those behaviors. We imitate things God does, following in God's ways, as ministers of God's love—regardless of how we feel. Over time, as we act lovingly toward other human beings (*mitzvot bein adam la-chaveiro*) and toward God (*mitzvot bein adam la-makom*), we come to develop actual loving emotions in those relationships—which, in turn, further motivates us to engage in such loving behaviors. Judaism nurtures this virtuous cycle, says Held.

This matters, Held claims, not merely because love is a worthy end in and of itself, but because it leads us to behave in kinder ways and to feel more compassion for one another. It leads to a gentler and more loving world, one in which we "create moments of redemption even in the midst of this impossibly broken, thoroughly unredeemed world" (260).

There is much in *Judaism Is About Love* that speaks to our current historical moment. Though it does not refer to the October 7, 2023 Hamas attack and subsequent war, the book happened to be published within the first six months of that Israel-Hamas conflict. Reading it in this context, I found solace in Held's discussion of love expressed both particularly and universally. Held wholeheartedly endorses Jewish partiality, giving both theological and psychosocial arguments for why it is both natural and good to care for one's own tribe as distinct from care for all humans. In a time when many Jews struggle to hold and express concern for all innocents, both Israeli and Gazan, Held's words give readers language for understanding the legitimacy of privileging one's own group while maintaining concern for another. Judaism commands us to love our neighbors, while also commanding us to love everyone else too. These are separate commands, claims Held, but both are nonetheless real.

One of the most remarkable aspects of Held's writing is his reference to and conversation with an immense number of thinkers, whose works span centuries. *Judaism Is About Love* includes numerous Biblical citations, Rabbinic *midrashim*, and classical commentaries. It also includes the more recent works of countless scholars: Jewish, secular, and even Christian. As he notes in his introduction, Held clearly takes seriously Maimonides' dictum to "learn the truth from whoever says it" (18). At other times, he cites thinkers for the sake of critique, such as in his extended evaluation of Mordecai Kaplan's resistance to chosenness. While Held self-consciously selects the sources that help him build his argument, he still offers readers a broad survey of thought on the subject of love in Judaism.

My one gripe with the book is with its introductory framing. Held opens with something to prove, as reflected in his opening line: "Judaism is not what you think it is" (3). Bothered by the (mis)conception that Judaism privileges justice while Christianity privileges love, Held laments that even learned Jews seem to have internalized this perspective. In Held's view, this conceptualization is a result of dual phenomena: American Jews defining themselves as "not Christian" on the one hand, and polemical Christian supersessionism on the other. He positions his project as a corrective to both, but I wish he had not introduced them with such oppositionality. Held's points are persuasive enough on their own.

Judaism Is About Love is a worthwhile read for anyone interested in understanding how love permeates all aspects of Jewish life. Because of its wide-ranging, scholarly explorations of so many theological, philosophical, and spiritual concepts in Judaism, however, the book is likely most accessible to readers familiar with a breadth of Jewish thought already—such as clergy or learned laypeople. *Judaism Is About Love* is less useful as a first journey through Jewish thought than it is as a guidebook for retracing that journey with love at the lead. Held's insights themselves, though, *are* accessible—and worthwhile—for a wide audience, and his frequent use of Biblical and Rabbinic texts makes the book a valuable resource for teachers and preachers to draw inspiration and mine for sources. I recommend that whoever reads the book do so with a pencil in hand; readers will want to jot notes and questions in conversation with Held as they read.

As I wrote above, I can sense already that *Judaism Is About Love* will have a lasting impact on my life: both on my Judaism personally and on my work as a rabbi and educator. I expect to return to its pages time and again. Throughout the book, Held continually invites his readers to imagine a life in which love animates and pervades our relationships and our actions, our ethics and our theology. With gratitude for this invitation, I am now asking myself what it means to have a rabbinate centered on love, to cultivate educational programs that nurture love, and to act in ways large and small that are motivated by love. I do not yet have my own responses to these questions, but the fact that I am moved to ask them at all shows the influence Held's book is having on me already.[1]

Not that questions like these have easy responses; it would be simpler for us all to maintain our typical modes of operation, without holistically reorienting our lives and our work around love. But that's Held's point exactly. As he says: "I am advocating for how I believe religion *should* function, not portraying how it always *does* function.…My goal is to make life harder for believers, not easier: make sure your religious life in general, and your religious study in particular, make you kinder and more present, because after all, *that's ultimately what it's all about*" (240; emphasis in original).

Judaism Is About Love really is about love, through and through. Despite its length, it remains focused on conveying its titular message. Rabbi Shai Held's readers will find meaning in this extended meditation on love, and they will likely close the book inspired to bring love more to the fore in their lives and in the world.

Notes

1. I do not mean to imply that love is absent from my life! Only that I fit well into Held's imagined audience, meaning that I have not centered love in my Judaism the way he advocates.

RABBI SAM POLLAK (C '17) currently serves as Director of Youth and Family Education at Temple Isaiah in Lexington, Massachusetts. He previously served congregations in Concord, Massachusetts and Port Washington, New York, and he is proud to have grown up in Cincinnati, Ohio.

Books Like Sapphires: From the Library of Congress Judaica Collection
by Ann Brener
(Brandeis University Press, 2024), 272 pp.

Ann Brener's *Books Like Sapphires* provides an expertly curated and handsomely illustrated tour through the treasures of the Judaica

Collection held by the Library of Congress. As the rare book librarian of the Klau Library (Hebrew Union College), I am familiar with many of these gems. I agreed to review this book because I thought I would have some critical distance. However, since *Books Like Sapphires* is so beautiful a book, all dispassion was lost.

Let us begin at the beginning. In an infamous act of cultural vandalism, much of the original collection of the Library of Congress, little over a decade into its existence, was burned by British troops during the War of 1812. To replace that loss, 6,487 volumes were purchased from Thomas Jefferson, forming the seed of the current collection. While Brener notes that "there were certainly no Hebrew books in the collection that Thomas Jefferson sold" (2), there were in point of fact three: two Bible-related books (a Hexapla and a Pseudepigrapha) and a copy of the Mishnaic tractate *Bava Kama* in Hebrew and Latin. In fact, the percentage of Hebrew books in Jefferson's collection is almost exactly the same as that of Jews in the population of the United States at the time of the purchase. Proportional representation indeed!

With *Bava Kama* on the shelf, the Judaica Collection came into its own with a related series of purchase-donations between 1912 and 1920. These collections were amassed by the bookman and adventurer Ephraim Deinard over the course of a lively career. Deinard originally proposed selling his collections directly to the Library, arguing that as every other great library had a Hebraica collection, if the Library of Congress wanted to be great it had better get in on the act. While the will was there—in the person of Herbert Putnam, the Librarian of Congress—the money was not. Great library collections are so often the products not only of great book collectors but also of great book donors. It was banker-turned-philanthropist Jacob Schiff who would purchase Deinard's several collections and donate their more than 10,000 volumes to the Library. Schiff had internalized the Aristotelian ideal: "The magnificent man is an artist in expenditure: he can discern what is suitable, and spend great sums with good taste."[1] Schiff's "artistry" lay in his ability to envision simultaneously how such a growing collection would redound to the prestige of the nation's library as well as the boon such a collection would represent to the nation's scholarship. And as Brener is right to point out, the Library's Judaica collecting has steadily built on Schiff and Putnam's foresightful foundation.

It is easy for me, a rare book librarian, to argue why Hebrew Union College's library should house one of the finest collections of Judaica in the country: we hold our books in trust for the Jewish people. But what is the rationale for the United States' national library to do the same? Why the exemplary collection of 16th-century Hebrew imprints, or one of the finest late-medieval illuminated Haggadot in the world? It's more than that the Library of Congress similarly holds its collections in trust for the American people. The impetus behind a great research collection is the Terentian verity that, being human, nothing human ought be foreign. To understand the Jewish roles in the American pageant means understanding Jews. *Books Like Sapphires* is a splendid tableau laying bare Jewish book culture as an integral part of Jewish culture.

The book is organized into seven categories, beginning with Biblical and Rabbinic material, followed by liturgy, Hebrew literature, children's literature (*en passant*, an important and welcome addition to the usual cast of characters), and communal life. It ends with books from Jewish Cultural Reconstruction, that is, orphaned volumes saved from Nazi looting. These are serviceable rubrics as they encompass much of the treasures of the collection. Divided amongst these categories are forty-seven individual items from the collection, each of which gets its own chapter. In these lovely exposés, each accompanied by excellent photographs, Brener ably captures the substance and context of each work. Once the reader has perused the four dozen jewels on offer, the contours of the diadem become clear.

Take the very first example in the book: the *chumash* printed in Bologna in 1482, the first printed Hebrew Pentateuch. Not only does it include an Aramaic translation parallel to the text as well as Rashi's commentary in the margins above and below—in a separate typeface no less—but it also represents one of the first significant deployments of vowel signs and cantillation marks in print. This a scant generation after the advent of European movable type. Brener rightly makes much of the paratextual elements, the printer's colophon and the proofreader's note, to highlight the great skill of the craftsmen who produced this book. Notable, too, is that the Library of Congress's copy is printed on vellum—a deluxe edition if ever there was one. But this is where working in an exceptional Judaica collection amplifies the joy of browsing *Books Like Sapphires*, because the Klau Library holds two copies of this text, one on paper and the other, likewise, on vellum. There is an ineffable joy in letting one's hands play across the ripple of the vellum, and a frisson in realizing that, no, that's not discolored ink from printing, rather those vowels and cantillation marks, prevented by that selfsame rippled vellum from taking to the page, were added later by hand. So inured to mass production are we that we can easily overlook how even a printed book can be unique.

Or take what is perhaps the most storied part of the collection, the *Washington Haggadah*. Produced by Yoel ben Shimon in 1478, in either Germany or northern Italy, it represents the high-water mark of Ashkenazic illuminated Haggadot. Filled with sumptuous illustrations and exquisite scribal art, this manuscript is a stunner, a museum piece. Yet how to understand a book that speaks to us from more than half a millennium away? Just look at the bibliographical references, at the facsimile editions and scholarly essays that this one book has spawned, and you will get some impression of the scholarly, intellectual, artistic, and cultural potential all held within a single volume. Now multiply that across the whole of the Judaica Collection and you will get a sense of what *Books Like Sapphires* is actually offering: not only hours of edification and pleasure, but more importantly a challenge to the People of the Book both to love their books and to learn from them; to support their libraries and to use them.

Note

1. Aristotle, *Nicomachean Ethics*, trans. H. Rackham (Harvard University Press, 1934), 207.

JORDAN FINKIN is Rare Book and Manuscript Librarian at Hebrew Union College in Cincinnati. A scholar of modern and modernist Jewish literature, he is also a literary translator from Yiddish, German, and French, as well as the Director of Naydus Press, which publishes Yiddish literature in English translation.

Holy Rebellion: Religious Feminism and the Transformation of Judaism and Women's Rights in Israel By Ronit Irshai and Tanya Zion-Waldoks (Brandeis University Press, 2024), 400 pp.

Most of us are familiar with the works of central liberal Jewish feminist authors such as Rachel Adler and Judith Plaskow. Many of us have read Tamar Ross, Tova Hartman, and Blu Greenberg, who approach Jewish feminism from an Orthodox perspective. Irshai and Zion-Waldoks follow in the footsteps of these matriarchs in their new work of feminist history and scholarship, *Holy Rebellion: Religious Feminism and the Transformation of Judaism and Women's Rights in Israel*. One of the newest installations in the field of Jewish critical feminist research, this densely packed tome focuses especially on the evolutions and revolutions within the Religious Zionist branch of Israeli Judaism.

Holy Rebellion is a historical and theoretical exploration of the last fifty years of Religious Zionist feminism and its impact on Israeli Orthodoxy writ large. It describes and explains the interaction between religion and feminism, as well as the social and legal context in which this plays out—with an acknowledgment that these changes happen in the triple realms of theology, sociology, and halachah. Irshai and Zion-Waldoks identify both the grassroots Orthodox feminist activist groups and spaces (i.e., Pelech, Kehilat Yedidya, Women of the Wall) and the ways in which they interact with the *rabbanut* (Israeli High Religious Court) and the democratic state. They argue that Religious Zionist feminism is "evolutionary" rather than "revolutionary" and seeks to change Orthodoxy from within halachah and Orthodox tradition, contrasting the movement from the beginning as fundamentally different from liberal feminist endeavors.

This book is a history of Religious Zionist feminist thought, method, and progress written by Religious Zionist feminists. Both authors discuss in the preface the differences in access to learning that exist between their grandmothers and their daughters, and it is clear that this project is much more than simply a scholarly endeavor for them. It is a hopeful study that doesn't flinch from the real illiberal headwinds that Religious Zionist feminism faces within Israeli society. The authors argue that this pushback is evidence of the success of their "evolutionary" approach, and they even go so far as to define subgroups of Religious Zionism based on the stances they take on these specific gendered issues—arguing that in the future, their methodology will help women gain halachically-adherent equality at greater scale and with wider Orthodox acceptance.

Chapter 1, "Nomos and Narrative: A Story of Law and Culture," goes back to the seminal 1982 law article by Robert Cover of the same name and applies his methodology and thought to Religious Zionism's status of a "minority within the minority." Interestingly, the authors mention the work of Rachel Adler very briefly, but instead of tracing their influence through her work, they jump back in history to Cover himself and work their own thoughts through his argumentation rather than through Adler's. (A seeming discomfort with being linked to liberal Jewish feminism seems to permeate the book.) In this chapter, they identify the values, beliefs, stories, halachot, customs, and structural biases within Israeli Orthodoxy that feminism challenges.

The next chapter, "Homes: Renewing Orthodoxy from Within," uses the collective *"bayit"* to discuss the loci of these evolutionary trends and transformations. Areas discussed include the influence of Religious Zionist feminism on the *beit k'neset* (synagogue), *beit midrash* (yeshivot), and *beit din* (religious courts), and also on secular Israeli state law, the family home, and the physical bodies of women in Israel. They argue that through these transformations, these "homes" grow to include women in their fullness, rather than excluding or rendering them invisible. Each of these homes and the transformations of the last fifty years is explored in detail, constituting the bulk of the book.

Chapter 3, "Rabbinic Illiberal Backlash," outlines what Irshai and Zion-Waldoks calls "five obstructive mechanisms" that have resulted in the Israeli *rabbanut* due to the success of feminism's influence. The first of these they call "Akedah theology," a tendency for Orthodox men to invoke submission and sacrifice to religious authority when pushed to consider a feminist point of view. They also discuss the "slippery slope" argument, where the authors finally discuss rabbinic fears of the "deterioration of religious standards." Interestingly, this is the only place where an acknowledgement of the Reform Movement's feminist and LGBTQ+ stances and its influence on Judaism writ large is discussed. The other three reasons—essentialism, nationalism, and "normalcy" and family values—are obstructions that imagine the breakdown of the state and family by permitting any egalitarian values to be expressed in Orthodox spaces.

A case study follows in Chapter 4, "Judicial Encounters: Narrative Ripeness and Dignity Tests," and this is the section that I found the most interesting and ground-breaking. In it, Irshai and

Zion-Waldoks make the case that when women cannot be heard in religious courts, they go to the secular state for redress. They explore a selection of case law in Israel's High Court that shows the interaction between the state and religion in these instances, and they present a new theoretical framework for when the state should intervene in religious matters (and when and how it might succeed in enforcing needed feminist change). They come up with two tests: the "Narrative Ripeness Test," which identifies tipping points within the religious minority's discourse that favor the change, and the "Dignity Test," which fronts human rights and the state's mandate to protect women from harm and the violation of their (secular) rights to be full citizens of the state. This exploration runs from divorce to women in the rabbinate to kashrut supervision to the visibility of women in public space, and shows where and when these tests have succeeded in enacting and enforcing change within Israeli Orthodoxy from the outside.

While this book could make for a fascinating graduate-level class on Religious Zionist feminism, it is far too scholarly to be useful outside of the classroom. Its authors also seem reluctant to acknowledge the debt they owe to liberal Jewish feminist scholars, and it was mildly off-putting that rather than build solidarity between women in Jewish feminist spaces, they preferred to work from and with the men inside their community, even those obstructing their progress. Whatever its few flaws, this book is a pivotal reference for the last fifty years of Religious Zionist feminism in Israeli society.

RABBI SARA ZOBER (C '18) is a writer and congregational rabbi in Reno, Nevada.

Reading Reform Responsa: Jewish Tradition, Reform Rabbis, and Today's Issues by Mark Washofsky
(CCAR Press, 2024), 288 pp.

The Reform Movement can take great pride in the fact that two of our own, Rabbis David Ellenson and Mark Washofsky, have made significant contributions to English-language scholarship of the Jewish literary genre known as "responsa" (*sh'elot ut'shuvot*). Though many readers' impulse might be to read responsa with an eye toward the bottom-line ruling on the halachic question at hand, both Ellenson and Washofsky have demonstrated that it is the *body* of the responsum that deserves greater attention. This is because it is through the *posek*'s argumentation, rhetorical style, analysis of sources, use of precedents, and framing of the case that the responsum makes its real impact. Without understanding these and other literary, historical, and cultural elements of a responsum, a reader will miss the deeper significance of the final ruling.

Based on the academic contributions of Ellenson and Washofsky, we can identify four key features of responsa that are discernible across the denominational spectrum. First, responsa seek to persuade their intended audience to see the case in a particular way—to convince them, as Washofsky puts it, that "this particular answer is the best available solution to the question and why other answers, even if plausible, are not as good" (6). Second, responsa aim to lead the community toward a particular way of thinking and living Jewishly. They do so, Ellenson explains, by "mediat[ing] between a received religious tradition, on the one hand, and the inescapable demands of a contemporary cultural, social, and political context…on the other"[1] in a way that resonates with intended readers. Third, responsa try to persuade and/or reinforce for readers that halachah is relevant to their communal and individual lives. This is a particularly salient feature of Reform responsa because of the force of the claim made by many that Reform Judaism is a "non-halachic" movement. Washofsky strongly rejects that claim, arguing that "a good Reform Jewish decision" is always the product of "exercising [our] autonomy in thoughtful conversation with the Jewish tradition" (11), and "if we want to know how the 'Jewish tradition' addresses any question of ritual or ethical practice, then we have no option but to consult and study the halachic literature" (13). And fourth, responsa teach Torah by presenting Biblical, Rabbinic, and other relevant Jewish sources to the reader in the course of building their case. Thus responsa are texts for sacred study in their own right.

Mark Washofsky's outstanding new book, *Reading Reform Responsa*, demonstrates how these features manifest in the Reform Movement's particular approach to *sh'eilot ut'shuvot*. By teaching reading strategies to draw out the complex dynamics of the lived Reform Jewish community contained in this literature, Washofsky does for modern Reform responsa what David Ellenson did for nineteenth- and twentieth-century Orthodox responsa. Whereas Ellenson's approach is sociological and historical, however,

Washofsky's method "resembles 'literary criticism'" (16). Reading Reform responsa as literary compositions—or, what he has elsewhere called "rhetorical performances"[2]—Washofsky asks questions of the text like: What kind of community does the *posek* think we ought to be? Who does the *posek* see as the ideal reader of this text, and what role does he[3] want the ideal reader to play in the community he is envisioning? Fundamentally, what does he believe the case at hand to be *about*? Who are the "characters" in the story the *posek* is telling, and how does he portray them? How does the *posek* use rhetoric and halachic sources to invite readers into the decision-making process and persuade them to see the case as he sees it? In this way, Washofsky's approach is inspired by the modern school of secular legal theory known as "Law and Literature," which uses the same tools to analyze legal texts that literary critics use to analyze novels, poems, and short stories.

Indeed, the ability to apply complex secular legal theories to the reading of halachic texts in a clear and accessible way is one of Washofsky's great strengths and most important contributions to the field. David Ellenson once referred to Washofsky as a genuine halachic *ilui* (genius),[4] and it is evident that this book is a deeply learned work of an extraordinary legal mind. Academics and lawyers will be impressed by Washofsky's strong grasp of the work of theorists like Ronald Dworkin, James Boyd White, Stanley Fish, and others, and how he integrates them into the classical halachic conversation. At the same time, lay readers will appreciate how he is able to distill and translate these esoteric ideas, which are generally the province of law schools and dense legal-philosophy books, into concepts they can understand and put to use. By combining his extensive knowledge of legal theory, classical halachic literature, and Reform Jewish culture with his characteristic dry wit and engaging writing style, Washofsky offers compelling analyses of some of the Reform Movement's most important responsa. Each of the book's ten chapters analyzes a responsum or cluster of responsa on a particular issue. A brief look at one of these chapters will illustrate Washofsky's approach.

In Chapter 2, Washofsky examines a responsum that he himself authored as Chairman of the CCAR Responsa Committee entitled "Orthodox Minyan in a Reform Synagogue." As the title suggests, the rabbi of a Reform temple in Jackson, Mississippi—the only synagogue of any denomination in that city—asked if it would be appropriate for the congregation to allow an Orthodox minyan that was looking for a place to pray to meet in its building. The *sho'el* expresses reservation about agreeing to this because the Orthodox group would not count women in the minyan or permit them to participate fully in the service, and that would violate the Reform Movement's commitment to gender egalitarianism. At the same time, he wonders whether the obligation to welcome guests (*hachnasat orchim*) should override this concern.

Washofsky begins his analysis by pointing out a subtle yet critical rhetorical-interpretive move in how the responsum "frames" what the case is about. He notes that whereas the questioner describes the dilemma as a conflict between the core values of gender egalitarianism, on the one hand, and hospitality, on the other, "the responsum declares at the outset that it will rewrite the *sh'eilah*" by "identif[ying] the clashing values as 'Jewish pluralism' and 'Reform Jewish integrity'" (33). As Washofsky explains, "Jewish pluralism" is the conviction that "there is more than one legitimate approach to Jewish religion," whereas "Reform Jewish integrity" means adhering to "affirmations without which Reform Judaism as we know it could scarcely exist," with gender equality being one such affirmation (34). The responsum reframes the case this way, he says, because it "wants to tackle a more difficult—and therefore more interesting—question" (32–33) than the one originally posed by the *sho'el*. As the Responsa Committee saw it, the dilemma of whether to host an Orthodox minyan in a Reform synagogue was in fact a symptom of a larger philosophical tension in Reform Judaism, and the *sh'eilah* presented an opportunity to address that tension. In so doing, the responsum makes a profound statement about what it means to be a Reform community.

Washofsky walks the reader through not only the responsum's arguments and the sources it employs, but also its rhetorical structure. He notes that it begins by defining "Jewish pluralism" and "Reform Jewish integrity" in a way that makes it clear that both these values are essential to the Reform religious outlook. Rhetorically, the responsum prepares the reader to think that the only way to answer the *sh'eilah* is to choose one of these core values over the other: either the Reform congregation should refuse to host the Orthodox minyan on the grounds that excluding women violates

Reform Jewish integrity (a decidedly non-pluralist position), or it should agree to host the minyan because Jewish pluralism means we cannot require other Jews to adhere to our particular way of practicing Judaism (requiring the congregation to compromise its Reform Jewish integrity). But it is here, as the tension reaches its crescendo, that the responsum makes a critical and unexpected turn: "The responsum...does not attempt to argue against either of those positions," Washofsky explains. Instead, it "asks us to imagine ourselves as a different kind of Reform Jewish community, one whose members wish to uphold both principles....*This* is the responsum's 'intended audience,' the audience for whom the depiction of the question as a 'hard' one will resonate..." (35).

In his trademark colloquial and conversational manner, Washofsky explains how the responsum constructs an argument using both classical Rabbinic sources and persuasive narrative to bring the reader along in how it thinks about the case. The halachic argument is based on a Talmudic story about Beit Hillel and Beit Shammai, two different schools of thought that nevertheless co-existed in the same community. Yet, more important to the responsum's *persuasive* argument than these classical Rabbinic figures are the modern "characters" in the story—Orthodox Jews, on the one hand, who, due to their non-pluralistic religious philosophy, we should not expect to accord Reform Judaism respect and legitimacy, and Reform Jews, on the other hand, who are *required* by "the values that make us who and what we are...to make room for the practices of the other 'school'—the Orthodox minyan—in our building" (42). At the same time, the responsum insists that this accommodation can and must be made in a way that also upholds Reform Jewish integrity. Therefore, its bottom-line ruling is that a Reform synagogue may host an Orthodox minyan in its space, provided that it takes clear and public steps to indicate that the Orthodox minyan is a separate entity that is not affiliated with the Reform temple, so that no one will conclude that it is in any way sponsoring non-egalitarian prayer.

Washofsky's discussion of this responsum demonstrates how it uses the vocabulary and analytical tools of halachic discourse to engage in a broader project of partnering with readers to realize the *posek*'s vision for the community. The Reform community that the Responsa Committee envisions is one that is confident enough in what it stands for to show respect for and hospitality to Jews whose beliefs are diametrically opposed to its own—and who might not show it the same respect in return. It is a community that judges its own legitimacy and authenticity not by standards put forth by someone else, but by the way it lives out its own values, both internally and in relationship with others who see the world differently. And, in the spirit of the legal theorist Ronald Dworkin[5] (whose influence on Washofsky is evident throughout his oeuvre), it is a community that knows its core values are fundamentally coherent and in harmony with each other, and that thinking intentionally about how to make that coherence manifest in the world is the key to living with integrity.

I remember, as a second-year rabbinic student at HUC Cincinnati, asking Professor Washofsky why we should study halachic texts at all. His answer: "Because they teach you how to think." Perhaps the greatest contribution of *Reading Reform Responsa* to the field generally, and to the Reform Movement specifically, is that it teaches us how to think halachically in a uniquely Reform way.

Notes

1. David Ellenson and Daniel Gordis, Pledges of Jewish Allegiance: Conversion, Law, and Policymaking in Nineteenth- and Twentieth-Century Orthodox Responsa (Stanford University Press, 2012), 8.
2. See Mark Washofsky, "Responsa and Rhetoric: On Law, Literature, and the Rabbinic Decision," in John C. Reeves and John Kampen, eds., *Pursuing the Text: Studies in Honor of Ben Zion Wacholder on the Occasion of His Seventieth Birthday* (Sheffield Academic Press, 1994), 385.
3. I use the masculine pronoun "he" in this context because all of the responsa analyzed in Washofsky's book were written by male *poskim*. It is a particular point of pride for Reform Judaism that, today, the CCAR Responsa Committee is chaired by—and most of its responsa are written by—its first female *posek*, Rabbi Joan Friedman.
4. Rabbi Ellenson made this remark to me in conversation.
5. See Ronald Dworkin, *Justice for Hedgehogs* (The Bellknap Press of Harvard University Press, 2011). In this book, Dworkin argues that a political/legal community should strive for a "unified theory of values," in which all of the community's core values are interrelated and support, rather than contradict, each other.

RABBI A. BRIAN STOLLER (C '08) is Senior Rabbi of Temple Beth-El of Great Neck and an adjunct professor at HUC-JIR (New York).

Poetry

Wicked Problems

Miriam Flock

During the Holocaust, 27-year-old Rabbi Ephraim Oshry of Lithuania was asked to decide several questions of Jewish Law. These poems are based on his rulings.

1. On Washing a Dead Body

It was the time of mourning
for the destruction of the First Temple
and the destruction of the Second Temple.
The rabbi was chanting Lamentations,
when Reb Zalman's daughter
burst into the house of learning, shrieking:
her husband and three children
had been slaughtered by the Nazis.

But that was not the problem
the rabbi had to solve nor even
that Reb Zalman teetered
on the spot and fell, life wafting
from him like smoke from a sacrifice.

The question came from Leib, the tailor:
"If we report Reb Zalman's death,
the Nazis will forbid us
to put him in the ground today—
our law since Moses taught,
the hanged man shall not remain all night
dangling from the tree. But if we wait

MIRIAM FLOCK's work has appeared in *Poetry*, the *Berru* Poetry Series, *Lifecycles: Jewish Women on Biblical Themes in Contemporary Life*, and other publications. She was the 2019 winner of the Anna Davidson Rosenberg Award for poems on the Jewish experience.

to wash the body till the Nazis (may their names
be blotted out) release it, we, too,
may be dead, and no one will be left
to do our friend this final service."

The rabbi helped them clear the table,
where they had just dissected
the passage, "Alas! lonely
sits the city once great with people!"
They laid the corpse out like a scroll.
They bathed the head, and then the right arm,
and then the right side, and then
the left arm, and then the left side.
And they poured nine buckets of water
over Reb Zalman without ceasing,
and they said, together, "He is pure."

2. On Using the Clothes of the Murdered Dead

At Rosh HaShanah, because they were praying
for a sweet new year
and that God might deliver them,
they could not deliver
enough workers for the quota.

So the Nazis dragged them from the benches
by their forelocks, like wanton boys
yanking the tails of cats.
Yitzchok Baum and Berel Mendelevitch
were too slow. The Nazis gunned them down,
the shots popping like the bangers
their non-Jewish neighbors set off
to mark their own new year.

Lithuanians say, "The way you meet the year
is how you'll spend it."
The Jews spent theirs digging graves.
Ordering them to strip the bodies,
drop them in the earth like turnips,
the Nazis offered them the garments
of the dead—gag gifts.

By Jewish law, the murdered are buried
in their clothes; not even shoes should be removed.
But Rabbi Oshry ruled, Yitzchok and Berel
were already in the ground,
and their children needed coats.

3. On Eating in the Presence of the Dead

Already pressed together like cattle
on a train, the Jews lived
many to a room. On Jurbako Street,
a certain Rabinowitz died—typhus?
broken spirit? Who kept track?

"Rabbi," the roommates pleaded,
"we must report to work by dawn.
Our shoulders have no flesh
to cushion the concrete sacks we carry;
our stomachs whine like wind
through a rattling sash. May we eat
our soup of peelings and flaccid cabbage
in the presence of the corpse?"

The rabbi wished no precedents—
no sieges, no pogroms—had ever squeezed
this self-same question from the clenched teeth
of earlier hungry Jews.
But the Talmud teaches, "He whose dead
lie before him, eats in another house;
if he has no other house, he eats
in the house of a neighbor; if the neighbor's house
is not available, he erects a partition
between himself and the corpse;
if he has nothing to make a partition,
he turns his back and eats."

4. On Committing Suicide

Two days before the liquidation,
the conscripts from the daily quota,
who'd been digging peat and sowing barley
at the Ninth Fort, finished the last

of fourteen pits, too deep for planting anything
but bodies. They knew their fate.
The Germans enjoyed killing
the babies first, slinging them against a wall,
accompanied by their parents' wailing;
it was like Wagner to them.

Despite the curfew, one father ventured out,
like a starving man for bread,
to ask the rabbi, "Is it permissible
to exterminate myself?"

Rav Oshry began, as always, with the word
of God. "Did the Holy One not say to Noah,
'Surely the blood of your lives
will I require'? From this we reason,
in so far as it is in our power (and what,
in Kovno—now like the valley
of Gehenna, where ancient kings
sacrificed their children in the fire—
is in our power?) we must return our bodies
as God gave them (though we know
the Nazi beasts descend on us and leave shreds).

"Thus, to take your own life is forbidden—
in most cases.
But there is Saul, who fell upon his sword;
Zedekiah, the final king of Judah, who knew,
as you do, he was closer to death
than life, imploring Nebuchadnezzar,
'Kill me first so I won't see my children's blood.'
What of Asher ben Jehiel, who teaches
in 'The Incense of Spices,'
a Jew does not transgress by suicide
if he's beset by sorrow?

"And still, I rule, you mustn't.
Suicide is surrender
to our enemies. The Germans
might imagine we don't trust in God's deliverance.
Did God not lead the Hebrew children
through the parting sea?

Surely the Straightener of the Bent,
the Clother of the Naked, the God Who Sees,
the Holy Name *Ein Sof*
will not forsake God's people."

In Kovno Ghetto, only three
put themselves down,
as they might have one of their horses
who had broken a leg.
The rest believed
in the coming of the Messiah,
and every day they waited.

Jacob in Luz

Janet Ruth Heller

After he left home,
young Jacob slept in a field
near the town of Luz,
known for its almond trees
but otherwise obscure.

He dreamed about a staircase
stretching from the ground
to the highest heavens
with angels climbing
and angels descending.

Then God appeared to Jacob,
promised the lonely shepherd
a large family
and many acres of land.
God pledged to protect the lad.

God said that Jacob's children
would bless those around them.
In awe, Jacob re-named Luz,
calling it Beit-El
in honor of his vision.

Many centuries have passed.
We can't see that stairwell
and God hides
from us mortals.
Heaven seems very distant.

JANET RUTH HELLER is the past president of the Michigan College English Association and the Society for the Study of Midwestern Literature. She has a PhD in English Language and Literature from the University of Chicago. She has published four poetry books.

Bring us closer, like Jacob,
and restore the flight of steps.
Talk to us often like an old friend.
Transform our drab cities
into sites of revelation.

POETRY

To See the Divine Face and Live—Or Not!

Rabbi Stephen S. Pearce

Shut your eyes, Marion,
whatever you do, don't look at it…but
I don't know,
I'm making this up as I go!
       Indiana Jones in Steven
        Spielberg's *Raiders of*
        the Lost Ark

When standing before the Burning Bush,
Moses heard God calling:
Moses, Moses…do not come closer.
Remove your sandals from your feet,
for the place on which you stand is holy ground,
…And Moses hid his face
for he was afraid to look at God.
       Exodus 3:5–6

Nevertheless, Moses pleaded,
Oh, let me behold Your Presence
       Exodus 33:18

in a Grain of Sand,
and Heaven in a Wild Flower.
(Let me) hold Infinity in my palm,
       William Blake, *Auguries of*
       Innocence

RABBI STEPHEN S. PEARCE, PhD (NY '72) is senior rabbi emeritus and the Taube Emanu-El Scholar at Congregation Emanu-El of San Francisco. He is the author of *Flash of Insight: Metaphor and Narrative in Therapy* and the recently published, *I Wish I'd Said That: A Guide for Writers, Speakers, and Healers.*

I will put you in the cleft of the rock
and shield you...
My posterior can be seen,
But not My anterior.
                                      Exodus 33:22

To what may this tension
between
closeness and distance,
the visual and hidden,
the back and front
be compared?
To porcupines in winter—
They prick each other when they draw too close;
And freeze when too distant from one another.
                            Schopenhauer, *Parerga und*
                                     Paralipomena

A sweet punim contains God's image,
in spite of hearing the sound of words
but seeing no image;
nothing but a voice,
                                     Deuteronomy 4:12

heeding the warning:
"Do not make for yourself
any carved image or likeness
in the form of any creature
of what is in heavens above
or in the waters beneath the earth."
                                        Exodus 20:4

Patriarch Jacob named the place of contention, *Peniel*—
meaning
I have seen a divine being
face to face,
yet my life was preserved.
                                      Genesis 32:31

(And) Moses, Aaron, (novice priests) Nadab and Abihu,
and the seventy elders ascended;
and they saw the God of Israel:
(and) under God's feet there was
the likeness of a pavement of sapphire,

like the very sky for purity...
and they beheld God, ate, and drank.

                                      Exodus 24:9

(Then) Aaron's sons,
Nadav and Abihu
offered "alien" fire

                                      Leviticus 10:1

and perished when they drew too close
to the presence of the Lord.

                                      Leviticus 16:1

God spoke to Moses face to face
as an individual speaks to another.

                                      Exodus 33:11

(Thus) when Moses and Aaron
then went inside the Tent of Meeting.
When they came out,
they blessed the people;
and the Presence of the Lord
appeared to all the people.

                                      Leviticus 9:23

Since you (Moses) saw no shape
when the Holy One
spoke to you at Horeb out of the fire...

                                      Deuteronomy 4:15

you nevertheless, spoke to (Moses)
face to face
on the mountain
out of the fire.

                                      Deuteronomy 5:4

When again a prophet of the Lord arises among You,
I make Myself known in a vision,
I (will) speak in a dream.
Not so with My servant Moses;
he is trusted throughout My household.
With him I speak
mouth to mouth,

plainly
and not in riddles,
and he beholds the likeness of the God

                                                              Numbers 12: 5-8

Never again did there arise in Israel
a prophet like Moses—
whom God singled out,
face to face…

                                                      Deuteronomy 34:10

except…
in the year that King Uzziah died,
I beheld God seated on a high and lofty throne;
and the skirts of His robe filled the Temple."

                                                            Isaiah 6:1

I don't believe in magic,
but a few times in my life
I've seen things,
things I can't explain.
But after a life wrestling with sacred mysteries,
it's not so much what you believe.
It's about how hard you believe it.

                                        Indiana Jones in Steven
                                        Spielberg's
                                        Raiders of the Lost Ark: The
                                        Dial of Destiny

Springtime

Wayne Norman Cochran

Don't be so still and careful with yourself.
Walk barefoot around bulbs broken in the ground.
Take pleasure in the crocuses, the tulips, the daffodils
on a field of old defeats.

Pull back bark;
taste the sap of sassafras;
pick a pussy willow for
tracing smiles on the fuzzy jowls of spring.
Reach up through winter's gray husk
while stretching towards the sun.

Spring thinly masks the greater source for your resurrection.

WAYNE NORMAN COCHRAN lives in Schaghticoke, New York. He is a member at Congregation Berith Sholom in Troy, New York.

POETRY

1 Tishrei

Jessica Greenbaum

I don't know how the first day of the first day
looked to those authors who stood in the center
of a turning season, what fell from trees
or sprang from dirt to spangle a reflection calling
for a holiday, but where I am you can't deny
the shift—boughs afluff with wind, the swinging
hummingbird feeders now half-full until March
returns, the lake glittering more in privacy
than invitation—and as I often sing with others
when I rarely do alone, I'll follow this calendar
around the curve with the congregation who stand
when the ark is opened and when it is closed
who consider forgiveness to have been created
before the world itself, and this first day will mirror
my instruction to rise, insistent, from time's detritus
of experience; I'll try to learn to begin again
out of the little junk yard at my feet—like that
orange mushroom, a home birth in fallen leaves.

JESSICA GREENBAUM is the co-editor, with Rabbi Hara Person, of the first-ever poetry Haggadah, *Mishkan HaSeder* (CCAR, 2021). Her last book of poems, *Spilled and Gone*, was named a Best Book of Poetry by the Boston Globe in 2021.

POETRY

A Poem for Purim

Rabbi Natalie Louise Shribman

We are caught up in a lost world,
swirling around in the chaos of terror.
Every day I search for hope under the snow
and in the water trenches in my neighborhood,
but just like God, hope is hiding.

Perhaps, "we were born for such a time as this"?
These words haunt me,
What can I do in this time of violence and disruption?
Aren't there other times we could be witnessing?
This life is hard to bear, and it feels upside down too often.

Sometimes I feel like Esther, hiding my Judaism.
Other days, I feel courageous like Esther,
and I proudly show my Hebrew necklace.
Maybe I can be both Vashti and Esther—
they both stood up for themselves and principles.

I assemble *mishloach manot* for those I do not know:
Hamantaschen, flowers, and masks,
and hidden beneath, a smile.
As the gift is exchanged, a hand is held.
Perhaps the hope is between our fingers.

This year as I stare at the megillah,
I am searching for the little *alef*.
I know it's in a different scroll.
But I will still look for that the little piece,
the little reminder,
that things can get better.

RABBI NATALIE LOUISE SHRIBMAN (C '20) is the rabbi of Temple Kol Ami in West Bloomfield, Michigan.

As I pour my drink, I think about Haman and Mordecai,
and what we are carrying on from their time in this world.
We all need a little celebration so we can see the daily miracles.

This Purim, have a drink in celebration or
in sadness or in commemoration.
Make a basket for another.
Help those around you.
And be grateful. Maybe all of this will
make a better time for us to be in.

The Synagogue of the Sea

Roger Nash

And God saw all God had made, and found it very good.
—Genesis 1:31

In the surging synagogue of the sea,
prayers merge waves, countlessly.
No other synagogue to attend.
In the blue zion of sky,
no more zions to find
or deny: one zion
shining over everywhere.
On the ancient scrolls stored
in cells of each grain of wheat,
a quick-sprouting truth,
as old as history can scribe itself:
"It's *all* very good. Indivisibly."
If we can all live here, indivisibly, too.

Elegy: Forest Wildfires 2023

Hoofed forests leap,
deer race trees
with antlers flaring, birds
ignite in songs of flame,
wood-mice roar clearly,
boars hubbub
their unhewn hullabaloos,
pines fall heavy
as bent anvils, fire-breaks
wrangle and tilt their own
headstones, even cooling boulders
bleed unstaunched heat.

ROGER NASH is a past-president of the League of Canadian Poets. Literary awards include the Canadian Jewish Book Award for Poetry. He is professor emeritus in Philosophy at Laurentian University.

No ark built yet
to float on fast floods
of fire from fountainheads
of our highly molten ignorance.
Noah, too, knelled daily
in bells of black ash.

Saving Eden

A nonstop threat of skies full
of mushroom clouds. It out-elbows
all tales of new beginnings
and hopeful endurance. Incinerates even Eden
by firing a blazing end into what the Garden
began. No more beginnings to be seen
in the cracked and rimless spectacles of time.
We try to tell new parables,
but they're like riding an unstoppable windmill
on a wooden horse: the horse turns
to ashes as quickly as anything else.
Can we save the epic messaging from Eden
that guides us forward? Only if we bring
nuclear disarmament towards its fragile birth.
Eden isn't safe around nuclear stockpiles.

POETRY

Kfar Aza

Sharon Rogoff

So many birds.
In this lush and Edenic place
where the brutality was unspeakable
I first notice the birds.

Half a tree is charred
black from fire
the other half green with life.
Branches crowded with birds.

Most survivors can't come home
not now, maybe never.
One couple has returned.
We talk.

They try to put the terror into words for me.

Inside a small room for hours and hours and hours
they stayed.
Hearts racing
explosions and fire and gunfire all around
people yelling, people screaming
sweat, confusion, and the unknowing.
The horror of unknowing.

I try to imagine the terror through their words. I can't.
So much chaos numbs me.

SHARON ROGOFF retired from the healthcare field and has been involved in the Sacramento Jewish community for about ten years. She served as the JCRC Chair from 2020 to 2022 and currently serves as a member-at-large on the board of the Jewish Federation of the Sacramento Region.

Signs on homes say, *cleared* —
cleared of blood
of bodies
of body parts.

Names of those who lived in the homes
written in red if murdered
yellow if taken hostage.

I can't feel the terror
only a sadness so deep, I'm numb.

The birds sing as I leave.

The Diameter of the Massacres*

Rabbi Karen Bender

The diameter of the **massacres**
was the length of Israel
and the depth of the universe.
It stretched to every continent,
college campuses and social media.
It spread information and disinformation
Twisting and distorting morality
And redefining madness.
It wreaked havoc and wrecked lives
In Israel and Gaza
In kitchens and living rooms
In bedrooms and porches
In souls and hearts.

The diameter of the **visit**
was the length of Israel
the distance to California
and everyone and everywhere
we will speak of it.
The mission stretched
our compassion and minds
and challenged our faith
in human nature.
It struck us with awe
in every cell of our being
as we saw the resiliency of our people
and as we strove together to answer
the unspoken question:
Where shall we place all the pain?
We were messengers and witnesses,
representatives with wishes to help
and we did and we will.

The diameter of the **hugs**
is the length of an Israeli flag
and the width of a tallit large enough
to enwrap every Israeli who hurts right now
and therefore every Israeli
with the comfort of our love

and with a strand of *t'chelet* turquoise
in the tzitzit to remind us all that
the morning will come and
we will say the *Sh'ma* someday with one voice.

*A reprise of Yehudah Amichai's poem, "The Diameter of the Bomb."

RABBI KAREN BENDER (NY '94), born and raised in Los Angeles to Israeli parents, earned her degree in political science from the University of California at Berkeley. Following two decades of pulpit work in New York and Los Angeles, Rabbi Bender now serves as Chief Mission Officer at Los Angeles Jewish Health. Passionate about social justice, she champions causes such as racial equality and Israel and interfaith dialogue, while also enjoying music, outdoor adventures, and quality time with her three children, Holden, Bot, and Shoshie.

Poor God

Paul Raboff

Poor God
He's looking
He's begging
For people
In His image
After all
To believe in Him
Even just a little
Even less
He can't find them
He has to settle
For someone
Like me
And because
Of that
Just a little.
Poor God.
I'm sorry
You can't
Do better than me
But here I am
Filling this space
The only space
Available for me.

PAUL RABOFF, a poet, is a resident of Jerusalem whose poetry has been published for over fifty years.

POETRY

Englischer Garten, 1922

Nathaniel Lachenmeyer

Regarding the sun flashing through the trees
and the young girls playing among dappled shadows

cast by so many and such bright green leaves,
and the small dog running happily after a ball,

and the dignified gentleman with his cane,
and the young couple sitting on the gray bench

with only true love for company in the glory
of that once-day, I would like to ask you,

who painted such a day so prettily and well,
even if it were all true, even if the gentleman

and the couple in love and the dog and the girls
and the leaves were exactly that, exactly

how and what your living eyes and hands captured
in that moment on that sunny day long ago,

would you have painted it like this, or painted this
place at all, if you had known what in two decades

NATHANIEL LACHENMEYER is an award-winning author of books for children and adults. His first book, *The Outsider*, which takes as its subject his late father's struggles with schizophrenia and homelessness, was published by Broadway Books. His most recent book, an all-ages graphic novel called *The Singing Rock & Other Brand-New Fairy Tales*, was published by First Second/Macmillan. Nathaniel lives outside Atlanta with his family.

would become of you and almost everyone you knew?
Would you have used your paints to keep this bright place,

this moment, nearly alive for more than a hundred years,
or would you have painted something entirely different,

something new and very old, which your eyes had not yet
met, something unexpected and infinitely darker?

Savta

Rinat Harel

I can hear your pain lifting
from beneath the earth.
A slight tremor under my feet.
Savta, the memories your brain devoured,
your wrongs, your ghosts—are mine now.

If I only had the courage
to hold tight as life seeped out
of your frail flesh, the flaking skin,
the thinning hair.
If I could only mend your hunched back,
your mangled toes, the wrinkled brow.

Your family, cindered in the Camps, lived
in the blue depths of your sad eyes.
I now collect their ashes with my bare hands—a tiny
Fuji Mountain—purify them with my breath,
and watch the diamond sprout.

It will sprout and grow, grow and swell,
crystalizing into pure love,
holding our dead in its luminous folds.

Oh, Savta, you can rest now.

RINAT HAREL holds a PhD in Creative Writing from the University of Exeter in England, and her poetry has been published in various literary magazines.

War and All

After the War,
my grandfather had to decide:
United States of America,
or Israel.
(Or so the story goes.)
And he chose,
and his choice became mine by default.

He had great dreams,
they all had great dreams:
Rebellion;
Redemption;
Resurrection.
Shedding the old to embrace
the new,
to start anew,
in the Newland.

It took me twenty-six years to overturn
his decision.
(I recently read that America is the real home of the Jews. Not sure about that, but the living here, summertime and all, *is* easy.)

The darn thing is this: Europe begs my return.
War and all.

POETRY

Love and Lice

Rabbi Dr. Israel Zoberman

In the 1947 photo, Wetzlar, Germany,
Displaced Persons Camp,
At about age one I am held high

Like an adored *sefer Torah* by
My grandparents Rachel and Zvi,
With my little refugee head adorned
By a white cap soon turning black
By lurching envious lice,
Yet my family's love for their
Surviving little scroll colorless remained.

RABBI DR. ISRAEL BOBROV ZOBERMAN (C '74) is founder of Temple Lev Tikvah, and Honorary Senior Rabbi Scholar at Eastern Shore Chapel Episcopal Church, both in Virginia Beach.

Dead Sons

Rabbi Adam D. Fisher

When Aaron's sons,
Nadab and Abihu,
were killed by God,
Moses told him
not to mourn.
Aaron, speechless,
told his wife, Elisheva,
who screamed her grief,
then shaking with anger
turned on Aaron:
"Why were you silent? Why did

that *pisher* of a little brother of yours
tell you not to mourn? Go tell
him that we are finished with him
and his cruel god who thinks
he becomes holy by killing my boys.
Go tell him or don't come back."

What Happened On Mount Sinai

I need to write rules
for this unruly people,
so I hike up a mountain
slipping on rocks and sandy soil,
sending down small avalanches.
At the top I look over the scrub
and barren soil below: not promising
but we will manage.
I find a few large flat rocks

RABBI ADAM D. FISHER (NY '67), rabbi emeritus of Temple Isaiah, Stony Brook, NY is the author of numerous articles and two books of liturgy. He is also the author of a book of short fiction, and four books of poetry. He was the Poetry Editor of the *CCAR Journal* from 2006-2014.

and begin writing feeling
the Presence—
I am taking dictation.
As it will later say,
"with the light of Your Presence,
You give us instruction." (Prayer Book)

POETRY

Elegy in Reverse for Yom Kippur

Rabbi William Cutter

It came to me the other day
As I thought about Yom Kippur (penultimate accent)
that maybe we should have a day
For Praise that makes us chipper.

Then I might say on such a day
"Sometimes I've been exceptional;
I've helped an elder cross the street
and made my life receptional.

I'd balance all the sins I've done
I've surely managed plenty,
I'd think of days of ruth and fun
Until a hundred-twenty.

For good I did when I helped out
and shared some of my riches,
A time to say, "How goes YOUR day"
You sinning sons of breaches.

Forgive me not, I'll do the same,
I'll celebrate the sun.
That's left to me, you'll join the game
to cook beef on the bun.

So I will say on such a day
I'll fail to make complaint.
I'll take in all my energy and
I'll use it for restraint.

RABBI WILLIAM (BILL) CUTTER (C '65), is Emeritus Professor of Hebrew Literature and Human Relations, at HUC-JIR, Los Angeles. He is writing a series of poems, light verse, and rhyming amplifications of Jewish holy days.

Just one lone day, when I can ask
"I've really been a hero?"
I'll take off my confession mask
And think about it Zero.

Fidelity to spouse and home,
A virtue sentimental,
And virtually, its graces good,
Sometimes it's regimental.

For honoring my parents, and
For stifling my temper
I'll honor all my teachers, then,
And keep fidele semper.

Today I may be very sad, tomorrow
I'll remember
that on the other side of bad
I'm still a happy member.

Of Jewish groups—they're happy troops,
They think of many good times;
I'll think about the happy rest,
the loving and the food times.

This day of awe which haunts us all
is surely necessary;
It's ballast for the other times
that aren't awe-filled and scary.

It's hard to live a happy life
to praise one's own achievements;
to fret about the greedy folks
and folks in their bereavements.

Remember, then, your synagogue's
a place to bring together
the sunny days with rainy days
And other kinds of whether.

Shanah tovah success and then,
So happy it should be,
To struggle with all people then,
Our friends and enemies.

Shanah tovah to friends and colleagues!

Call for Papers: *Maayanot*

The *CCAR Journal: The Reform Jewish Quarterly* is committed to serving its readers' professional, intellectual, and spiritual needs. In pursuit of that objective, the *Journal* created a new section known as *Maayanot* (Primary Sources), which made its debut in the Spring 2012 issue.

We continue to welcome proposals for *Maayanot* —translations of significant Jewish texts, accompanied by an introduction as well as annotations and/or commentary. *Maayanot* aims to present fresh approaches to materials from any period of Jewish life, including but not confined to the biblical or Rabbinic periods. When appropriate, it is possible to include the original document in the published presentation.

Please submit proposals, inquiries, and questions to *Maayanot* editor Rabbi Daniel F. Polish, dpolish@optonline.net.

Along with submissions for *Maayanot*, the *Journal* encourages the submission of scholarly articles in fields of Jewish studies, as well as other articles that fit within our Statement of Purpose.

The *CCAR Journal: The Reform Jewish Quarterly*
Published quarterly by the Central Conference of American Rabbis

Volume LXXI No. 4 Issue Number: Two hundred seventy-nine
Fall 2024

STATEMENT OF PURPOSE

The *CCAR Journal: The Reform Jewish Quarterly* seeks to explore ideas and issues of Judaism and Jewish life, primarily—but not exclusively—from a Reform Jewish perspective. To fulfill this objective, the *Journal* is designed to:

1. provide a forum to reflect the thinking of informed and concerned individuals—especially Reform rabbis—on issues of consequence to the Jewish people and the Reform movement;

2. increase awareness of developments taking place in fields of Jewish scholarship and the practical rabbinate, and to make additional contributions to these areas of study;

3. encourage creative and innovative approaches to Jewish thought and practice, based upon a thorough understanding of the traditional sources.

The views expressed in the *Journal* do not necessarily reflect the position of the Editorial Board or the Central Conference of American Rabbis.

The *CCAR Journal: The Reform Jewish Quarterly* (ISSN 1058-8760) is published quarterly by the Central Conference of American Rabbis, 355 Lexington Avenue, 8th Floor, New York, NY 10017.

Subscriptions should be sent to CCAR Executive Offices, 355 Lexington Avenue, 8th Floor, New York, NY 10017. Subscription rate as set by the Conference is $140 for a one-year subscription, $250 for a two-year subscription. Overseas subscribers should add $36 per year for postage. POSTMASTER: Please send address changes to *CCAR Journal: The Reform Jewish Quarterly*, c/o Central Conference of American Rabbis, 355 Lexington Avenue, 8th Floor, New York, NY 10017.

Typesetting services provided by Westchester Publishing Services.

Copyediting services provided by Michelle Kwitkin.

The *CCAR Journal: The Reform Jewish Quarterly* is indexed in the *Index to Jewish Periodicals*. Articles appearing in it are listed in the *Index of Articles on Jewish Studies* (of *Kirjath Sepher*) and in *Religious and Theological Abstracts*.

© Copyright 2024 by the Central Conference of American Rabbis
All rights reserved.
ISSN 1058-8760

ISBN: 978-0-88123-650-7

GUIDELINES FOR SUBMITTING MATERIAL

1. The *CCAR Journal* welcomes submissions that fulfill its Statement of Purpose whatever the author's background or identification. Inquiries regarding publishing in the *CCAR Journal* and submissions for possible publication (including poetry) should be sent to the editor, Rabbi Edwin Goldberg, at rabbi@cbsw.org.

2. Other than commissioned articles, submissions to the *CCAR Journal* are sent out to a member of the editorial board for anonymous peer review. Thus submitted articles and poems should be sent to the editor with the author's name omitted. Please use MS Word format for the attachment. The message itself should contain the author's name, phone number, and e-mail address, as well as the submission's title and a brief author biography.

3. Books for review and inquiries regarding submitting a review should be sent directly to the book review editor, Rabbi Ari Lorge, at alorge6@gmail.com.

4. Inquiries concerning or submissions for poetry should be directed to the editor, Rabbi Edwin Goldberg, at rabbi@cbsw.org.

5. Inquiries concerning or submissions for *Maayanot* (Primary Sources) should be directed to the *Maayanot* editor, Rabbi Daniel F. Polish, at dpolish@optonline.net.

6. Based on Reform Judaism's commitment to egalitarianism, we request that articles be written in gender-inclusive language.

7. The *Journal* publishes reference notes at the end of articles, but submissions are easier to review when notes come at the bottom of each page. If possible, keep this in mind when submitting an article. Notes should conform to the following style:

a. Rachel Adler, *Engendering Judaism: An Inclusive Theology and Ethics* (Philadelphia: Jewish Publication Society, 1999), 101–6. **[book]**

b. Lawrence A. Hoffman, "The Liturgical Message," in *Gates of Understanding*, ed. Lawrence A.Hoffman (New York: CCAR Press, 1977), 147–48, 162–63. **[chapter in a book]**

c. Richard Levy, "The God Puzzle," *Reform Judaism* 28 (Spring 2000): 18–22. **[article in a periodical]**

d. Adler, *Engendering,* 102. **[short form for subsequent reference]**

e. Levy, "God Puzzle," 20. **[short form for subsequent reference]**

f. Ibid., 21. **[short form for subsequent reference]**

8. If Hebrew script is used, please include an English translation. If transliteration is used, follow the guidelines in the **Master Style Sheet**, available on the CCAR website at www.ccarnet.org.

To You I Call
Psalms Throughout Our Lives
Rabbi Jade Sank Ross

Psalms have been part of Jewish ritual and liturgy for centuries, expressing praise to God, feelings of sorrow and longing, and much more. In *To You I Call*, Rabbi Jade Sank Ross invites us to make the ancient words of psalms part of our daily lives. The book pairs seventy-two psalms with a range of life moments, from giving birth to retirement to experiencing antisemitism—times of grief and gratitude, anticipation and despair, pain and relief. With sensitivity and vulnerability, *To You I Call* brings the psalms to life for our lives, today.

Through her pastoral sensitivity and creative readings, Rabbi Sank Ross powerfully brings these ancient words to life, inviting us to recite them with true connection and devotion.—**Rabbi Elie Kaunfer**, CEO of the Hadar Institute

toyouicall.ccarpress.org

www.ingramcontent.com/pod-product-compliance
Lightning Source LLC
Chambersburg PA
CBHW070405240426
43661CB00056B/2538